On Literature and Art

Lenin

On Literature and Art

WILDSIDE PRESS

www.wildsidepress.com

PUBLISHERS' NOTE

The translations are taken from the Progress
Publishers' edition of V. I. Lenin's *Collected Works*
in 45 volumes, except where otherwise indicated.

CONTENTS

DECREES AND DECISIONS
SIGNED BY LENIN

From What the "Friends of the People" Are and How They Fight the Social-Democrats

(A Reply to Articles in *Russkoye Bogatstvo* [1] Opposing the Marxists)

... And as far as humbleness is concerned, one must do *Russkoye Bogatstvo* justice: truly, it stands out even among the Russian liberal press for its inability to display the slightest independence. Judge for yourselves:

"The abolition of the salt tax, the abolition of the poll-tax and the reduction of the land redemption payments" [2] are described by Mr. Yuzhakov as "a considerable relief to people's farming". Well, of course! But was not the abolition of the salt tax accompanied by the imposition of a host of new indirect taxes and an increase in the old ones? Was not the abolition of the poll-tax accompanied by an increase in the payments made by the former state peasants, under guise of placing them on a redemption basis? And is there not even now, after the famous reduction of redemption payments (by which the government did not even return to the peasants the profit it had made out of the redemption operations), a discrepancy between the payments and the income from the land, i. e., a direct survival of feudal quitrent? Never mind! What is important, you see, is "the first step", the "principle". As for the rest ... the rest we can plead for later on!

These, however, are only the blossoms. Now for the fruit.

"The eighties eased the people's burden" (that's by the above measures!) "and thus saved them from utter ruin."

This is another phrase classic for its shameless servility, one that can only be placed, say, alongside Mr. Mikhailovsky's statement, quoted above, that we have still to create a proletariat. One cannot help recalling in this connection Shchedrin's incisive description of the evolution of the Russian liberal! This liberal starts out by pleading with the authorities to grant reforms "as far as possible", then he goes on to beg for "well, at least something", and ends by taking up an eternal and unshakable stand on "anything, however mean". And what else can one say of the "friends of the people" but that they have adopted this eternal and unshakable stand when, fresh from the impressions of a famine affecting millions of people, towards which the government's attitude was first one of a huckster's stinginess and then of a huckster's cowardice, they say in print that the government has saved the people from utter ruin!! Several years more will pass, marked by the still more rapid expropriation of the peasantry; the government, in addition to establishing a Ministry of Agriculture, will abolish one or two direct and impose several new indirect taxes; the famine will then affect 40 million people — and these gentlemen will write in the same old way: you see, 40 and not 50 million are starving, that is because the government has eased the people's burden and has saved them from utter ruin; it is because the government has hearkened to the "friends of the people" and established a Ministry of Agriculture!

Another example:

In *Russkoye Bogatstvo* No. 2, the chronicler of home affairs arguing that Russia is "fortunately" (sic!) a backward country, "which has preserved elements that enable her to base her economic system on the principle of solidarity",* says that she is therefore able to act "in international affairs as an exponent of economic solidarity" and that Russia's chances for this are enhanced by her undeniable "political might"!!

It is the gendarme of Europe, that constant and most reliable bulwark of all reaction, who has reduced the Russian people, themselves oppressed at home, to the shameful position of serving as an instrument for oppressing the peoples in the West — it is this gendarme who is described as an exponent of economic solidarity!

This is indeed beyond all limit! Messrs. the "friends of the people" will outdo all liberals. They not only plead with the government, they not only eulogise it, they positively pray to it, pray with such obeisance, with such zeal that a stranger cannot help feeling eerie at the sound of their loyal foreheads cracking on the flagstones.

Do you remember the German definition of a philistine?

---

* Between whom? The landlord and the peasant, the enterprising muzhik and the tramp, the mill-owner and the worker? To understand what this classical "principle of solidarity" means, we must remember that solidarity between the employer and the workman is achieved by "a reduction in wages".

Was ist der Philister?
Ein hohler Darm,
Voll Furcht und Hoffnung,
*Dass Gott erbarm.**

This definition does not quite apply to our affairs. God ...
God takes a back seat with us. But the authorities ... that's a
different matter. And if in this definition we substitute the
word "authorities" for the word "God" we shall get an exact
description of the ideological stock-in-trade, the moral level
and the civic courage of the Russian humane and liberal
"friends of the people".

To this absolutely preposterous view of the government, the
"friends of the people" add a corresponding attitude toward
the so-called "intelligentsia". Mr. Krivenko writes: "Literature
..." should "appraise phenomena according to their social
meaning and encourage every active effort to do good. It has
harped, and continues to harp, on the shortage of teachers,
doctors, technicians, on the fact that the people are sick, poor"
(there are few technicians), "illiterate, etc.; and when people
come forward who are weary of sitting at card tables,
participating in private theatricals and eating sturgeon patties
at parties given by Marshals of Nobility, and who go out to
work with rare self-sacrifice and in face of numerous obstacles"
(think of it: they have sacrificed card tables, theatricals and
patties!), "literature should welcome them".

Two pages later, with the business-like air of an old
campaigner grown wise by experience, he reproves those who
"wavered when confronted with the question whether or not to
accept office as Zemsky Nachalniks,[3] town mayors, or chairmen
or members of Zemstvo Boards under the new regulations. In
a society with a developed consciousness of civic requirements
and duties" (really, gentlemen, this is as good as the speeches
of famous Russian Jacks-in-office like the Baranovs and
Kosiches!), "such wavering and such an attitude to affairs
would be inconceivable, because it would assimilate in its own
way every reform that had any vital side to it at all, that is,
would take advantage of and develop those sides of the reform
that are expedient; as to the undesirable sides, it would convert
them into a dead letter; and if there were nothing whatever
vital in the reform it would remain an entirely alien body."

---

* What is a philistine? A hollow gut, full of fear and of hope in God's mercy
(Goethe).— *Ed.*

What on earth do you make of that! What miserable
twopenny-ha'penny opportunism, what indulgence in self-admiration! The task of literature is to collect all the drawing-
room gossip about the wicked Marxists, to bow and cringe to
the government for saving the people from utter ruin, to
welcome people who have grown weary of sitting at card tables,
to teach the "public" not to fight shy even of such posts as that
of Zemsky Nachalnik.... What is this I am reading—*Nedelya*,[4]
or *Novoye Vremya*[5]? No, it is *Russkoye Bogatstvo*, the organ of the
advanced Russian democrats....

And such gentlemen talk about the "ideals of their fathers",
claim that they, and they alone, guard the traditions of the days
when France poured the ideas of socialism all over
Europe[6]—and when, in Russia, the assimilation of these ideas
produced the theories and teachings of Herzen and Chernyshevsky. This is a downright disgrace and would be
positively outrageous and offensive—if *Russkoye Bogatstvo*
were not so utterly amusing, if such statements in the columns
of a magazine of this type did not arouse Homeric laughter,
and nothing else. Yes, indeed, you are besmirching those
ideals! What were actually the ideals of the first Russian
socialists, the socialists of the epoch which Kautsky so aptly
described in the words:

"When every socialist was a poet and every poet a socialist."

*Faith in a special social order, in the communal system of Russian
life; hence—faith in the possibility of a peasant socialist revolution*—that is what inspired them and roused dozens and
hundreds of people to wage a heroic struggle against the
government. And you, you cannot reproach the Social-
Democrats with failing to appreciate the immense historical
services of these, the finest people of their day, with failing to
respect their memory profoundly. But I ask you, where is that
faith now? It has vanished. So utterly, that when Mr. V. V.
tried to argue last year that the village commune trains the
people to common effort and is a centre of altruistic
sentiments, etc.,[7] even Mr. Mikhailovsky's conscience
was pricked and he shamefacedly began to lecture Mr. V. V.
and to point out that "no *investigation* has shown a
connection between our village commune and altruism".[8]
And, indeed, no investigation has. Yet there was a time
when people had faith, implicit faith, without making any
investigation.

How? Why? On what grounds?...

"Every socialist was a poet and every poet a socialist"....

* * *

... Let us take another example, one from opinions on the peasant Reform. What attitude towards it had Chernyshevsky, a democrat of that epoch, when democracy and socialism were undivided? Unable to express his opinion openly, he *kept silent*, but gave the following roundabout description of the contemplated reform:

"Suppose I was interested in taking measures to protect the provisions out of which your dinner is made. It goes without saying that if I was prompted to do so by my kind disposition towards you, then my zeal was based on the assumption that the provisions belonged to you and that the dinner prepared from them would be wholesome and beneficial to you. Imagine my feelings, then, when I learn that the provisions do not belong to you at all, and that for every dinner prepared from them you are charged a price which n o t o n l y e x c e e d s t h e c o s t o f t h e d i n n e r" (this was written *before* the Reform. Yet the Messrs. Yuzhakovs assert now that its fundamental principle was to give security to the peasants!!) *"but which you are not able to pay at all without extreme hardship. What thoughts enter my head when I make such strange discoveries?... How stupid I was to bother about the matter when the conditions did not exist to ensure its usefulness! Who but a fool would bother about the retention of property in certain hands without first satisfying himself that those hands will receive the property, and on favourable terms?... Far better if all these provisions are lost, for they w i l l o n l y c a u s e h a r m to my dear friend! F a r better be done with the whole business, for it will only cause your ruin!"*

I have emphasised the passages which show most saliently how profoundly and splendidly Chernyshevsky understood the realities of his time, how he understood the significance of the peasants' payments, how he understood the antagonism between the social classes in Russia. It is also important to note his ability to expound such purely revolutionary ideas in the censored press. He wrote the same thing in his illegal works, but without circumlocution. In *A Prologue to the Prologue*, Volgin (into whose mouth Chernyshevsky puts his ideas) says: *"Let the emancipation of the peasant be placed in the hands of the landlords' party. It won't make much difference."* * And in reply to his interlocutor's remark that, on the contrary, the difference

---

* I quote from Plekhanov's article "N. G. Chernyshevsky", in *Sotsial-Demokrat.*[9]

would be tremendous, because the landlords' party was opposed to allotting land to the peasants, he replies emphatically:

"No, not tremendous, but insignificant. It would be tremendous if the peasants obtained the land without redemption payments. There is a difference between taking a thing from a man and leaving it with him, but if you take payment from him it is all the same. The only difference between the plan of the landlords' party and that of the progressists is that the former is simpler and shorter. That is why it is even better. Less red tape and, in all probability, less of a burden on the peasants. Those peasants who have money will buy land. As to those who have none—there's no use compelling them to buy it. It will only ruin them. Redemption is nothing but purchase."

It required the genius of a Chernyshevsky to understand so clearly at that time, when the peasant Reform was only being introduced (when it had not yet been properly elucidated even in Western Europe), its fundamentally bourgeois character, to understand that already at that time Russian "society" and the Russian "state" were ruled and governed by social classes that were irreconcilably hostile to the working people and that undoubtedly predetermined the ruin and expropriation of the peasantry. Moreover, Chernyshevsky understood that the existence of a government that screens our antagonistic social relations is a terrible evil, which renders the position of the working people ever so much worse.

"To tell the truth," Volgin continues, *"it would be better if they were emancipated without land."* (That is, since the feudal landlords in this country are so strong, it would be better if they acted openly, straightforwardly, and said all they had in mind, instead of hiding their interests as serf owners behind the compromises of a hypocritical absolute government.)

"The matter is put in such a way that I see no reason for getting excited, even over whether the peasants are emancipated or not, let alone over whether the liberals or the landlords are to emancipate them. To my mind it is all the same. It will even be better if the landlords do it."

Here is a passage from "Unaddressed Letters": *"They say: emancipate the peasants.... Where are the forces for it? Those forces do not yet exist. It is useless tackling a job when the forces for it are lacking. Yet you see the way things are going. They will start emancipating. But what will come of it? Well, judge for yourself what comes of tackling a job which is beyond your powers. You just botch it — and the result will be vile."*

Chernyshevsky understood that the Russian feudal, bureaucratic state was incapable of emancipating the peasants, that is, of overthrowing the feudal serf owners, that it was only capable of something "vile", of a miserable compromise between the interests of the liberals (redemption is nothing but purchase) and of the landlords, a compromise employing the illusion of security and freedom to deceive the peasants, but actually ruining them and completely betraying them to the landlords. And he protested, execrated the Reform, wanted it to fail, wanted the government to get tied up in its equilibristics between the liberals and the landlords, and wanted a crash to take place that would bring Russia out on the high road of open class struggle.

Yet *today*, when Chernyshevsky's brilliant predictions have become fact, when the history of the past thirty years has ruthlessly shown up all economic and political illusions, our contemporary "democrats" sing the praises of the Reform, regard it as a sanction for "people's" production, contrive to draw proof from it of the possibility of finding a way which would *get around* the social classes hostile to the working people. I repeat, their attitude towards the peasant Reform is most striking proof of how profoundly bourgeois our democrats have become. These gentlemen have learned nothing, but have forgotten very, very much.

Written in the spring
and summer of 1894

Hectographed in 1894

Collected Works,
Vol. 1, pp. 260-64,
280-83

Svoboda is a worthless little rag. Its author—indeed, this is precisely the impression it creates, that one person has written it all, from beginning to end—claims to write popularly "for the workers". But what we have here is not popularisation, but talking down in the worst sense of the term. There is not one simple word, everything is twisted.... The author cannot write a single phrase without embellishments, without "popular" similes and "popular" catchwords such as "theirn". Outworn socialist ideas are chewed over in this ugly language without any new data, any new examples, any new analysis, and the whole thing is deliberately vulgarised. Popularisation, we should like to inform the author, is a long way from vulgarisation, from talking down. The popular writer leads his reader towards profound thoughts, towards profound study, proceeding from simple and generally known facts; with the aid of simple arguments or striking examples he shows the main *conclusions* to be drawn from those facts and arouses in the mind of the thinking reader ever newer questions. The popular writer does not presuppose a reader that does not think, that cannot or does not wish to think; on the contrary, he assumes in the undeveloped reader a serious intention to use his head and *aids* him in his serious and difficult work, *leads* him, helps him over his first steps, and *teaches* him to go forward independently. The vulgar writer assumes that his reader does not think and is incapable of thinking; he does not lead him in his first steps towards serious knowledge, but in a distortedly simplified form, interlarded with jokes and facetiousness, hands out "ready-made" *all* the conclusions of a known theory, so that the reader does not even have to chew but merely to swallow what he is given.

Written in the autumn of 1901
First published in the magazine
Bolshevik No. 2, 1936

Collected Works,
Vol. 5, pp. 311-12

From Demonstrations Have Begun

A fortnight ago we observed the twenty-fifth anniversary of the first social-revolutionary demonstration in Russia, which took place on December 6, 1876, on Kazan Square in St. Petersburg,[11] and we pointed to the enormous upswing in the number and magnitude of the demonstrations at the beginning of the current year. We urged that the demonstrators should advance a political slogan more clearly defined than "Land and Freedom"[12] (1876), and a more far-reaching demand than "Repeal the Provisional Regulations" (1901). Such a slogan must be: *political freedom*; and the demand to be put forward by the entire people has to be *the demand for the convocation of the people's representatives.*

We see now that demonstrations are being revived on the most varied grounds in Nizhni-Novgorod, in Moscow, and in Kharkov. Public unrest is growing everywhere, and more and more imperative becomes the necessity to unify it into one single current directed *against the autocracy,* which everywhere sows tyranny, oppression, and violence. On November 7, a small but successful demonstration was held in Nizhni-Novgorod, which arose out of a farewell gathering in honour of Maxim Gorky. An author of European fame, whose only weapon was free speech (as a speaker at the Nizhni-Novgorod demonstration aptly put it), was being banished by the autocratic government from his home town without trial or investigation. The bashibazouks accuse him of exercising a harmful influence on us, said the speaker in the name of all Russians in whom but a spark of striving towards light and liberty is alive, but we declare that his influence has been a good one. The myrmidons of the tsar perpetrate their outrages in secret, and we will expose their outrages publicly and openly. In Russia, workers are assaulted for demanding their right to a better life; students are assaulted for protesting against tyranny. Every honest and bold utterance is suppressed! The demonstration, in which workers took part, was concluded by a student reciting: "Tyranny shall fall, and the people shall rise — mighty, free, and strong!"

In Moscow, hundreds of students waited at the station to greet Gorky. Meanwhile, the police, scared out of their wits, *arrested* him on the train *en route* and (despite the special permission previously granted him) prohibited his entering Moscow, forcing him to change directly from the Nizhni-Novgorod to the Kursk line. The demonstration against Gorky's banishment failed; but on the eighteenth of November, without any preparation, a small demonstration of students and "strangers" (as our Ministers put it) took place in front of the Governor General's house against the prohibition of a social evening arranged for the previous day to commemorate the fortieth anniversary of the death of N. A. Dobrolyubov. The representative of the autocracy in Moscow was howled down by people who, in unison with all educated and thinking people in Russia, held dear the memory of a writer who had passionately hated tyranny and passionately looked forward to a people's uprising against the "Turks at home", i.e., against the autocratic government.[13]

Iskra No. 13,   *Collected Works*,
December 20, 1901   Vol. 5, pp. 322-23

From What Is To Be Done?

Burning Questions of Our Movement

"We should dream!" I wrote these words and became alarmed. I imagined myself sitting at a "unity conference" and opposite me were the *Rabocheye Dyelo*[14] editors and contributors. Comrade Martynov rises and, turning to me, says sternly: "Permit me to ask you, has an autonomous editorial board the right to dream without first soliciting the opinion of the Party committees?" He is followed by Comrade Krichevsky, who (philosophically deepening Comrade Martynov, who long ago rendered Comrade Plekhanov more profound) continues even more sternly: "I go further. I ask, has a Marxist any right at all to dream, knowing that according to Marx mankind always sets itself the tasks it can solve and that tactics is a process of the growth of Party tasks which grow together with the Party?"

The very thought of these stern questions sends a cold shiver down my spine and makes me wish for nothing but a place to hide in. I shall try to hide behind the back of Pisarev.

"There are rifts and rifts," wrote Pisarev of the rift between dreams and reality. "My dream may run ahead of the natural march of events or may fly off at a tangent in a direction in which no natural march of events will ever proceed. In the first case my dream will not cause any harm; it may even support and augment the energy of the working men.... There is nothing in such dreams that would distort or paralyse labour-power. On the contrary, if man were completely deprived of the ability to dream in this way, if he could not from time to time run ahead and mentally conceive, in an entire and completed picture, the product to which his hands are only just beginning to lend shape, then I cannot at all imagine what stimulus there would be to induce man to undertake and complete extensive and strenuous work in the sphere of art, science, and practical endeavour.... The rift between dreams and reality causes no harm if only the person dreaming believes seriously in his dream, if he attentively observes life, compares his observations with his castles in the air, and if, generally speaking, he works conscientiously for the achievement of his fantasies. If there is some connection between dreams and life then all is well." [15]

Of this kind of dreaming there is unfortunately too little in our movement. And the people most responsible for this are those who boast of their sober views, their "closeness" to the "concrete", the representatives of legal criticism and of illegal "tail-ism".

Written between the autumn of
1901 and February 1902

Published in book form   *Collected Works,*
in Stuttgart in March 1902   Vol. 5, pp. 509-10

Party Organisation
and Party Literature [16]

The new conditions for Social-Democratic work in Russia which have arisen since the October Revolution [17] have brought the question of party literature to the fore. The distinction between the illegal and the legal press, that melancholy heritage of the epoch of feudal, autocratic Russia, is beginning to disappear. It is not yet dead, by a long way. The hypocritical government of our Prime Minister is still running amuck, so much so that *Izvestia Soveta Rabochikh Deputatov* [18] is printed "illegally"; but apart from bringing disgrace on the government, apart from striking further moral blows at it, nothing comes of the stupid attempts to "prohibit" that which the government is powerless to thwart.

So long as there was a distinction between the illegal and the legal press, the question of the party and non-party press was decided extremely simply and in an extremely false and abnormal way. The entire illegal press was a party press, being published by organisations and run by groups which in one way or another were linked with groups of practical party workers. The entire legal press was non-party — since parties were banned — but it "gravitated" towards one party or another. Unnatural alliances, strange "bed-fellows" and false cover-devices were inevitable. The forced reserve of those who wished to express party views merged with the immature thinking or mental cowardice of those who had not risen to these views and who were not, in effect, party people.

An accursed period of Aesopian language, literary bondage, slavish speech, and ideological serfdom! The proletariat has put an end to this foul atmosphere which stifled everything living and fresh in Russia. But so far the proletariat has won only half freedom for Russia.

The revolution is not yet completed. While tsarism is *no longer* strong enough to defeat the revolution, the revolution is *not yet* strong enough to defeat tsarism. And we are living in times when everywhere and in everything there operates this unnatural combination of open, forthright, direct and consistent party spirit with an underground, covert, "diplomatic" and dodgy "legality". This unnatural combination makes itself felt even in our newspaper: for all Mr. Guchkov's witticisms about Social-Democratic tyranny forbidding the publication of moderate liberal-bourgeois newspapers, the fact remains that *Proletary*, [19] the Central Organ of the Russian Social-Democratic Labour Party, still remains outside the locked doors of *autocratic*, police-ridden Russia.

Be that as it may, the half-way revolution compels all of us to set to work at once organising the whole thing on new lines. Today literature, even that published "legally", can be nine-tenths party literature. It must become party literature. In contradistinction to bourgeois customs, to the profit-making, commercialised bourgeois press, to bourgeois literary careerism and individualism, "aristocratic anarchism" and drive for profit, the socialist proletariat must put forward the principle of *party literature*, must develop this principle and put it into practice as fully and completely as possible.

What is this principle of party literature? It is not simply that, for the socialist proletariat, literature cannot be a means of enriching individuals or groups; it cannot, in fact, be an individual undertaking, independent of the common cause of the proletariat. Down with non-partisan writers! Down with literary supermen! Literature must become *part* of the common cause of the proletariat, "a cog and a screw" of one single great Social-Democratic mechanism set in motion by the entire politically-conscious vanguard of the entire working class. Literature must become a component of organised, planned and integrated Social-Democratic Party work.

"All comparisons are lame," says a German proverb. So is my comparison of literature with a cog, of a living movement with a mechanism. And I daresay there will even be hysterical intellectuals to raise a howl about such a comparison, which degrades, deadens, "bureaucratises" the free battle of ideas, freedom of criticism, freedom of literary creation, etc., etc. Such outcries, in point of fact, would be nothing more than an expression of bourgeois-intellectual individualism. There is no question that literature is least of all subject to mechanical adjustment or levelling, to the rule of the majority over the minority. There is no question, either, that in this field greater scope must undoubtedly be allowed for personal initiative, individual inclination, thought and fantasy, form and content.

All this is undeniable; but all this simply shows that the literary side of the proletarian party cause cannot be mechanically identified with its other sides. This, however, does not in the least refute the proposition, alien and strange to the bourgeoisie and bourgeois democracy, that literature must by all means and necessarily become an element of Social-Democratic Party work, inseparably bound up with the other elements. Newspapers must become the organs of the various party organisations, and their writers must by all means become members of these organisations. Publishing and distributing centres, bookshops and reading-rooms, libraries and similar establishments — must all be under Party control. The organised socialist proletariat must keep an eye on all this work, supervise it in its entirety, and, from beginning to end, without any exception, infuse into it the life-stream of the living proletarian cause, thereby cutting the ground from under the old, semi-Oblomov,[20] semi-shopkeeper Russian principle: the writer does the writing, the reader does the reading.

We are not suggesting, of course, that this transformation of literary work, which has been defiled by the Asiatic censorship and the European bourgeoisie, can be accomplished all at once. Far be it from us to advocate any kind of standardised system, or a solution by means of a few decrees. Cut-and-dried schemes are least of all applicable here. What is needed is that the whole of our Party, and the entire politically-conscious Social-Democratic proletariat throughout Russia, should become aware of this new problem, specify it clearly and everywhere set about solving it. Emerging from the captivity of the feudal censorship, we have no desire to become, and shall not become, prisoners of bourgeois-shopkeeper literary relations. We want to establish, and we shall establish, a free press, free not simply from the police, but also from capital, from careerism, and what is more, free from bourgeois-anarchist individualism.

These last words may sound paradoxical, or an affront to the reader. What! some intellectual, an ardent champion of liberty, may shout. What, you want to impose collective control on such a delicate, individual matter as literary work! You want workmen to decide questions of science, philosophy, or aesthetics by a majority of votes! You deny the absolute freedom of absolutely individual ideological work!

Calm yourselves, gentlemen! First of all, we are discussing

party literature and its subordination to party control. Everyone is free to write and say whatever he likes, without any restrictions. But every voluntary association (including the party) is also free to expel members who use the name of the party to advocate anti-party views. Freedom of speech and the press must be complete. But then freedom of association must be complete too. I am bound to accord you, in the name of free speech, the full right to shout, lie and write to your heart's content. But you are bound to grant me, in the name of freedom of association, the right to enter into, or withdraw from, association with people advocating this or that view. The party is a voluntary association, which would inevitably break up, first ideologically and then physically, if it did not cleanse itself of people advocating anti-party views. And to define the border-line between party and anti-party there is the party programme, the party's resolutions on tactics and its rules and, lastly, the entire experience of international Social-Democracy, the voluntary international associations of the proletariat, which has constantly brought into its parties individual elements and trends not fully consistent, not completely Marxist and not altogether correct and which, on the other hand, has constantly conducted periodical "cleansings" of its ranks. So it will be with us too, supporters of bourgeois "freedom of criticism", *within* the Party. We are now becoming a mass party all at once, changing abruptly to an open organisation, and it is inevitable that we shall be joined by many who are inconsistent (from the Marxist standpoint), perhaps we shall be joined even by some Christian elements, and even by some mystics. We have sound stomachs and we are rock-like Marxists. We shall digest those inconsistent elements. Freedom of thought and freedom of criticism within the Party will never make us forget about the freedom of organising people into those voluntary associations known as parties.

Secondly, we must say to you bourgeois individualists that your talk about absolute freedom is sheer hypocrisy. There can be no real and effective "freedom" in a society based on the power of money, in a society in which the masses of working people live in poverty and the handful of rich live like parasites. Are you free in relation to your bourgeois publisher, Mr. Writer, in relation to your bourgeois public, which demands that you provide it with pornography in frames * and

---

* There must be a misprint in the source, which says *ramkakh* (frames), while the context suggests *romanakh* (novels).— *Ed.*

paintings, and prostitution as a "supplement" to "sacred" scenic art? This absolute freedom is a bourgeois or an anarchist phrase (since, as a world outlook, anarchism is bourgeois philosophy turned inside out). One cannot live in society and be free from society. The freedom of the bourgeois writer, artist or actress is simply masked (or hypocritically masked) dependence on the money-bag, on corruption, on prostitution.

And we socialists expose this hypocrisy and rip off the false labels, not in order to arrive at a non-class literature and art (that will be possible only in a socialist extra-class society), but to contrast this hypocritically free literature, which is in reality linked to the bourgeoisie, with a really free one that will be *openly* linked to the proletariat.

It will be a free literature, because the idea of socialism and sympathy with the working people, and not greed or careerism, will bring ever new forces to its ranks. It will be a free literature, because it will serve, not some satiated heroine, not the bored "upper ten thousand" suffering from fatty degeneration, but the millions and tens of millions of working people — the flower of the country, its strength and its future. It will be a free literature, enriching the last word in the revolutionary thought of mankind with the experience and living work of the socialist proletariat, bringing about permanent interaction between the experience of the past (scientific socialism, the completion of the development of socialism from its primitive, utopian forms) and the experience of the present (the present struggle of the worker comrades).

To work, then, comrades! We are faced with a new and difficult task. But it is a noble and grateful one — to organise a broad, multiform and varied literature inseparably linked with the Social-Democratic working-class movement. All Social-Democratic literature must become Party literature. Every newspaper, journal, publishing house, etc., must immediately set about reorganising its work, leading up to a situation in which it will, in one form or another, be integrated into one Party organisation or another. Only then will "Social-Democratic" literature really become worthy of that name, only then will it be able to fulfil its duty and, even within the framework of bourgeois society, break out of bourgeois slavery and merge with the movement of the really advanced and thoroughly revolutionary class.

Novaya Zhizn No. 12,
November 13, 1905
Signed: *N. Lenin*

Collected Works,
Vol. 10, pp. 44-49

Leo Tolstoy
As the Mirror of the Russian Revolution

To identify the great artist with the revolution which he has obviously failed to understand, and from which he obviously stands aloof, may at first sight seem strange and artificial. A mirror which does not reflect things correctly could hardly be called a mirror. Our revolution, however, is an extremely complicated thing. Among the mass of those who are directly making and participating in it there are many social elements which have also obviously not understood what is taking place and which also stand aloof from the real historical tasks with which the course of events has confronted them. And if we have before us a really great artist, he must have reflected in his work at least some of the essential aspects of the revolution.

The legal Russian press, though its pages teem with articles, letters and comments on Tolstoy's eightieth birthday, is least of all interested in analysing his works from the standpoint of the character of the Russian revolution and its motive forces. The whole of this press is steeped to nausea in hypocrisy, hypocrisy of a double kind: official and liberal. The former is the crude hypocrisy of the venal hack who was ordered yesterday to hound Leo Tolstoy, and today to show that Tolstoy is a patriot, and to try to observe the decencies before the eyes of Europe. That the hacks of this kind have been paid for their screeds is common knowledge and they cannot deceive anybody. Much more refined and, therefore, much more pernicious and dangerous is liberal hypocrisy. To listen to the Cadet Balalaikins [21] of Rech, [22] one would think that their sympathy for Tolstoy is of the most complete and ardent kind. Actually, their calculated declamations and pompous phrases about the "great seeker after God" are false from beginning to end, for no Russian liberal believes in Tolstoy's God, or sympathises with Tolstoy's criticism of the existing social order. He associates himself with a popular name in order to increase his political capital, in order to pose as a leader of the nation-wide opposition; he seeks, with the din and thunder of claptrap, to *drown* the demand for a straight and clear answer to the question: what are the glaring contradictions of "Tolstoyism" due to, and what shortcomings and weaknesses of our revolution do they express?

The contradictions in Tolstoy's works, views, doctrines, in his school, are indeed glaring. On the one hand, we have the great artist, the genius who has not only drawn incomparable pictures of Russian life but has made first-class contributions to world literature. On the other hand, we have the landlord obsessed with Christ. On the one hand, the remarkably powerful, forthright and sincere protest against social falsehood and hypocrisy; and on the other, the "Tolstoyan", i. e., the jaded, hysterical sniveller called the Russian intellectual, who publicly beats his breast and wails: "I am a bad wicked man, but I am practising moral self-perfection; I don't eat meat any more, I now eat rice cutlets." On the one hand, merciless criticism of capitalist exploitation, exposure of government outrages, the farcical courts and the state administration, and unmasking of the profound contradictions between the growth of wealth and achievements of civilisation and the growth of poverty, degradation and misery among the working masses. On the other, the crackpot preaching of submission, "resist not evil" with violence. On the one hand, the most sober realism, the tearing away of all and sundry masks; on the other, the preaching of one of the most odious things on earth, namely, religion, the striving to replace officially appointed priests by priests who will serve from moral conviction, i. e., to cultivate the most refined and, therefore, particularly disgusting clericalism. Verily:

> *Thou art a pauper, yet thou art abundant,*
> *Thou art mighty, yet thou art impotent —*
> *— Mother Russia!*[23]

That Tolstoy, owing to these contradictions, could not possibly understand either the working-class movement and its role in the struggle for socialism, or the Russian revolution, goes without saying. But the contradictions in Tolstoy's views and doctrines are not accidental; they express the contradictory conditions of Russian life in the last third of the nineteenth century. The patriarchal countryside, only recently emancipated from serfdom, was literally given over to the capitalist and the tax-collector to be fleeced and plundered. The ancient foundations of peasant economy and peasant life, foundations that had really held for centuries, were broken up for scrap with extraordinary rapidity. And the contradictions in Tolstoy's views must be appraised not from the standpoint of the present-day working-class movement and present-day socialism (such an appraisal is, of course, needed, but it is not enough), but from the standpoint of protest against advancing capitalism, against the ruining of the masses, who are being dispossessed of their land — a protest which had to arise from the patriarchal Russian countryside. Tolstoy is absurd as a prophet who has discovered new nostrums for the salvation of mankind — and therefore the foreign and Russian "Tolstoyans" who have sought to convert the weakest side of his doctrine into a dogma, are not worth speaking of. Tolstoy is great as the spokesman of the ideas and sentiments that emerged among the millions of Russian peasants at the time the bourgeois revolution was approaching in Russia. Tolstoy is original, because the sum total of his views, taken as a whole, happens to express the specific features of our revolution as a *peasant* bourgeois revolution. From this point of view, the contradictions in Tolstoy's views are indeed a mirror of those contradictory conditions in which the peasantry had to play their historical part in our revolution. On the one hand, centuries of feudal oppression and decades of accelerated post-Reform pauperisation piled up mountains of hate, resentment, and desperate determination. The striving to sweep away completely the official church, the landlords and the landlord government, to destroy all the old forms and ways of landownership, to clear the land, to replace the police-class state by a community of free and equal small peasants — this striving is the keynote of every historical step the peasantry has taken in our revolution; and, undoubtedly, the message of Tolstoy's writings conforms to this peasant striving far more than it does to abstract "Christian Anarchism", as his "system" of views is sometimes appraised.

On the other hand, the peasantry, striving towards new ways of life, had a very crude, patriarchal, semi-religious idea of what kind of life this should be, by what struggle could liberty be won, what leaders it could have in this struggle, what was the attitude of the bourgeoisie and the bourgeois intelligentsia towards the interests of peasant revolution, why the forcible overthrow of tsarist rule was needed in order to abolish landlordism. The whole past life of the peasantry had taught it to hate the landowner and the official, but it did not, and could not, teach it where to seek an answer to all these questions. In our revolution a minor part of the peasantry really did fight, did organise to some extent for this purpose; and a very small part indeed rose up in arms to exterminate its enemies, to destroy the tsar's servants and protectors of the landlords. Most of the peasantry wept and prayed, moralised and dreamed, wrote petitions and sent "pleaders" — quite in the vein of Leo Tolstoy! And, as always happens in such cases, the effect of this Tolstoyan abstention from politics, this Tolstoyan renunciation of politics, this lack of interest in and understanding of politics, was that only a minority followed the lead of the class-conscious revolutionary proletariat, while the majority became the prey of those unprincipled, servile, bourgeois intellectuals who under the name of Cadets hastened from a meeting of Trudoviks[24] to Stolypin's ante-room, and begged, haggled, reconciled and promised to reconcile — until they were kicked out with a military jackboot. Tolstoy's ideas are a mirror of the weakness, the shortcomings of our peasant revolt, a reflection of the flabbiness of the patriarchal countryside and of the hidebound cowardice of the "enterprising muzhik".

Take the soldiers' insurrections in 1905-06. In social composition these men who fought in our revolution were partly peasants and partly proletarians. The proletarians were in the minority; therefore the movement in the armed forces does not even approximately show the same nation-wide solidarity, the same party consciousness, as were displayed by the proletariat, which became Social-Democratic as if by the wave of a hand. Yet there is nothing more mistaken than the view that the insurrections in the armed forces failed because no officers had led them. On the contrary, the enormous progress the revolution had made since the time of the Narodnaya Volya[25] was shown precisely by the fact that the "grey herd" rose in arms against their superiors, and it was this self-dependency of theirs that so frightened the liberal landlords and the liberal officers. The common soldier fully sympathised with the peasants' cause; his eyes lit up at the very mention of land. There was more than one case when authority in the armed forces passed to the mass of the rank and file, but determined use of this authority was hardly made at all; the soldiers wavered; after a couple of days, in some cases a few hours, after killing some hated officer, they released the others who had been arrested, parleyed with the authorities and then faced the firing squad, or bared their backs for the birch, or put on the yoke again — quite in the vein of Leo Tolstoy!

Tolstoy reflected the pent-up hatred, the ripened striving for a better lot, the desire to get rid of the past — and also the immature dreaming, the political inexperience, the revolutionary flabbiness. Historical and economic conditions explain both the inevitable beginning of the revolutionary struggle of the masses and their unpreparedness for the struggle, their Tolstoyan non-resistance to evil, which was a most serious cause of the defeat of the first revolutionary campaign.

It is said that beaten armies learn well. Of course, revolutionary classes can be compared with armies only in a very limited sense. The development of capitalism is hourly changing and intensifying the conditions which roused the millions of peasants — united by their hatred for the feudalist landlords and their government — for the revolutionary-democratic struggle. Among the peasantry themselves the growth of exchange, of the rule of the market and the power of money is steadily ousting old-fashioned patriarchalism and the patriarchal Tolstoyan ideology. But there is one gain from the first years of the revolution and the first reverses in mass revolutionary struggle about which there can be no doubt. It is the mortal blow struck at the former softness and flabbiness of the masses. The lines of demarcation have become more distinct. The cleavage of classes and parties has taken place. Under the hammer blows of the lessons taught by Stolypin, and with undeviating and consistent agitation by the revolutionary Social-Democrats not only the socialist proletariat but also the democratic masses of the peasantry will inevitably advance from their midst more and more steeled fighters who will be less capable of falling into our historical sin of Tolstoyism!

Proletary No. 35,   *Collected Works,*
September 11 (24), 1908   Vol. 15, pp. 202-09

The Bourgeois Press Fable
about the Expulsion of Gorky [26]

For several days now the bourgeois newspapers of France (*L'Eclair, Le Radical*), Germany (*Berliner Tageblatt*) and Russia (*Utro Rossii, Rech, Russkoye Slovo, Novoye Vremya*) have been smacking their lips over a most sensational piece of news: the expulsion of Gorky from the Social-Democratic Party. *Vorwärts* [27] has already published a refutation of this nonsensical report. The editorial board of *Proletary* has also sent a denial to several newspapers, but the bourgeois press ignores it and continues to boost the libel.

It is easy to see how it originated: some penny-a-liner overheard a whisper of the dissensions about otzovism [28] and god-building [29] (a question which has been discussed openly for almost a year in the Party in general and in *Proletary* [30] in particular), made an unholy mess in weaving together his fragments of information and "earned a pretty penny" out of imaginary "interviews", etc.

The aim of this slanderous campaign is no less clear. The bourgeois parties *would like* Gorky to leave the Social-Democratic Party. The bourgeois newspapers are sparing no effort to fan the dissensions in the Social-Democratic Party and to give a distorted picture of them.

Their labour is in vain. Comrade Gorky by his great works of art has bound himself too closely to the workers' movement in Russia and throughout the world to reply with anything but contempt.

Proletary No. 50,
November 28 (December 11),
1909

Collected Works,
Vol. 16, p. 106

Concerning *Vekhi*[31]

The well-known symposium *Vekhi,* compiled from contributions by the most influential Constitutional-Democratic publicists, which has run through several editions in a short time and has been rapturously received by the whole reactionary press, is a real sign of the times. However much the Cadet newspapers do to "rectify" particular passages in *Vekhi* that are excessively nauseating, however much it is repudiated by some Cadets who are quite powerless to influence the policy of the Constitutional-Democratic Party as a whole or are aiming to deceive the masses as to the true significance of this policy, it is an unquestionable fact that *"Vekhi" has expressed the unmistakable essence of modern Cadetism.* The party of the Cadets is the party of *Vekhi.*

Prizing above everything the development of the political and class consciousness of the masses, working-class democrats should welcome *Vekhi* as a magnificent exposure of the essence of the political trend of the Cadets by their ideological leaders. The gentlemen who have written *Vekhi* are: Berdayev, Bulgakov, Herschensohn, Kistyakovsky, Struve, Frank and Izgoyev. The very names of these well-known deputies, well-known renegades and well-known Cadets, are eloquent enough. The authors of *Vekhi* speak as real ideological leaders of a whole social trend. They give us in concise outline a complete encyclopaedia on questions of philosophy, religion, politics, publicist literature, and appraisals of the whole liberation movement and the whole history of Russian democracy. By giving *Vekhi* the subtitle "A Collection of Articles on the Russian Intelligentsia" the authors understate the actual subject-matter of their publication, for, with them, the "intelligentsia" in fact appears as the spiritual leader, inspirer and mouthpiece of the whole Russian democracy and the whole Russian liberation movement. *Vekhi* is a most significant landmark on the road of Russian Cadetism and Russian liberalism in general towards a *complete break* with the Russian liberation movement, with all its main aims and fundamental traditions.

I

This *encyclopaedia of liberal renegacy* embraces three main subjects: (1) the struggle against the ideological principles of the whole world outlook of Russian (and international) democracy; (2) repudiation and vilification of the liberation movement of recent years; (3) an open proclamation of its "flunkey" sentiments (and a corresponding "flunkey" policy) in relation to the Octobrist bourgeoisie, the old regime and the entire old Russia in general.

The authors of *Vekhi* start from the philosophical bases of the "intellectualist" world outlook. The book is permeated through and through with bitter opposition to materialism, which is qualified as nothing but dogmatism, metaphysics, "the most elementary and lowest form of philosophising" (p. 4 — references are to the first edition of *Vekhi*). Positivism is condemned because "for us" (i.e., the Russian "intelligentsia" that *Vekhi* annihilates) it was "identified with materialist metaphysics" or was interpreted "exclusively in the spirit of materialism" (15), while "no mystic, no believer, can deny scientific positivism and science" (11). Don't laugh! "Hostility to idealist and religious mystical tendencies" (6) — such is the charge with which *Vekhi* attacks the "intelligentsia". "Yurkevich, at any rate, was a real philosopher in comparison with Chernyshevsky" (4).

Holding this point of view, *Vekhi* very naturally thunders incessantly against the atheism of the "intelligentsia" and strives with might and main to re-establish the religious world outlook in its entirety. Having demolished Chernyshevsky as a philosopher it is quite natural that *Vekhi* demolishes Belinsky as a publicist. Belinsky, Dobrolyubov and Chernyshevsky were the leaders of the "intellectuals" (134, 56, 32, 17 and elsewhere). Chaadayev, Vladimir Solovyov, Dostoyevsky were "not intellectuals at all". The former were the leaders of a trend against which *Vekhi* is fighting to the death. The latter "tirelessly maintained" the very same things that *Vekhi* stands for today, but "they were unheeded, the intelligentsia passed them by", declares the preface to *Vekhi*.

The reader can already see from this that it is not the "intelligentsia" that *Vekhi* is attacking. This is only an artificial and misleading manner of expression. The attack is being pursued all along the line against democracy, against the democratic world outlook. And since it is inconvenient for the ideological leaders of a party that advertises itself as "constitutional" and "democratic" to call things by their true names, they have borrowed their terminology from *Moskovskiye Vedomosti*.[32] They are not renouncing democracy (what a scandalous libel!) but only "intellectualism".

Belinsky's letter to Gogol,[33] declares *Vekhi*, is a "lurid and classical expression of intellectualist sentiment" (56). "The history of our publicist literature, after Belinsky, in the sense of an understanding of life, is a sheer nightmare" (82).

Well, well. The serf peasants' hostility to serfdom is obviously an "intellectualist" sentiment. The history of the protest and struggle of the broadest masses of the population from 1861 to 1905 against the survivals of feudalism throughout the whole system of Russian life is evidently a "sheer nightmare". Or, perhaps, in the opinion of our wise and educated authors, Belinsky's sentiments in the letter to Gogol did not depend on the feelings of the serf peasants? The history of our publicist literature did not depend on the indignation of the popular masses against the survivals of feudal oppression?

Moskovskiye Vedomosti has always tried to prove that Russian democracy, beginning with Belinsky at least, in no way expresses the interests of the broadest masses of the population in the struggle for the elementary rights of the people, violated by feudal institutions, but expresses only "intellectualist sentiments".

Vekhi has the same programme as *Moskovskiye Vedomosti* both in philosophy and in publicist matters. In philosophy, however, the liberal renegades decided to tell the whole truth, to reveal *all* their programme (war on materialism and the materialist interpretation of positivism, restoration of mysticism and the mystical world outlook), whereas on publicist subjects they prevaricate and hedge and Jesuitise. They have broken with the most fundamental ideas of democracy, the most elementary democratic tendencies, but pretend that they are breaking only with "intellectualism". The liberal bourgeoisie has decisively turned away from defence of popular rights to defence of institutions hostile to the people. But the liberal politicians want to retain the title of "democrats".

The same trick that was performed with Belinsky's letter to Gogol and the history of Russian publicist literature is being applied to the history of the recent movement.

II

As a matter of fact *Vekhi* attacks only the intelligentsia that was a voice of the democratic movement and only for that which showed it to be a real participant in this movement. *Vekhi* furiously attacks the intelligentsia precisely because this "little underground sect came out into the broad light of day, gained a multitude of disciples and for a time became ideologically influential and even actually powerful" (176). The liberals sympathised with the "intelligentsia" and sometimes supported it secretly *as long as* it remained *merely* a little underground sect, until it gained a multitude of disciples and became actually powerful; that is to say, the liberals sympathised with democracy as long as it did not set in motion the real masses, for, as long as the masses were not drawn in, it only served the self-seeking aims of liberalism, it only helped the upper section of the liberal bourgeoisie to climb a little nearer to power. The liberal turned his back on democracy when it drew in the masses, who began to realise their *own* aims and uphold their *own* interests. Under the cover of outcries against the democratic "intelligentsia" *the war of the Cadets is in fact being waged against the democratic movement of the masses.* One of the innumerable and obvious revelations of this in *Vekhi* is its declaration that the great social movement of the end of the eighteenth century in France was "an example of a sufficiently prolonged intellectualist revolution, displaying all its spiritual potentialities" (57).

Good, is it not? The French movement of the end of the eighteenth century, please note, was not an example of the democratic movement of the masses in its profoundest and broadest form, but an example of "intellectualist" revolution! Since democratic aims have never anywhere in the world been achieved without a movement of a *homogeneous* type it is perfectly obvious that the ideological leaders of liberalism are breaking with democracy.

The feature of the Russian intelligentsia that *Vekhi* inveighs against is the *necessary* accompaniment and expression of *any* democratic movement. "The admixture of the political radicalism of intellectualist ideas to the social radicalism of popular

2*

instincts* was achieved with amazing rapidity" (141) — and this
was "not simply a political mistake, not simply an error of
tactics. The mistake here was a moral one." Where there are no
martyred popular masses, there can be no democratic movement. And what distinguishes a democratic movement from a
mere "riot" is that it proceeds under the banner of certain
radical political ideas. Democratic movements and democratic
ideas are not only politically erroneous, are not only out of
place tactically but are morally sinful — such in essence is the
real opinion of *Vekhi*, which does not differ one iota from the
real opinions of Pobedonostsev. Pobedonostsev only said more
honestly and candidly what Struve, Izgoyev, Frank and Co. are
saying.

When *Vekhi* proceeds to define more precisely the substance
of the hateful "intellectualist" ideas, it naturally speaks about
"Left" ideas in general and Narodnik and Marxist ideas in particular. The Narodniks [34] are accused of "spurious love for
the peasantry" and the Marxists "for the proletariat" (9). Both
are blasted to smithereens for "idolisation of the people" (59,
59-60). To the odious "intellectual" "god is the people, the
sole aim is the happiness of the majority" (159). "The stormy
oratory of the atheistic Left bloc" (29) — this is what impressed
itself most on the memory of the Cadet Bulgakov in the Second
Duma [35] and particularly aroused his indignation. And there is
not the slightest doubt that Bulgakov has expressed here,
somewhat more conspicuously than others, the general Cadet
psychology, he has voiced the cherished thoughts of the whole
Cadet Party.

That for a liberal the distinction between Narodism and
Marxism is obliterated is not accidental, but inevitable. It is not
the "trick" of the writer (who is perfectly aware of the
distinction) but a logical expression of the present nature of
liberalism. At the *present* time what the liberal bourgeoisie in
Russia dreads and abominates is not so much the socialist
movement of the working class in Russia as the democratic
movement both of the workers and the peasants, i.e., it dreads
and abominates what Narodism and Marxism have in common, their defence of democracy by appealing to the masses. It
is characteristic of the present period that liberalism in Russia
has decisively turned against democracy; quite naturally it is
not concerned either with the distinctions within democracy or

---

* "Of the martyred popular masses" is the phrase used on the same page,
two lines down.

with the further aims, vistas and prospects which will be unfolded when democracy is achieved.

Vekhi simply teems with catchwords like "idolisation of the people". This is not surprising, for the liberal bourgeoisie, which has become frightened of the people, has no alternative but to shout about the democrats' "idolisation of the people". The retreat cannot but be covered by an extra loud roll of the drums. In point of fact, it is impossible to deny outright that it was in the shape of the workers and peasants' deputies that the first two Dumas expressed the real interests, demands and views of the mass of the workers and peasants. Yet it was just these "intellectualist"* deputies who infected the Cadets with their abysmal *hatred of the "Lefts"* because of the exposure of the Cadets' everlasting retreats from democracy. In point of fact, it is impossible to deny outright the justice of the "four-point electoral system" [36] demand; yet no political leader who is at all honest has the slightest doubt that in contemporary Russia elections on the "four-point" system, really democratic elections, would give an overwhelming majority to the Trudovik deputies together with the deputies of the workers' party.

Nothing remains for the back-sliding liberal bourgeoisie but to conceal its break with democracy by means of catchwords from the vocabulary of *Moskovskiye Vedomosti* and *Novoye Vremya* [37]; the whole symposium *Vekhi* positively teems with them.

Vekhi is a veritable torrent of reactionary mud poured on the head of democracy. Of course the publicists of *Novoye Vremya* — Rozanov, Menshikov and A. Stolypin — have hastened to salute *Vekhi* with their kisses. Of course, Anthony, Bishop of Volhynia, is enraptured with this publication of the leaders of liberalism.

"When the intellectual," says *Vekhi*, "reflected upon his duty to the people, he never arrived at the thought that the idea of personal responsibility expressed in the principle of duty must be applied not only to him, the intellectual, but to the people as well" (139). The democrat reflected on the extension of the rights and liberty of the people, clothing this thought in words

---

* *Vekhi's* distortion of the ordinary meaning of the word "intellectual" is really laughable. We have only to look through the list of deputies in the first two Dumas to see at once the overwhelming majority of peasants among the Trudoviks, the predominance of workers among the Social-Democrats and the concentration of the mass of the bourgeois intelligentsia among the Cadets.

about the "duty" of the upper classes to the people. The
democrat could never and will never arrive at the thought that
in a country prior to reform or in a country with a June 3
constitution [38] there could be any question of "responsibility"
of the people to the ruling classes. To arrive at this thought the
democrat, or so-called democrat, must be completely converted into a counter-revolutionary liberal.

"Egoism, self-assertion is a great power," we read in *Vekhi*,
"this is what makes the Western bourgeoisie a mighty
unconscious instrument of God's will on earth" (95). This is
nothing more than a paraphrase flavoured with incense of the
celebrated "Enrichissez-vous!— enrich yourselves!"— or of
our Russian motto: "We put our stake on the strong!" [39] When
the bourgeoisie were helping the people to fight for freedom
they declared this struggle to be a divine cause. When they
became frightened of the people and turned to supporting all
kinds of medievalism against the people, they declared as a
divine cause "egoism", self-enrichment, a chauvinistic foreign
policy, etc. Such was the case all over Europe. It is being
repeated in Russia.

"The revolution should virtually and formally have culmi-
nated with the edict of October 17" (136). This is the alpha and
omega of Octobrism, i.e., of the programme of the counter-
revolutionary bourgeoisie. The Octobrists have always said this
and acted openly in accordance with it. The Cadets acted
surreptitiously in the same way (beginning from October 17), but
at the same time wanted to keep up the pretence of being
democrats. If the cause of democracy is to be successful, a
complete, clear and open demarcation between the democrats
and the renegades is the most effective and necessary thing.
Vekhi must be utilised for this necessary act. "We must have the
courage to confess at last," writes the renegade Izgoyev, "that
in our State Dumas the vast majority of the deputies, with the
exception of three or four dozen Cadets and Octobrists, have
not displayed knowledge required for the government and
reformation of Russia" (208). Well, of course, how could
clod-hopping Trudovik deputies or some sort of working men
undertake such a task? It needs a majority of Cadets and
Octobrists and that needs a Third Duma....

And so that the people and their idolaters should realise
their "responsibility" to the bosses in the Third Duma and
Third Duma Russia the people must be taught — with the
assistance of Anthony, Bishop of Volhynia — "repentance"
(*Vekhi*, 26), "humility" (49), opposition to "the pride of the

intellectual" (52) "obedience" (55), "the plain, coarse food of
old Moses' Ten Commandments" (51), struggle against "the
legion of devils who have entered the gigantic body of Russia"
(68). If the peasants elect Trudoviks and the workers elect
Social-Democrats, this of course is just such devils' work, for
by their true nature the people, as Katkov and Pobedonostsev
discovered long ago, entertain "hatred for the intelligentsia"
(87; read for democracy).

Therefore, *Vekhi* teaches us, Russian citizens must "bless this
government which alone with its bayonets and prisons still
protects us ["the intellectuals"]* from popular fury" (88).

This tirade is good because it is frank; it is useful because it
reveals the truth about the real essence of the policy of the
whole Constitutional-Democratic Party throughout the period
1905-09. This tirade is good because it reveals concisely and
vividly the whole spirit of *Vekhi*. And *Vekhi* is good because it
discloses the whole spirit of the *real* policy of the Russian
liberals and of the Russian Cadets included among them. That
is why the Cadet polemic with *Vekhi* and the Cadet renunciation of *Vekhi* are nothing but hypocrisy, sheer idle talk, for in
reality the Cadets collectively, as a party, as a social force, have
pursued and are pursuing the policy of *Vekhi* and *no other*. The
calls to take part in the elections to the Bulygin Duma in
August and September 1905,[40] the betrayal of the cause of
democracy at the end of the same year, their persistent fear of
the people and the popular movement and systematic opposition to the deputies of the workers and peasants in the first two
Dumas, the voting for the budget, the speeches of Karaulov on
religion and Berezovsky on the agrarian question in the Third
Duma, the visit to London[41]—these are only a few of the
innumerable *landmarks* of just *that* policy which has been
ideologically proclaimed in *Vekhi*.

Russian democracy cannot make a single step forward until
it understands the essence of this policy and the class roots of it.

Novy Dyen No. 15,
December 13, 1909
Signed: *V. Ilyin*

Collected Works,

Vol. 16, pp. 123-31

---

* Interpolations in square brackets (within passages quoted by Lenin) have
been introduced by Lenin, unless otherwise indicated.— *Ed.*

From Notes of a Publicist

I
The "Platform" of the Adherents
and Defenders of Otzovism [42]

...The present inter-revolutionary period cannot be explained away as a mere accident. There is no doubt now that we are confronted by a special stage in the development of the autocracy, in the development of the bourgeois monarchy, bourgeois Black-Hundred [43] parliamentarism and the bourgeois policy of tsarism in the countryside, and that the counter-revolutionary bourgeoisie is supporting all this. The present period is undoubtedly a *transitional* period "between two waves of the revolution", but in order to prepare for the second revolution we must master the peculiarities of this transition, we must be able to adapt our tactics and organisation to this difficult, hard, sombre transition forced on us by the whole trend of the "campaign". Using the Duma tribune, as well as all other legal opportunities, is one of the humble methods of struggle which do not result in anything "spectacular". But the transitional period is transitional precisely because its specific task is to prepare and rally the *forces*, and not to bring them into immediate and decisive action. To know how to organise this work, which is devoid of outward glamour, to know how to utilise for this purpose all those semi-legal institutions which are peculiar to the period of the Black-Hundred-Octobrist Duma, [44] to know how to uphold *even on this basis* all the traditions of revolitionary Social-Democracy, all the slogans of its recent heroic past, the entire spirit of its work, its irreconcilability with opportunism and reformism — such is the *task of the Party*, such is the task of the moment.

We have examined the new platform's first deviation from the tactics set out in the resolution of the December Conference of 1908. [45] We have seen that it is a deviation towards otzovist ideas, ideas that have nothing in common

either with the Marxist analysis of the present situation or with
the fundamental premises of revolutionary Social-Democratic
tactics in general. Now we must examine the second original
feature of the new platform.

This feature is the task, proclaimed by the new group, of
"creating" and "disseminating among the masses a new,
proletarian" culture: "of developing proletarian science, of
strengthening genuine comradely relations among the proletarians, of developing a proletarian philosophy, of directing
art towards proletarian aspirations and experience"
(p. 17).

Here you have an example of that naïve diplomacy which in
the new platform serves to cover up the essence of the matter!
Is it not really naïve to insert *between* "science" and
"philosophy" the "strengthening of genuine comradely relations"? The new group introduces into the *platform* its
supposed *grievances,* its accusations against the other groups
(namely, against the orthodox Bolsheviks in the first place) that
they have broken "genuine comradely relations" Such is
precisely the *real* content of this amusing clause.

Here "proletarian science" also looks "sad and out of place".
First of all, we know now of only one proletarian science — Marxism. For some reason the authors of the platform
systematically avoid this, the only precise term, and everywhere
use the words "scientific socialism" (pp. 13, 15, 16, 20, 21). It is
common knowledge that even outright opponents of Marxism
lay claim to this latter term in Russia. In the second place, if the
task of developing "proletarian science" is introduced in the
platform, it is necessary to state plainly just what ideological
and theoretical struggle of our day is meant here and whose
side the authors of the platform take. Silence on this point is a
naïve subterfuge, for the *essence of the matter* is obvious to
everyone who is acquainted with the Social-Democratic literature of 1908—09. In *our* day a struggle between the Marxists
and the Machists[46] has come to the fore and is being waged in
the domain of science, philosophy and art. It is ridiculous, to
say the least, to shut one's eyes to this commonly known fact.
"Platforms" should be written not in order to gloss over
differences but in order to explain them.

Our authors clumsily give themselves away by the above-
quoted passage of the platform. Everyone knows that it is
Machism that is *in fact* implied by the term "proletarian
philosophy" — and every intelligent Social-Democrat will at
once decipher the "new" *pseudonym.* There was no point in

inventing this pseudonym, no point in trying to hide behind it. In actual fact, the most influential literary nucleus of the new group is Machist, and it regards non-Machist philosophy as non-"proletarian".

Had they wanted to speak of it in the platform, they should have said: the new group unites those who will fight against non-"proletarian", i.e., non-Machist, theories in philosophy and art. That would have been a straightforward, truthful and open declaration of a well-known *ideological* trend, an open challenge to the other tendencies. When an ideological struggle is held to be of great importance for the Party, one does not hide but comes out with an open declaration of war.

And we shall call upon everyone to give a definite and clear answer to the platform's veiled declaration of a philosophical struggle against Marxism. *In reality*, all the phraseology about "proletarian culture" is just a screen for the *struggle against Marxism*. The "original" feature of the new group is that it has introduced *philosophy* into the Party platform without stating frankly *what* tendency in philosophy it advocates.

Incidentally, it would be incorrect to say that the real content of the words of the platform quoted above is wholly negative. They have a certain positive content. This positive content can be expressed in one name: Maxim Gorky.

Indeed, there is no need to conceal the fact already proclaimed by the bourgeois press (which has distorted and twisted it), namely, that Gorky is one of the adherents of the new group. And Gorky is undoubtedly the greatest representative of *proletarian* art, one who has done a great deal for this art and is capable of doing still more in the future. Any faction of the Social-Democratic Party would be justly proud of having Gorky as a member, but to introduce "proletarian art" into the *platform* on this ground means giving this platform a certificate of poverty, means reducing one's group to a literary *circle*, which exposes itself as being precisely "authoritarian".... The authors of the platform say a great deal against recognising authorities, without explaining directly what it is all about. The fact is that they regard the Bolsheviks' defence of materialism in philosophy and the Bolsheviks' struggle against otzovism as the enterprise of individual "authorities" (a gentle hint at a serious matter) whom the enemies of Machism, they say, "trust blindly". Such sallies, of course, are quite childish. But it is precisely the Vperyodists[47] who mistreat authorities. Gorky is an authority in the domain of proletarian art — that is beyond dispute. The attempt to "utilise" (in the ideological sense, of course) *this* authority to bolster up Machism and otzovism is an *example* of how one should not treat *authorities*.

In the field of proletarian art Gorky is an enormous *asset* in spite of his sympathies for Machism and otzovism. But a *platform* which sets up within the Party a separate group of otzovists and Machists and advances the development of alleged "proletarian" art as a special task of the group is a *minus* in the development of the Social-Democratic proletarian movement; because this platform wants to consolidate and utilise the very features in the activities of an outstanding authority which represent his weak side and are a negative quantity in the enormous service he renders the proletariat.

Published March 6 (19)   *Collected Works*,
and May 25 (June 7), 1910   Vol. 16, pp. 204-07
in *Diskussionny Listok*
Nos. 1 and 2
Signed: *N. Lenin*

L. N. Tolstoy

Leo Tolstoy is dead. His universal significance as an artist and his universal fame as a thinker and preacher reflect, each in its own way, the universal significance of the Russian revolution. L. N. Tolstoy emerged as a great artist when serfdom still held sway in the land. In a series of great works, which he produced during the more than half a century of his literary activity, he depicted mainly the old, pre-revolutionary Russia which remained in a state of semi-serfdom even after 1861 — rural Russia of the landlord and the peasant. In depicting this period in Russia's history, Tolstoy succeeded in raising so many great problems and succeeded in rising to such heights of artistic power that his works rank among the greatest in world literature. The epoch of preparation for revolution in one of the countries under the heel of the serf-owners became, thanks to its brilliant illumination by Tolstoy, a step forward in the artistic development of humanity as a whole.

Tolstoy the artist is known to an infinitesimal minority even in Russia. If his great works are really to be made the possession of *all*, a struggle must be waged against the system of society which condemns millions and scores of millions to ignorance, benightedness, drudgery and poverty — a socialist revolution must be accomplished.

Tolstoy not only produced artistic works which will always be appreciated and read by the masses, once they have created human conditions of life for themselves after overthrowing the yoke of the landlords and capitalists; he succeeded in conveying with remarkable force the moods of the large masses that are oppressed by the present system, in depicting their condition and expressing their spontaneous feelings of protest and anger. Belonging, as he did, primarily to the era of 1861—1904, Tolstoy in his works—both as an artist and as a thinker and preacher—embodied in amazingly bold relief the specific historical features of the entire first Russian revolution, its strength and its weakness.

One of the principal distinguishing features of our revolution is that it was a *peasant* bourgeois revolution in the era of the very advanced development of capitalism throughout the world and of its comparatively advanced development in Russia. It was a bourgeois revolution because its immediate aim was to overthrow the tsarist autocracy, the tsarist monarchy, and to abolish landlordism, but not to overthrow the domination of the bourgeoisie. The peasantry in particular was not aware of the latter aim, it was not aware of the distinction between this aim and the closer and more immediate aims of the struggle. It was a peasant bourgeois revolution because objective conditions put in the forefront the problem of changing the basic conditions of life for the peasantry, of breaking up the old, medieval system of landownership, of "clearing the ground" for capitalism: the objective conditions were responsible for the appearance of the peasant masses on the arena of more or less independent historic action.

Tolstoy's works express both the strength and the weakness, the might and the limitations, precisely of the peasant mass movement. His heated, passionate, and often ruthlessly sharp protest against the state and the official church that was in alliance with the police conveys the sentiments of the primitive peasant democratic masses, among whom centuries of serfdom, of official tyranny and robbery, and of church Jesuitism, deception and chicanery had piled up mountains of anger and hatred. His unbending opposition to private property in land conveys the psychology of the peasant masses during that historical period in which the old, medieval landownership, both in the form of landed estates and in the form of state "allotments", definitely became an intolerable obstacle to the further development of the country, and when this old landownership was inevitably bound to be destroyed most summarily and ruthlessly. His unremitting accusations against capitalism—accusations permeated with most profound emotion and most ardent indignation—convey all the horror felt by the patriarchal peasant at the advent of the new, invisible, incomprehensible enemy coming from somewhere in the cities, or from somewhere abroad, destroying all the "pillars" of rural life, bringing in its train unprecedented ruin, poverty, starvation, savagery, prostitution, syphilis — all the calamities attending the "epoch of primitive accumulation", aggravated a hundredfold by the transplantation into Russian soil of the most modern methods of plunder elaborated by the all powerful Monsieur Coupon.[48]

But the vehement protestant, the passionate accuser, the great critic at the same time manifested in his works a failure to understand the causes of the crisis threatening Russia, and the means of escape from it, that was characteristic only of a patriarchal, naïve peasant, but not of a writer with a European education. His struggle against the feudal police state, against the monarchy turned into a repudiation of politics, led to the doctrine of "non-resistance to evil", and to complete aloofness from the revolutionary struggle of the masses in 1905-07. The fight against the official church was combined with the preaching of a new, purified religion, that is to say, of a new, refined, subtle poison for the oppressed masses. The opposition to private property in land did not lead to concentrating the struggle against the real enemy — landlordism and its political instrument of power, i.e., the monarchy — but led to dreamy, diffuse and impotent lamentations. The exposure of capitalism and of the calamities it inflicts on the masses was combined with a wholly apathetic attitude to the world-wide struggle for emancipation waged by the international socialist proletariat.

The contradictions in Tolstoy's views are not contradictions inherent in his personal views alone, but are a reflection of the extremely complex, contradictory conditions, social influences and historical traditions which determined the psychology of various classes and various sections of Russian society in the post-Reform, but pre-revolutionary era.

That is why a correct appraisal of Tolstoy can be made only from the viewpoint of the class which has proved, by its political role and its struggle during the first denouement of these contradictions, at a time of revolution, that it is destined to be the leader in the struggle for the people's liberty and for the emancipation of the masses from exploitation — the class which has proved its selfless devotion to the cause of democracy and its ability to fight against the limitations and inconsistency of bourgeois (including peasant) democracy; such an appraisal is possible only from the viewpoint of the Social-Democratic proletariat.

Look at the estimate of Tolstoy in the government newspapers. They shed crocodile tears, professing their respect for "the

great writer" and at the same time defending the "Holy"
Synod.[49] As for the holy fathers, they have just perpetrated a
particularly vile iniquity; they sent priests to the dying man in
order to hoodwink the people and say that Tolstoy had
"repented". The Holy Synod excommunicated Tolstoy. So
much the better. It will be reminded of this exploit when the
hour comes for the people to settle accounts with the officials
in cassocks, the gendarmes in Christ, the sinister inquisitors
who supported anti-Jewish pogroms and other exploits of the
Black-Hundred [50] tsarist gang.

Look at the estimate of Tolstoy in the liberal newspapers.
They confine themselves to those hollow, official-liberal,
hackneyed professorial phrases about the "voice of civilised
mankind", "the unanimous response of the world", the "ideas
of truth, good", etc., for which Tolstoy so castigated — and
justly castigated — bourgeois science. They *cannot* voice plainly
and clearly their opinion of Tolstoy's views on the state, the
church, private property in land, capitalism — not because they
are prevented by the censorship; on the contrary, the
censorship is helping them out of an embarrassing position!— but because each proposition in Tolstoy's criticism is a
slap in the face of bourgeois liberalism; because the very way in
which Tolstoy fearlessly, frankly and ruthlessly *poses* the sorest
and most vexatious problems of our day is a *rebuff* to the
commonplace phrases, trite quirks and evasive, "civilised"
falsehoods of our liberal (and liberal-Narodnik) publicists. The
liberals are all for Tolstoy, they are all against the
Synod — and, at the same time, they are for ... the Vekhists,[51]
with whom "it is possible to disagree", but with whom it is
"necessary" to live in harmony in one party, with whom it is
"necessary" to work together in literature and politics. And yet
the Vekhists are greeted with kisses by Anthony, Bishop of
Volhynia.

The liberals put in the forefront that Tolstoy is "the great
conscience". Is not this a hollow phrase which is repeated in a
thousand variations both by *Novoye Vremya* [52] and by all such
newspapers? Is this not an evasion of the *concrete* problems
of democracy and socialism which Tolstoy *posed?* Is this not
to put in the forefront the feature that expresses Tolstoy's
prejudice, not his intellect, the part of him that belongs to the
past and not to the future, his repudiation of politics and
his preaching of moral self-perfection, but not his vehement
protest against all class domination?

Tolstoy is dead, and the pre-revolutionary Russia whose

weakness and impotence found their expression in the
philosophy and are depicted in the works of the great artist,
has become a thing of the past. But the heritage which he has
left includes that which has not become a thing of the past, but
belongs to the future. This heritage is accepted and is being
worked upon by the Russian proletariat. The Russian proletariat will explain to the masses of the toilers and the
exploited the meaning of Tolstoy's criticism of the state, the
church, private property in land — not in order that the masses
should confine themselves to self-perfection and yearning for a
godly life, but in order that they should rise to strike a new
blow at the tsarist monarchy and landlordism, which were but
slightly damaged in 1905, and which must be destroyed. The
Russian proletariat will explain to the masses Tolstoy's criticism
of capitalism — not in order that the masses should confine
themselves to hurling imprecations at capital and the rule of
money, but in order that they should learn to utilise at every
step in their life and in their struggle the technical and social
achievements of capitalism, that they should learn to weld
themselves into a united army of millions of socialist fighters
who will overthrow capitalism and create a new society in which
the people will not be doomed to poverty, in which there will be
no exploitation of man by man.

Sotsial-Demokrat No. 18,   *Collected Works,*
November 16 (29), 1910   Vol. 16, pp. 323-27

L. N. Tolstoy
and the Modern Labour Movement

The Russian workers in practically all the large cities of Russia have already made their response in connection with the death of L. N. Tolstoy and, in one way or another, expressed their attitude to the writer who produced a number of most remarkable works of art that put him in the ranks of the great writers of the world, and to the thinker who with immense power, self-confidence and sincerity *raised* a number of questions concerning the basic features of the modern political and social system. All in all, this attitude was expressed in the telegram, printed in the newspapers, which was sent by the labour deputies in the Third Duma.[53]

L. Tolstoy began his literary career when serfdom still existed but at a time when it had already obviously come to the end of its days. Tolstoy's main activity falls in that period of Russian history which lies between two of its turning-points, 1861 and 1905. Throughout this period traces of serfdom, direct survivals of it, permeated the whole economic (particularly in the countryside) and political life of the country. And at the same time this was a period of the accelerated growth of capitalism from below and its implantation from above.

In what were the survivals of serfdom expressed? Most of all and clearest of all in the fact that in Russia, mainly an agricultural country, agriculture at that time was in the hands of a ruined, impoverished peasantry who were working with antiquated, primitive methods on the old feudal allotments which had been cut in 1861 for the benefit of the landlords. And, on the other hand, agriculture was in the hands of the landlords who in Central Russia cultivated the land by the labour, the wooden ploughs, and the horses of the peasants in return for the "cut-off lands",[54] meadows, access to watering-places, etc. To all intents and purposes this was the old feudal system of economy. Throughout this period the political system of Russia was also permeated with feudalism. This is evident from the constitution of the state prior to the first moves to change it in 1905, from the predominant influence of the landed nobility on state affairs and from the unlimited power of the officials, who also for the most part—especially the higher ranks—came from the landed nobility.

After 1861 this old partriarchal Russia began rapidly to disintegrate under the influence of world capitalism. The peasants were starving, dying off, being ruined as never before, fleeing to the towns and abandoning the soil. There was a boom in the construction of railways, mills and factories, thanks to the "cheap labour" of the ruined peasants. Big finance capital was developing in Russia together with large-scale commerce and industry.

It was this rapid, painful, drastic demolition of all the old "pillars" of old Russia that was reflected in the works of Tolstoy the artist, and in the views of Tolstoy the thinker.

Tolstoy had a surpassing knowledge of rural Russia, the mode of life of the landlords and peasants. In his artistic productions he gave descriptions of this life that are numbered among the best productions of world literature. The drastic demolition of all the "old pillars" of rural Russia sharpened his attention, deepened his interest in what was going on around him, and led to a radical change in his whole world outlook. By birth and education Tolstoy belonged to the highest landed nobility in Russia—he broke with all the customary views of this environment and in his later works attacked with fierce criticism all the contemporary state, church, social and economic institutions which were based on enslavement of the masses, on their poverty, on the ruin of the peasants and the petty proprietors in general, on the coercion and hypocrisy which permeated all contemporary life from top to bottom.

Tolstoy's criticism was not new. He said nothing that had not been said long before him both in European and in Russian literature by friends of the working people. But the uniqueness of Tolstoy's criticism and its historical significance lie in the fact that it expressed, with a power such as is possessed only by artists of genius, the radical change in the views of the broadest masses of the people in the Russia of this period, namely, rural, peasant Russia. For Tolstoy's criticism of contemporary institutions differs from the criticism of the same institutions by representatives of the modern labour movement in the fact that Tolstoy's point of view was that of the patriarchal, naïve peasant, whose psychology Tolstoy introduced into his criticism and his doctrine. Tolstoy's criticism is marked by such emotional power, such passion, convincingness, freshness, sincerity and fearlessness in striving to "go to the roots", to find the real cause of the afflictions of the masses, just because this criticism really expresses a sharp change in the ideas of millions of peasants, who had only just emerged from feudalism into freedom, and saw that this freedom meant new horrors of ruin, death by starvation, a homeless life among the lower strata of the city population, and so on and so forth. Tolstoy mirrored their sentiments so faithfully that he imported their naïveté into his own doctrine, their alienation from political life, their mysticism, their desire to keep aloof from the world, "non-resistance to evil", their impotent imprecations against capitalism and the "power of money". The protest of millions of peasants and their desperation—these were combined in Tolstoy's doctrine.

The representatives of the modern labour movement find that they have plenty to protest against but nothing to despair about. Despair is typical of the classes which are perishing, but the class of wage-workers is growing inevitably, developing and becoming strong in every capitalist society, Russia included. Despair is typical of those who do not understand the causes of evil, see no way out, and are incapable of struggle. The modern industrial proletariat does not belong to the category of such classes.

Nash Put No. 7,
November 28, 1910
Signed: V. I-in

Collected Works,
Vol. 16, pp. 330-32

Tolstoy and the Proletarian Struggle

Tolstoy's indictment of the ruling classes was made with tremendous power and sincerity; with absolute clearness he laid bare the inner falsity of all those institutions by which modern society is maintained: the church, the law courts, militarism, "lawful" wedlock, bourgeois science. But his doctrine proved to be in complete contradiction to the life, work and struggle of the grave-digger of the modern social system, the proletariat. Whose then was the point of view reflected in the teachings of Leo Tolstoy? Through his lips there spoke that multitudinous mass of the Russian people who *already* detest the masters of modern life but have not *yet* advanced to the point of intelligent, consistent, thoroughgoing, implacable struggle against them.

The history and the outcome of the great Russian revolution have shown that such precisely was the mass that found itself *between* the class-conscious, socialist proletariat and the out-and-out defenders of the old regime. This mass, consisting mainly of the peasantry, showed in the revolution how great was its hatred of the old, how keenly it felt all the inflictions of the modern regime, how great within it was the spontaneous yearning to be rid of them and to find a better life.

At the same time, however, this mass showed in the revolution that it was not politically conscious enough in its hatred, that it was not consistent in its struggle and that its quest for a better life was confined within narrow bounds.

This great human ocean, agitated to its very depths, with all its weaknesses and all its strong features found its reflection in the doctrine of Tolstoy.

By studying the literary works of Leo Tolstoy the Russian working class will learn to know its enemies better, but in examining the *doctrine* of Tolstoy, the whole Russian people will have to understand where their own weakness lies, the weakness which did not allow them to carry the cause of their emancipation to its conclusion. This must be understood in order to go forward.

This advance is impeded by all those who declare Tolstoy a "universal conscience", a "teacher of life". This is a lie that the liberals are deliberately spreading in their desire to utilise the anti-revolutionary aspect of Tolstoy's doctrine. This lie about Tolstoy as a "teacher of life" is being repeated after the liberals by some former Social-Democrats.

The Russian people will secure their emancipation only when they realise that it is not from Tolstoy they must learn to win a better life but from the class the significance of which Tolstoy did not understand, and which alone is capable of destroying the old world which Tolstoy hated. That class is the proletariat.

Rabochaya Gazeta No. 2,
December 18 (31), 1910

Collected Works,
Vol. 16, pp. 353-54

Leo Tolstoy and his Epoch

The epoch to which Leo Tolstoy belongs and which is reflected in such bold relief both in his brilliant literary works and in his teachings began after 1861 and lasted until 1905. True, Tolstoy commenced his literary career earlier and it ended later, but it was during this period, whose transitional nature gave rise to *all* the distinguishing features of Tolstoy's works and of Tolstoyism, that he fully matured both as an artist and as a thinker.

Through Levin, a character in *Anna Karenina*, Tolstoy very vividly expressed the nature of the turn in Russia's history that took place during this half-century.

"...Talk about the harvest, hiring labourers, and so forth, which, as Levin knew, it was the custom to regard as something very low, ... now seemed to Levin to be the only important thing. 'This, perhaps, was unimportant under serfdom, or is unimportant in England. In both cases the conditions are definite; but here today, when everything has been turned upside down and is only just taking shape again, the question of how these conditions will shape is the only important question in Russia,' mused Levin." (*Collected Works*, Vol. X, p. 137.)

"Here in Russia everything has now been turned upside down and is only just taking shape,"—it is difficult to imagine a more apt characterisation of the period 1861-1905. What "was turned upside down" is familiar, or at least well known, to every Russian. It was serfdom, and the whole of the "old order" that went with it. What "is just taking shape" is totally unknown, alien and incomprehensible to the broad masses of the population. Tolstoy conceived this bourgeois order which was "only just taking shape" vaguely, in the form of a bogey—England. Truly, a bogey, because Tolstoy rejects, on principle, so to speak, any attempt to investigate the features of the social system in this "England", the connection between this system and the domination of capital, the role played by money, the rise and development of exchange. Like the Narodniks,[55] he refuses to see, he shuts his eyes to, and dismisses the thought that what is "taking shape" in Russia is none other than the bourgeois system.

It is true that, if not the "only important" question, then certainly one of the most important from the standpoint of the immediate tasks of all social and political activities in Russia in the period of 1861-1905 (and in our times, too), was that of "what shape" this system would take, this bourgeois system that had assumed extremely varied forms in "England", Germany, America, France, and so forth. But such a definite, concretely historical presentation of the question was something absolutely foreign to Tolstoy. He reasons in the abstract, he recognises only the standpoint of the "eternal" principles of morality, the eternal truths of religion, failing to realise that this standpoint is merely the ideological reflection of the old ("turned upside down") order, the feudal order, the way of the life of the Oriental peoples.

In *Lucerne* (written in 1857), Tolstoy declares that to regard "civilisation" as a boon is an "imaginary concept" which "destroys in human nature the instinctive, most blissful primitive need for good". "We have only one infallible guide," exclaims Tolstoy, "the Universal Spirit that permeates us." *(Collected Works,* Vol. II, p. 125.)

In *The Slavery of Our Times* (written in 1900), Tolstoy, repeating still more zealously these appeals to the Universal Spirit, declares that political economy is a "pseudoscience" because it takes as the "pattern" "little England, where conditions are most exceptional", instead of taking as a pattern "the conditions of men in the whole world throughout the whole of history". What this "whole world" is like is revealed to us in the article "Progress and the Definition of Education" (1862). Tolstoy counters the opinion of the "historians" that progress is "a general law for mankind" by referring to "the whole of what is known as the Orient" (IV, 162). "There is no general law of human progress," says Tolstoy, "and this is proved by the quiescence of the Oriental peoples."

Tolstoyism, in its real historical content, is an ideology of an Oriental, an Asiatic order. Hence the asceticism, the non-resistance to evil, the profound notes of pessimism, the conviction that "everything is nothing, everything is a material

nothing" ("The Meaning of Life", p. 52), and faith in the
"Spirit", in "the beginning of everything", and that man, in his
relation to this beginning, is merely a "labourer ... allotted the
task of saving his own soul", etc. Tolstoy is true to this ideology
in his *Kreutzer Sonata* too when he says: "the emancipation of
woman lies not in colleges and not in parliaments, but in the
bedroom", and in the article written in 1862, in which he says
that universities train only "irritable, debilitated liberals" for
whom "the people have no use at all", who are "uselessly torn
from their former environment", "find no place in life", and
so forth (IV, 136-37).

Pessimism, non-resistance, appeals to the "Spirit" constitute
an ideology inevitable in an epoch when the whole of the old
order "has been turned upside down", and when the masses,
who have been brought up under this old order, who imbibed
with their mother's milk the principles, the habits, the
traditions and beliefs of this order, do not and cannot see *what
kind* of a new order is "taking shape", *what* social forces are
"shaping" it and how, what social forces are *capable* of bringing
release from the incalculable and exceptionally acute distress
that is characteristic of epochs of "upheaval".

The period of 1862-1904 was just such a period of upheaval
in Russia, a period in which before everyone's eyes the old
order collapsed, never to be restored, in which the new system
was only just taking shape; the social forces shaping the new
system first manifested themselves on a broad, nation-wide
scale, in mass public action in the most varied field only in
1905. And the 1905 events in Russia were followed by
analogous events in a number of countries in that very
"Orient" to the "quiescence" of which Tolstoy referred in
1862. The year 1905 marked the beginning of the end of
"Oriental" quiescence. Precisely for this reason that year
marked the historical end of Tolstoyism, the end of an epoch
that could give rise to Tolstoy's teachings and in which they
were inevitable, not as something individual, not as a caprice or
a fad, but as the ideology of the conditions of life under which
millions and millions actually found themselves for a certain
period of time.

Tolstoy's doctrine is certainly utopian and in content is
reactionary in the most precise and most profound sense of the
word. But that certainly does not mean that the doctrine was
not socialistic or that it did not contain critical elements capable
of providing valuable material for the enlightenment of the
advanced classes.

There are various kinds of socialism. In all countries where the capitalist mode of production prevails there is the socialism which expresses the ideology of the class that is going to take the place of the bourgeoisie; and there is the socialism that expresses the ideology of the classes that are going to be replaced by the bourgeoisie. Feudal socialism, for example, is socialism of the latter type, and the nature of *this* socialism was appraised long ago, over sixty years ago, by Marx, simultaneously with his appraisal of other types of socialism.[56]

Furthermore, critical elements are inherent in Tolstoy's utopian doctrine, just as they are inherent in many utopian systems. But we must not forget Marx's profound observation to the effect that the value of critical elements in utopian socialism "bears an inverse relation to historical development". The more the activities of the social forces which are "shaping" the new Russia and bringing release from present-day social evils develop and assume a definite character, the more rapidly is critical-utopian socialism "losing all practical value and all theoretical justification".[57]

A quarter of a century ago, the critical elements in Tolstoy's doctrine might at times have been of practical value for some sections of the population *in spite of* its reactionary and utopian features. This could not have been the case during, say, the last decade, because historical development had made considerable progress between the eighties and the end of the last century. In our days, since the series of events mentioned above has put an end to "Oriental" quiescence, in our days, when the consciously reactionary ideas of *Vekhi* (reactionary in the narrow-class, selfishly-class sense) have become so enormously widespread among the liberal bourgeoisie and when these ideas have infected even a section of those who were almost Marxists and have created a liquidationist trend[58]—in our days, the most direct and most profound harm is caused by every attempt to idealise Tolstoy's doctrine, to justify or to mitigate his "non-resistance", his appeals to the "Spirit", his exhortations for "moral self-perfection", his doctrine of "conscience" and universal "love", his preaching of asceticism and quietism, and so forth.

Zvezda No. 6, January 22,
1911
Signed: V. *Ilyin*

Collected Works,
Vol. 17, pp. 49-53

In Memory of Herzen

One hundred years have elapsed since Herzen's birth. The whole of liberal Russia is paying homage to him, studiously evading, however, the serious questions of socialism, and taking pains to conceal that which distinguished Herzen the *revolutionary* from a liberal. The Right-wing press, too, is commemorating the Herzen centenary, falsely asserting that in his last years Herzen renounced revolution. And in the orations on Herzen that are made by the liberals and Narodniks abroad, phrase-mongering reigns supreme.

The working-class party should commemorate the Herzen centenary, not for the sake of philistine glorification, but for the purpose of making clear its own tasks and ascertaining the place actually held in history by this writer who played a great part in paving the way for the Russian revolution.

Herzen belonged to the generation of revolutionaries among the nobility and landlords of the first half of the last century. The nobility gave Russia the Birons and Arakcheyevs, innumerable "drunken officers, bullies, gamblers, heroes of fairs, masters of hounds, roisterers, floggers, pimps", as well as amiable Manilovs.[59] "But," wrote Herzen, "among them developed the men of December 14,[60] a phalanx of heroes reared, like Romulus and Remus, on the milk of a wild beast.... They were veritable titans, hammered out of pure steel from head to foot, comrades-in-arms who deliberately went to certain death in order to awaken the young generation to a new life and to purify the children born in an environment of tyranny and servility."[61]

Herzen was one of those children. The uprising of the Decembrists awakened and "purified" him. In the feudal Russia of the forties of the nineteenth century, he rose to a height which placed him on a level with the greatest thinkers of

his time. He assimilated Hegel's dialectics. He realised that it
was "the algebra of revolution". He went further than Hegel,
following Feuerbach to materialism. The first of his *Letters on
the Study of Nature*, "Empiricism and Idealism", written in
1844, reveals to us a thinker who even now stands head and
shoulders above the multitude of modern empiricist natural
scientists and the host of present-day idealist and semi-idealist
philosophers. Herzen came right up to dialectical materialism,
and halted—before historical materialism.

It was this "halt" that caused Herzen's spiritual shipwreck
after the defeat of the revolution of 1848. Herzen had left
Russia, and observed this revolution at close range. He was at
that time a democrat, a revolutionary, a socialist. But his
"socialism" was one of the countless forms and varieties of
bourgeois and petty-bourgeois socialism of the period of 1848,
which were dealt their death-blow in the June days of that year.
In point of fact, it was not socialism at all, but so many
sentimental phrases, benevolent visions, which were the
expression *at that time* of the revolutionary character of the
bourgeois democrats, as well as of the proletariat, which had
not yet freed itself from the influence of those democrats.

Herzen's spiritual shipwreck, his deep scepticism and
pessimism after 1848, was a shipwreck of the *bourgeois illusions*
of socialism. Herzen's spiritual drama was a product and
reflection of that epoch in world history when the revolutionary character of the bourgeois democrats was *already* passing
away (in Europe), while the revolutionary character of the
socialist proletariat had *not yet* matured. This is something the
Russian knights of liberal verbiage, who are now covering up
their counter-revolutionary nature by florid phrases about
Herzen's scepticism, did not and could not understand. With
these knights, who betrayed the Russian revolution of 1905,
and have even forgotten to think of the great name of
revolutionary, scepticism is a form of transition from democracy
to liberalism, to that toadying, vile, foul and brutal liberalism
which shot down the workers in 1848, restored the shattered
thrones and applauded Napoleon III, and which Herzen
cursed, unable to understand its class nature.

With Herzen, scepticism was a form of transition from the
illusion of a bourgeois democracy that is "above classes" to the
grim, inexorable and invincible class struggle of the proletariat.
The proof: the *Letters to an Old Comrade*—to Bakunin—written by Herzen in 1869, a year before his death. In them
Herzen breaks with the anarchist Bakunin. True, Herzen still

sees this break as a mere disagreement on tactics and not as a gulf between the world outlook of the proletarian who is confident of the victory of his class and that of the petty bourgeois who has despaired of his salvation. True enough, in these letters as well, Herzen repeats the old bourgeois-democratic phrases to the effect that socialism must preach "a sermon addressed equally to workman and master, to farmer and townsman". Nevertheless, in breaking with Bakunin, Herzen turned his gaze, not to liberalism, but to the *International*—to the International led by Marx, to the International which had begun to "*rally the legions*" of the proletariat, to unite "*the world of labour*", which is "abandoning the world of those who enjoy without working".[62]

Failing as he did to understand the bourgeois-democratic character of the entire movement of 1848 and of all the forms of pre-Marxian socialism, Herzen was still less able to understand the bourgeois nature of the Russian revolution. Herzen is the founder of "Russian" socialism, of "Narodism". He saw "socialism" in the emancipation of the peasants *with land*, in communal land tenure and in the peasant idea of "the right to land". He set forth his pet ideas on this subject an untold number of times.

Actually, there is *not a grain* of socialism in this doctrine of Herzen's, as, indeed, in the whole of Russian Narodism, including the faded Narodism of the present-day Socialist-Revolutionaries.[63] Like the various forms of "the socialism of 1848" in the West, this is the same sort of sentimental phrases, of benevolent visions, in which is expressed the *revolutionism* of the bourgeois peasant democracy in Russia. The more land the peasants would have received in 1861 and the less they would have had to pay for it, the more would the power of the feudal landlords have been undermined and the more rapidly, freely and widely would capitalism have developed in Russia. The idea of the "right to land" and of "equalised division of the land" is nothing but a formulation of the revolutionary aspiration for equality cherished by the peasants who are fighting for the complete overthrow of the power of the landlords, for the complete abolition of landlordism.

This was fully proved by the revolution of 1905: on the one hand, the proletariat came out quite independently at the head of the revolutionary struggle, having founded the Social-

Democratic Labour Party; on the other hand, the revolutionary peasants (the Trudoviks[64] and the Peasant Union[65]), who fought for every form of the abolition of landlordism even to "the abolition of private landownership", fought precisely as proprietors, as small entrepreneurs.

Today, the controversy over the "socialist nature" of the right to land, and so on, serves only to *obscure* and cover up the really important and serious historical question concerning the difference of *interests* of the liberal bourgeoisie and the revolutionary peasantry in the Russian *bourgeois* revolution; in other words, the question of the liberal and the democratic, the "compromising" (monarchist) and the republican trends manifested in that revolution. This is exactly the question posed by Herzen's *Kolokol*,[66] if we turn our attention to the essence of the matter and not to the words, if we investigate the class struggle as the basis of "theories" and doctrines and not vice versa.

Herzen founded a free Russian press abroad, and that is the great service rendered by him. *Polyarnaya Zvezda*[67] took up the tradition of the Decembrists. *Kolokol* (1857-67) championed the emancipation of the peasants with might and main. The slavish silence was broken.

But Herzen came from a landlord, aristocratic milieu. He left Russia in 1847; he had not seen the revolutionary people and could have no faith in it. Hence his liberal appeal to the "upper ranks". Hence his innumerable sugary letters in *Kolokol* addressed to Alexander II the Hangman, which today one cannot read without revulsion. Chernyshevsky, Dobrolyubov and Serno-Solovyevich, who represented the new generation of revolutionary raznochintsi,[68] were a thousand times right when they reproached Herzen for these departures from democracy *to* liberalism. However, it must be said in fairness to Herzen that, much as he vacillated between democracy and liberalism, the democrat in him gained the upper hand nonetheless.

When Kavelin, one of the most repulsive exponents of liberal servility — who at one time was enthusiastic about *Kolokol* precisely because of its *liberal* tendencies — rose in arms against a constitution, attacked revolutionary agitation, rose against "violence" and appeals for it, and began to preach tolerance, Herzen *broke* with that liberal sage. Herzen turned upon Kavelin's "meagre, absurd, harmful pamphlet" written "for the private guidance of a government pretending to be liberal"; he denounced Kavelin's "sentimen-

tal political maxims" which represented "the Russian people as brutes and the government as an embodiment of intelligence".
Kolokol printed an article entitled "Epitaph", which lashed out against "professors weaving the rotten cobweb of their superciliously paltry ideas, ex-professors, once open-hearted and subsequently embittered because they saw that the healthy youth could not sympathise with their scrofulous thinking".[69] Kavelin at once recognised himself in this portrait.

When Chernyshevsky was arrested, the vile liberal Kavelin wrote: "I see nothing shocking in the arrests ... the revolutionary party considers all means fair to overthrow the government, and the latter defends itself by its own means." As if in retort to this Cadet, Herzen wrote concerning Chernyshevsky's trial: "And here are wretches, weed-like people, jellyfish, who say that we must not reprove the gang of robbers and scoundrels that is governing us."[70]

When the liberal Turgenev wrote a private letter to Alexander II assuring him of his loyalty, and donated two goldpieces for the soldiers wounded during the suppression of the Polish insurrection, *Kolokol* wrote of "the grey-haired Magdalen (of the masculine gender) who wrote to the tsar to tell him that she knew no sleep because she was tormented by the thought that the tsar was not aware of the repentance that had overcome her".[71] And Turgenev at once recognised himself.

When the whole band of Russian liberals scurried away from Herzen for his defence of Poland, when the whole of "educated society" turned its back on *Kolokol*, Herzen was not dismayed. He went on championing the freedom of Poland and lashing the suppressors, the butchers, the hangmen in the service of Alexander II. Herzen saved the honour of Russian democracy. "We have saved the honour of the Russian name," he wrote to Turgenev, "and for doing so we have suffered at the hands of the slavish majority."[72]

When it was reported that a serf peasant had killed a landlord for an attempt to dishonour the serf's betrothed, Herzen commented in *Kolokol*: "Well done!" When it was reported that army officers would be appointed to supervise the "peaceable" progress of "emancipation", Herzen wrote: "The first wise colonel who with his unit joins the peasants instead of crushing them, will ascend the throne of the Romanovs." When Colonel Reitern shot himself in Warsaw (1860) because he did not want to be a helper of hangmen, Herzen wrote: "If there is to be any shooting, the ones to be shot should be the generals who give orders to fire upon unarmed people." When fifty peasants were massacred in Bezdna, and their leader, Anton Petrov, was executed (April 12, 1861), Herzen wrote in *Kolokol*:

> "If only my words could reach you, toiler and sufferer of the land of Russia!... How well I would teach you to despise your spiritual shepherds, placed over you by the St. Petersburg Synod and a German tsar.... You hate the landlord, you hate the official, you fear them, and rightly so; but you still believe in the tsar and the bishop ... do not believe them. The tsar is with them, and they are his men. It is him you now see — you, the father of a youth murdered in Bezdna, and you, the son of a father murdered in Penza.... Your shepherds are as ignorant as you, and as poor.... Such was another Anthony (not Bishop Anthony, but Anton of Bezdna) who suffered for you in Kazan.... The dead bodies of your martyrs will not perform forty-eight miracles, and praying to them will not cure a toothache; but their living memory may produce one miracle — your emancipation." [73]

This shows how infamously and vilely Herzen is being slandered by our liberals entrenched in the slavish "legal" press, who magnify Herzen's weak points and say nothing about his strong points. It was not Herzen's fault but his misfortune that he could not see the revolutionary people in Russia itself in the 1840s. When *in the sixties* he came to see the revolutionary people, he sided fearlessly with the revolutionary democracy against liberalism. He fought for a victory of the people over tsarism, not for a deal between the liberal bourgeoisie and the landlords' tsar. He raised aloft the banner of revolution.

In commemorating Herzen, we clearly see the three generations, the three classes, that were active in the Russian revolution. At first it was nobles and landlords, the Decembrists and Herzen. These revolutionaries formed but a narrow group. They were very far removed from the people. But their effort was not in vain. The Decembrists awakened Herzen. Herzen began the work of revolutionary agitation.

This work was taken up, extended, strengthened, and tempered by the revolutionary raznochintsi — from Chernyshevsky to the heroes of Narodnaya Volya.[74] The range of fighters widened; their contact with the people became closer. "The young helmsmen of the gathering storm" is what Herzen called them. But it was not yet the storm itself.

The storm is the movement of the masses themselves. The proletariat, the only class that is thoroughly revolutionary, rose at the head of the masses and for the first time aroused millions of peasants to open revolutionary struggle. The first onslaught in this storm took place in 1905. The next is beginning to develop under our very eyes.

In commemorating Herzen, the proletariat is learning from his example to appreciate the great importance of revolutionary theory. It is learning that selfless devotion to the revolution and revolutionary propaganda among the people are not wasted even if long decades divide the sowing from the harvest. It is learning to ascertain the role of the various classes in the Russian and in the international revolution. Enriched by these lessons, the proletariat will fight its way to a free alliance with the socialist workers of all lands, having crushed that loathsome monster, the tsarist monarchy, against which Herzen was the first to raise the great banner of struggle by addressing his *free Russian word* to the masses.

Sotsial-Demokrat No. 26,   *Collected Works*,
May 8 (April 25), 1912   Vol. 18, pp. 25-31

Lenin, Demyan Bedny and F. Panfilov, delegate
to the Congress
of the Russian Communist Party (Bolsheviks),
during the Congress. Photo, 1919

From Yet Another Anti-Democratic Campaign

That ill-famed publication, *Vekhi*,[75] which was a tremendous success in liberal-bourgeois society, a society thoroughly imbued with renegade tendencies, was not adequately countered, nor appraised deeply enough, in the democratic camp.

This was partly due to the fact that the success of *Vekhi* occurred at a time of almost complete suppression of the "open" democratic press.

Now Mr. Shchepetev comes forward in *Russkaya Mysl*[76] (August) with a refurbished edition of *Vekhi* ideas. This is perfectly natural on the part of a *Vekhi* organ edited by Mr. P. B. Struve, leader of the renegades. But it will be just as natural for the democrats, particularly the worker democrats, to make up now for at least a little of what they owe the *Vekhi* people.

I

Mr. Shchepetev's utterances take the form of a modest "Letter from France" — *about the Russians in Paris*. But behind this modest form there is actually a very definite "discussion" of the Russian revolution of 1905 and the Russian democracy.

"That disturbing [Oh! Disturbing *to whom*, esteemed liberal?], troubled and thoroughly confused year 1905 is fresh in everyone's memory...."

"Troubled and thoroughly confused"! What dirt and dregs a person must have in his soul to be able to write like that! The German opponents of the revolution of 1848 called that year the "crazy" year. The same idea, or rather the same dull, base fright, is expressed by the Russian Cadet writing in *Russkaya Mysl*.

3—70

We shall counter him only with a few facts, the most
objective and most "unpretentious" ones. That year wages
were rising as they had never done before. Land rent was
dropping. All forms of association of workers, including even
domestic servants, were making unprecedented progress.
Millions of inexpensive publications on political subjects were
being read by the people, the masses, the crowd, the "lower
ranks", as avidly as no one had ever read in Russia until then.
    Nekrasov exclaimed, in times long past:

> *Ah, will there ever be a time*
> *(Come soon, come soon, O longed-for day!)*
> *When people will not buy the books*
> *Of Blücher or some silly lord,*
> *But Gogol and Belinsky's works*
> *From market stalls bring home.* [77]

The "time" longed for by one of the old Russian democrats
came. Merchants stopped dealing in oats and engaged in more
profitable business — the sale of inexpensive democratic pamphlets. Democratic books became goods for the *market*. The
ideas of Belinsky and Gogol — which endeared these authors
to Nekrasov, as indeed to any decent person in Russia — ran
through the whole of that new market literature.
    How "troublesome"! cried the liberal pig, which deems itself
educated, but in fact is dirty, repulsive, overfat and smug,
when *in actual fact* it saw the "people" bringing home from the
market — Belinsky's letter to Gogol.
    And, strictly speaking, it is, after all, a letter from an
"intellectual", announced *Vekhi* to thunderous applause from
Rozanov of *Novoye Vremya* and from Anthony, Bishop of
Volhynia.
    What a disgraceful sight! a democrat from among the best
Narodniks will say. What an instructive sight! we will add. How
it sobers up those who took a *sentimental* view of democratic
issues, how it *steels* all the living and strong democratic
elements, mercilessly sweeping aside the rotten illusions of the
Oblomov-minded!
    It is very useful for anyone who has ever been enchanted
with liberalism to be disenchanted with it. And he who wishes
to recall the early history of Russian liberalism will certainly see
in the liberal Kavelin's attitude towards the democrat Chernyshevsky the exact prototype of the attitude adopted by the
Cadet *Party* of the liberal bourgeoisie towards the Russian
democratic *movement of the masses*. The liberal bourgeoisie in

Russia has "found itself", or rather its tail. Is it not time the democrats in Russia found their head?

It is particularly intolerable to see individuals like Shchepetev, Struve, Gredeskul, Izgoyev and the rest of the Cadet fraternity clutching at the coat-tails of Nekrasov, Shchedrin and others. Nekrasov, who was weak as a person, wavered between Chernyshevsky and the liberals, but all his sympathy went to Chernyshevsky. Out of the very same personal weakness, Nekrasov occasionally sounded the false note of liberal servility, but he himself bitterly deplored his "falsity" and *repented* of it *in public:*

> *I never sold my lyre, although at times,*
> *When pressed by unrelenting fate,*
> *False notes would sound among my rhymes.* [78]

"False notes" is what Nekrasov himself called the liberal servility he was occasionally guilty of. As for Shchedrin, he mocked mercilessly at the liberals, whom he branded for ever by the formula "conformably to villainy".[79]

How outdated this formula is as applied to Shchepetev, Gredeskul and the other * *Vekhi* people! The point now is by no means that these gentlemen must *conform* to villainy. Not by a long shot! They have created *their own theory* of "villainy" on their own initiative and in their own fashion, proceeding from neo-Kantianism [80] and other fashionable "European" theories.

III

Mr. Shchepetev devotes most space to sketches of life in exile. To find an analogy of these sketches, one would have to dig up *Russky Vestnik* [81] of Katkov's day and take from it novels portraying high-minded Marshals of the Nobility,[82] good-natured and contented muzhiks, and disgruntled brutes, scoundrels and monsters called revolutionaries.

Mr. Shchepetev has observed Paris (assuming that he has) with the eyes of a philistine embittered against the democratic movement, who could see nothing but "unrest" in the appearance in Russia of the first democratic pamphlets for the masses.

It is known that everyone sees abroad what he chooses to. Or, in other words, everyone sees in new conditions *his own self.*

---

* The objection will probably be raised that Gredeskul, as well as Milyukov and Co., *argued* with *Vekhi.* So they did, but they *remained* Vekhists for all that. See, inter alia, *Pravda* No. 85. (See Lenin, *Collected Works*, Vol. 18, pp. 254-55).— *Ed.*

3*

A member of the Black Hundreds sees abroad splendid landlords, generals and diplomats. A secret police agent sees there the noblest policemen. A liberal Russian renegade sees in Paris well-meaning concierges and "efficient" * shopkeepers who teach the Russian revolutionary that among them "humanitarian and altruistic sentiments had too much suppressed personal requirements, often to the detriment of the general progress and cultural advancement of the whole of our country".**

A lackey in spirit is naturally keen above all else on the gossip and petty scandals prevailing in the servants' room. It goes without saying that a shopkeeper or a lackey-minded concierge takes no notice of the ideological issues discussed at Paris meetings and in the Paris Russian-language press. How can he see, indeed, that this press raised, as early as 1908, for example, the very same questions concerning the social nature of the June Third regime,[83] the class roots of the new trends among the democrats, and so on, as found their way much later, and in much narrower and more distorted (and curtailed) form, into the press "protected" by reinforced security measures?

Shopkeepers and lackeys, however "intellectual" the garb in which people with such a mentality array themselves, cannot notice and grasp these questions. If a particular lackey is called a "publicist" contributing to a liberal magazine, he, that "publicist", will pass over in complete silence the great ideological questions which are posed openly and clearly nowhere but in Paris. On the other hand, this "publicist" will tell you in detail all that is well known in the servants' rooms.

He, this noble Cadet, will tell you in the magazine of the most noble Mr. Struve, that a hapless emigrant-prostitute was evicted from "the flat of a very well-known woman revolutionary in Paris", "not without help from the police"; that the "unemployed" again made a row at a charity ball; that a copyist in a house familiar to Mr. Shchepetev "had rather a considerable sum of money advanced to him and then began to absent himself"; that the exiles "rise at noon and go to bed after 1 or 2 a.m., and there are visitors and noise and arguments and disorder all day long".

All this the lackey magazine of the Cadet Mr. Struve will tell you in detail and with illustrations, with gusto and spiced with

---

* See Mr. Shchepetev's article, p. 139 (*Russkaya Mysl* No. 8, 1912).
** Ibid., p. 153.

pepper—just as well as Menshikov and Rozanov of *Novoye Vremya* do it.

"Give me money or I'll punch you on the jaw—this is the unambiguously hostile form which the relations between the upper and lower ranks of the exiles have taken. True, this formula has not become widespread, and 'the extreme trend among the lower ranks' has become represented [this is how the educated Cadet writes in Mr. Struve's magazine!] by a mere couple of dozens of very doubtful elements that are perhaps even guided by a skilful hand from outside."

Pause at this statement, reader, and think of the difference between an ordinary lackey and a lackey-minded publicist. Ordinary lackeys—meaning the bulk, of course, which does not include those politically-conscious elements that have already adopted a class point of view and are seeking a way out of their lackey's position—are unsophisticated, uneducated, and often illiterate and ignorant; it is pardonable for them to have a naïve passion for relating whatever reaches them more easily than anything else, and is closest and clearest to them. Lackey-minded publicists, on the other hand, are "educated" persons who are well received in all the finest drawing-rooms. They are aware that the number of common blackmailers among the exiles is very insignificant ("a couple of dozens" for *thousands* of exiles). They even realise that these blackmailers "are perhaps *guided*" by a *"skilful hand"*—from the tea-room of the Union of the Russian People.[84]

And because he realises all this, the lackey-minded publicist operates as befits the "educated". He certainly knows how to cover up his tracks and make the most of his goods! He is not a venal hack of the Black Hundreds [85]—nothing of the kind. He *"himself"* has even pointed out that *perhaps* someone is guiding the dozen or two of blackmailers, but at the same time it is *precisely* and *solely* those blackmailers rows and the absenteeism of copyists that he tells about!

The *Novoye Vremya* school for *"writers"* of *Russkaya Mysl* has not gone to waste. Suvorin of *Novoye Vremya* boasted that he had never received any subsidies—he *merely* "knew himself" how to hit the right tone.

Russkaya Mysl receives no subsidies—God forfend! It *merely* "knows itself" how to hit the right tone, a tone pleasing to the ear of the *Novoye Vremya* people and Guchkov's "stalwarts".

Nevskaya Zvezda Nos. 24 and 25, September 2 and 9, 1912 Signed: *V. I.*

Collected Works, Vol. 18, pp. 312-14, 317-19

Eugène Pottier

The 25th Anniversary of His Death

In November of last year — 1912 — it was twenty-five years since the death of the French worker-poet, Eugène Pottier, author of the famous proletarian song, the *Internationale* ("Arise ye starvelings from your slumbers", etc.). This song has been translated into all European and other languages. In whatever country a class-conscious worker finds himself, wherever fate may cast him, however much he may feel himself a stranger, without language, without friends, far from his native country — he can find himself comrades and friends by the familiar refrain of the *Internationale*.

The workers of all countries have adopted the song of their foremost fighter, the proletarian poet, and have made it the world-wide song of the proletariat.

And so the workers of all countries now honour the memory of Eugène Pottier. His wife and daughter are still alive and living in poverty, as the author of the *Internationale* lived all his life. He was born in Paris on October 4, 1816. He was 14 when he composed his first song, and it was called: *Long Live Liberty!* In 1848 he was a fighter on the barricades in the workers' great battle against the bourgeoisie.

Pottier was born into a poor family, and all his life remained a poor man, a proletarian, earning his bread as a packer and later by tracing patterns on fabrics.

From 1840 onwards, he responded to all great events in the life of France with militant songs, awakening the consciousness of the backward, calling on the workers to unite, castigating the bourgeoisie and the bourgeois governments of France.

In the days of the great Paris Commune (1871), Pottier was elected a member. Of the 3,600 votes cast, he received 3,352. He took part in all the activities of the Commune, that first proletarian government.

The fall of the Commune forced Pottier to flee to England, and then to America. His famous song, the *Internationale*, was written in *June 1871*—you might say, the day after the bloody defeat in May.

The Commune was crushed—but Pottier's *Internationale* spread its ideas throughout the world, and it is now more alive than ever before.

In 1876, in exile, Pottier wrote a poem, *The Workingmen of America to the Workingmen of France*. In it he described the life of workers under the yoke of capitalism, their poverty, their back-breaking toil, their exploitation, and their firm confidence in the coming victory of their cause.

It was only nine years after the Commune that Pottier returned to France, where he at once joined the Workers' Party. The first volume of his verse was published in 1884, the second volume, entitled *Revolutionary Songs*, came out in 1887.

A number of other songs by the worker-poet were published after his death. .

On November 8, 1887, the workers of Paris carried the remains of Eugène Pottier to the Père Lachaise cemetery, where the executed Communards are buried. The police savagely attacked the crowd in an effort to snatch the red banner. A vast crowd took part in the civic funeral. On all sides there were shouts of "Long live Pottier!"

Pottier died in poverty. But he left a memorial which is truly more enduring than the handiwork of man. He was one of the greatest *propagandists by song*. When he was composing his first song, the number of worker socialists ran to tens, at most. Eugène Pottier's historic song is now known to tens of millions of proletarians.

Pravda No. 2, January 3, 1913   *Collected Works,*
Signed: *N. L.*   Vol. 36, pp. 223-24

The Development of Workers' Choirs In Germany

The workers' choral societies of Germany recently celebrated a kind of jubilee: the number of worker-singers reached 100,000, with a total membership of 165,000 in these societies. The number of women workers in them is 11,000.

The workers' choirs have their own periodical, *Arbeiter-Sänger Zeitung*, which began to appear regularly only in 1907.

The beginnings of the workers' choral societies date back to the 1860s. A choral section was founded in the Leipzig Artisans' Educational Society, and one of its members was August Bebel.

Ferdinand Lassalle attached great importance to the organising of workers' choirs. At his insistence, members of the General Association of German Workers[86] founded, at Frankfurt am Main in 1863, a workers' society called the Choral Union. This Union held its meetings in the dark and smoky back room of a Frankfurt tavern. The room was lit with tallow candles.

There were 12 members of the Union. Once, when Lassalle, on one of his speaking tours, stayed overnight at Frankfurt, these 12 worker-singers sang him a song by the well-known poet Herwegh, whom Lassalle had long been urging to write the words for a workers' chorus.

In 1892, after the repeal of the Anti-Socialist Law,[87] there were 180 workers' choral societies in Germany with 4,300 members. In 1901, the membership reached 39,717, in 1907, 93,000, and by 1912, 165,000. Berlin is said to have 5,352 members of workers' choral societies; Hamburg, 1,628; Leipzig, 4,051; Dresden, 4,700, etc.

We recently reported how the workers of France and other Romance countries had marked the 25th anniversary of the death of Eugène Pottier (1816-1887), the author of the famous

*Internationale.** In Germany, the propaganda of socialism by workers' songs is much more recent, and the "Junker" (landowners', Black-Hundred) government of Germany has been throwing up many more foul police obstacles to such propaganda.

But no amount of police harassment can prevent the singing of the hearty proletarian song about mankind's coming emancipation from wage-slavery in all the great cities of the world, in all the factory neighbourhoods, and more and more frequently in the huts of village labourers.

Written after January 3 (16), 1913
First published in 1954
in the journal *Kommunist* No. 6
Signed: *T.*

Collected Works,
Vol. 36, pp. 225-26

---

* See pp. 70-71.— *Ed.*

From Critical Remarks on the National Question

1. Liberals and Democrats on the Language Question

On several occasions the newspapers have mentioned the report of the Governor of the Caucasus, a report that is noteworthy, not for its Black-Hundred spirit, but for its timid "liberalism". Among other things, the Governor objects to artificial Russification of non-Russian nationalities. Representatives of non-Russian nationalities in the Caucasus are *themselves* striving to teach their children Russian; an example of this is the Armenian church schools, in which the teaching of Russian is not obligatory.

Russkoye Slovo[88] (No. 198), one of the most widely circulating liberal newspapers in Russia, points to this fact and draws the correct conclusion that the hostility towards the Russian language in Russia "stems exclusively from" the "artificial" (it should have said "forced") implanting of that language.

"There is no reason to worry about the fate of the Russian language. It will itself win recognition throughout Russia," says the newspaper. This is perfectly true, because the requirements of economic exchange will always compel the nationalities living in one state (as long as they wish to live together) to study the language of the majority. The more democratic the political system in Russia becomes, the more powerfully, rapidly and extensively capitalism will develop, the more urgently will the requirements of economic exchange impel various nationalities to study the language most convenient for general commercial relations.

The liberal newspaper, however, hastens to slap itself in the face and demonstrate its liberal inconsistency.

"Even those who oppose Russification," it says, "would hardly be likely to deny that in a country as huge as Russia there must be one single official language, and that this language can be only Russian."

Logic turned inside out! Tiny Switzerland has not lost anything, but has gained from having not *one single* official language, but three — German, French and Italian. In Switzerland 70 per cent of the population are Germans (in Russia 43 per cent are Great Russians), 22 per cent French (in Russia 17 per cent are Ukrainians) and 7 per cent Italians (in Russia 6 per cent are Poles and 4.5 per cent Byelorussians). If Italians in Switzerland often speak French in their common parliament they do not do so because they are menaced by some savage police law (there are none such in Switzerland), but because the civilised citizens of a democratic state themselves prefer a language that is understood by a majority. The French language does not instil hatred in Italians because it is the language of a free civilised nation, a language that is not imposed by disgusting police measures.

Why should "huge" Russia, a much more varied and terribly backward country, *inhibit* her development by the retention of any kind of privilege for any one language? Should not the contrary be true, liberal gentlemen? Should not Russia, if she wants to overtake Europe, put an end to every kind of privilege as quickly as possible, as completely as possible and as vigorously as possible?

If all privileges disappear, if the imposition of any one language ceases, all Slavs will easily and rapidly learn to understand each other and will not be frightened by the "horrible" thought that speeches in different languages will be heard in the common parliament. The requirements of economic exchange will themselves *decide* which language of the given country it is to the *advantage* of the majority to know in the interests of commercial relations. This decision will be all the firmer because it is adopted voluntarily by a population of various nationalities, and its adoption will be the more rapid and extensive the more consistent the democracy and, as a consequence of it, the more rapid the development of capitalism.

The liberals approach the language question in the same way as they approach all political questions — like hypocritical hucksters, holding out one hand (openly) to democracy and the other (behind their backs) to the feudalists and police. We are against privileges, shout the liberals, and under cover they haggle with the feudalists for first one, then another, privilege.

Such is the nature of *all* liberal-bourgeois nationalism — not only Great-Russian (it is the worst of them all because of its violent character and its kinship with Messrs. Purishkeviches), but Polish, Jewish, Ukrainian, Georgian and every other nationalism. Under the slogan of "national culture" the bourgeoisie of *all* nations, both in Austria and in Russia, are *in fact* pursuing the policy of splitting the workers, emasculating democracy and haggling with the feudalists over the sale of the people's rights and the people's liberty.

The slogan of working-class democracy is not "national culture" but the international culture of democracy and the world-wide working-class movement. Let the bourgeoisie deceive the people with various "positive" national programmes. The class-conscious worker will answer the bourgeoisie — there is only one solution to the national problem (insofar as it can, in general, be solved in the capitalist world, the world of profit, squabbling and exploitation), and that solution is consistent democracy.

The proof — Switzerland in Western Europe, a country with an old culture and Finland in Eastern Europe, a country with a young culture.

The national programme of working-class democracy is: absolutely no privileges for any one nation or any one language; the solution of the problem of the political self-determination of nations, that is, their separation as states by completely free, democratic methods; the promulgation of a law for the whole state by virtue of which any measure (rural, urban or communal, etc., etc.) introducing any privilege of any kind for one of the nations and militating against the equality of nations or the rights of a national minority, shall be declared illegal and ineffective, and any citizen of the state shall have the right to demand that such a measure be annulled as unconstitutional, and that those who attempt to put it into effect be punished.

Working-class democracy contraposes to the nationalist wrangling of the various bourgeois parties over questions of language, etc., the demand for the unconditional unity and complete amalgamation of workers of *all* nationalities in *all* working-class organisations — trade union, co-operative, consumers', educational and all others — in contradistinction to any kind of bourgeois nationalism. Only this type of unity and amalgamation can uphold democracy and defend the interests of the workers against capital — which is already international and is becoming more so — and promote the development of mankind towards a new way of life that is alien to all privileges and all exploitation.

2. "National Culture"

As the reader will see, the article in *Severnaya Pravda*[89] made use of a particular example, i.e., the problem of the official language, to illustrate the inconsistency and opportunism of the liberal bourgeoisie, which, in the national question, extends a hand to the feudalists and the police. Everybody will understand that, apart from the problem of an official language, the liberal bourgeoisie behaves just as treacherously, hypocritically and stupidly (even from the standpoint of the interests of liberalism) in a number of other related issues. The conclusion to be drawn from this? It is that *all* liberal-bourgeois nationalism sows the greatest corruption among the workers and does immense harm to the cause of freedom and the proletarian class struggle. This bourgeois (and bourgeois-feudalist) tendency is all the more dangerous for its *being concealed* behind the slogan of "national culture". It is under the guise of national culture — Great-Russian, Polish, Jewish, Ukrainian, and so forth — that the Black Hundreds and the clericals, and also the bourgeoisie of *all* nations, are doing their dirty and reactionary work.

Such are the facts of the national life of today, if viewed from the Marxist angle, i.e., from the standpoint of the class struggle, and if the slogans are compared with the interests and policies of classes, and not with meaningless "general principles", declamations and phrases.

The slogan of national culture is a bourgeois (and often also a Black-Hundred and clerical) fraud. Our slogan is: the international culture of democracy and of the world working-class movement.

Here the Bundist[90] Mr. Liebman rushes into the fray and annihilates me with the following deadly tirade:

"Anyone in the least familiar with the national question knows that international culture is not non-national culture (culture without a national form); non-national culture, which must not be Russian, Jewish, or Polish, but only pure culture, is nonsense; international ideas can appeal to the working class only when they are adapted to the language spoken by the worker, and to the concrete national conditions under which he lives; the worker should not be indifferent to the condition and development of his national culture, because it is through it, and only through it, that he is able to participate in the 'international culture of democracy and of the world working-class movement'. This is well known, but V. I. turns a deaf ear to it all...."

Ponder over this typically Bundist argument, designed, if you please, to demolish the Marxist thesis that I advanced. With the air of supreme self-confidence of one who is "familiar with the national question", this Bundist passes off ordinary bourgeois views as "well-known" axioms.

It is true, my dear Bundist, that international culture is not non-national. Nobody said that it was. Nobody has proclaimed a "pure" culture, either Polish, Jewish, or Russian, etc., and your jumble of empty words is simply an attempt to distract the reader's attention and to obscure the issue with tinkling words.

The *elements* of democratic and socialist culture are present, if only in rudimentary form, in *every* national culture, since in *every* nation there are toiling and exploited masses, whose conditions of life inevitably give rise to the ideology of democracy and socialism. But *every* nation also possesses a bourgeois culture (and most nations a reactionary and clerical culture as well) in the form, not merely of "elements", but of the *dominant* culture. Therefore, the general "national culture" *is* the culture of the landlords, the clergy and the bourgeoisie. This fundamental and, for a Marxist, elementary truth, was kept in the background by the Bundist, who "drowned" it in his jumble of words, i.e., *instead of* revealing and clarifying the class gulf to the reader, he in fact obscured it. *In fact*, the Bundist acted like a bourgeois, whose every interest requires the spreading of a belief in a non-class national culture.

In advancing the slogan of "the international culture of democracy and of the world working-class movement", we take *from each* national culture *only* its democratic and socialist elements; we take them *only* and *absolutely* in opposition to the bourgeois culture and the bourgeois nationalism of *each* nation. No democrat, and certainly no Marxist, denies that all languages should have equal status, or that it is necessary to polemise with one's "native" bourgeoisie in one's native language and to advocate anti-clerical or anti-bourgeois ideas among one's "native" peasantry and petty bourgeoisie. That goes without saying, but the Bundist uses these indisputable truths to obscure the point in dispute, i.e., the real issue.

The question is whether it is permissible for a Marxist, directly or indirectly, to advance the slogan of national culture, or whether he should *oppose* it by advocating, in all languages, the slogan of workers' *internationalism* while "adapting" himself to all local and national features.

The significance of the "national culture" slogan is not determined by some petty intellectual's promise, or good intention, to "interpret" it as "meaning the development through it of an international culture". It would be puerile subjectivism to look at it in that way. The significance of the slogan of national culture is determined by the objective alignment of all classes in a given country, and in all countries of the world. The national culture of the bourgeoisie is a *fact* (and, I repeat, the bourgeoisie everywhere enters into deals with the landed proprietors and the clergy). Aggressive bourgeois nationalism, which drugs the minds of the workers, stultifies and disunites them in order that the bourgeoisie may lead them by the halter — such is the fundamental fact of the times.

Those who seek to serve the proletariat must unite the workers of all nations, and unswervingly fight bourgeois nationalism, *domestic* and foreign. The place of those who advocate the slogan of national culture is among the nationalist petty bourgeois, not among the Marxists.

Take a concrete example. Can a Great-Russian Marxist accept the slogan of national, Great-Russian, culture? No, he cannot. Anyone who does that should stand in the ranks of the nationalists, not of the Marxists. Our task is to fight the dominant, Black-Hundred and bourgeois national culture of the Great Russians, and to develop, exclusively in the internationalist spirit and in the closest alliance with the workers of other countries, the rudiments also existing in the history of our democratic and working-class movement. Fight your own Great-Russian landlords and bourgeoisie, fight their "culture" in the name of internationalism, and, in so fighting, "adapt" yourself to the special features of the Purishkeviches and Struves — that is your task, not preaching or tolerating the slogan of national culture.

The same applies to the most oppressed and persecuted nation — the Jews. Jewish national culture is the slogan of the rabbis and the bourgeoisie, the slogan of our enemies. But there are other elements in Jewish culture and in Jewish history as a whole. Of the ten and a half million Jews in the world, somewhat over a half live in Galicia and Russia, backward and semi-barbarous countries, where the Jews are *forcibly* kept in the status of a caste. The other half lives in the civilised world, and there the Jews do not live as a segregated caste. There the great world-progressive features of Jewish culture stand clearly revealed: its internationalism, its identification with the advanced movements of the epoch (the percentage of Jews in the democratic and proletarian movements is everywhere higher than the percentage of Jews among the population).

Whoever, directly or indirectly, puts forward the slogan of
Jewish "national culture" is (whatever his good intentions may
be) an enemy of the proletariat, a supporter of all that is
outmoded and connected with *caste* among the Jewish people; he
is an accomplice of the rabbis and the bourgeoisie. On the
other hand, those Jewish Marxists who mingle with the
Russian, Lithuanian, Ukrainian and other workers in international Marxist organisations, and make their contribution (both
in Russian and in Yiddish) towards creating the international
culture of the working-class movement—those Jews, despite
the separatism of the Bund, uphold the best traditions of Jewry
by fighting the slogan of "national culture".

Bourgeois nationalism and proletarian internationalism—these are the two irreconcilably hostile slogans that
correspond to the two great class camps throughout the
capitalist world, and express the *two* policies (nay, the two
world outlooks) in the national question. In advocating the
slogan of national culture and building up on it an entire plan
and practical programme of what they call "cultural-national
autonomy", the Bundists are *in effect* instruments of bourgeois
nationalism among the workers.

3. The Nationalist Bogey of "Assimilation"

The question of assimilation, i.e., of the shedding of national
features, and absorption by another nation, strikingly illus-
trates the consequences of the nationalist vacillations of the
Bundists and their fellow-thinkers.

Mr. Liebman, who faithfully conveys and repeats the stock
arguments, or rather, tricks, of the Bundists, has qualified as
"the *old assimilation story*" the demand for the unity and
amalgamation of the workers of all nationalities in a given
country in united workers' organisations (see the concluding
part of the article in *Severnaya Pravda*).

"Consequently," says Mr. F. Liebman, commenting on the
concluding part of the article in *Severnaya Pravda*, "if asked
what nationality he belongs to, the worker must answer: I am a
Social-Democrat."

Our Bundist considers this the acme of wit. As a matter of
fact, he gives himself away completely by *such* witticisms and
outcries about "assimilation", *levelled against* a consistently
democratic and *Marxist* slogan.

Developing capitalism knows two historical tendencies in the
national question. The first is the awakening of national life

and national movements, the struggle against all national oppression, and the creation of national states. The second is the development and growing frequency of international intercourse in every form, the break-down of national barriers, the creation of the international unity of capital, of economic life in general, of politics, science, etc.

Both tendencies are a universal law of capitalism. The former predominates in the beginning of its development, the latter characterises a mature capitalism that is moving towards its transformation into socialist society. The Marxists' national programme takes both tendencies into account, and advocates, firstly, the equality of nations and languages and the impermissibility of all *privileges* in this respect (and also the right of nations to self-determination, with which we shall deal separately later); secondly, the principle of internationalism and uncompromising struggle against contamination of the proletariat with bourgeois nationalism, even of the most refined kind.

The question arises: what does our Bundist mean when he cries out to heaven against "assimilation"? He *could not* have meant the oppression of nations, or the *privileges* enjoyed by a particular nation, because the word "assimilation" here does not fit at all, because all Marxists, individually, and as an official, united whole, have quite definitely and unambiguously condemned the slightest violence against and oppression and inequality of nations, and finally because this general Marxist idea, which the Bundist has attacked, is expressed in the *Severnaya Pravda* article in the most emphatic manner.

No, evasion is impossible here. In condemning "assimilation" Mr. Liebman had in mind, *not* violence, *not* inequality, and *not* privileges. Is there anything real left in the concept of assimilation, after all violence and all inequality have been eliminated?

Yes, there undoubtedly is. What is left is capitalism's world-historical tendency to break down national barriers, obliterate national distinctions, and to *assimilate* nations — a tendency which manifests itself more and more powerfully with every passing decade, and is one of the greatest driving forces transforming capitalism into socialism.

Whoever does not recognise and champion the equality of nations and languages, and does not fight against all national oppression or inequality, is not a Marxist; he is not even a democrat. That is beyond doubt. But it is also beyond doubt that the pseudo-Marxist who heaps abuse upon a Marxist of another nation for being an "assimilator" is simply a *nationalist philistine*. In this unhandsome category of people are all the Bundists and (as we shall shortly see) Ukrainian nationalist-socialists such as L. Yurkevich, Dontsov and Co.

To show concretely how reactionary the views held by these nationalist philistines are, we shall cite facts of three kinds.

It is the Jewish nationalists in Russia in general, and the Bundists in particular, who vociferate most about Russian orthodox Marxists being "assimilators". And yet, as the afore-mentioned figures show, out of the ten and a half million Jews all over the world, *about half* that number live in the *civilised* world, where conditions favouring "assimilation" are *strongest*, whereas the unhappy, downtrodden, disfranchised Jews in Russia and Galicia, who are crushed under the heel of the Purishkeviches (Russian and Polish), live where conditions for "assimilation" *least* prevail, where there is most segregation, and even a "Pale of Settlement", [91] a *numerus clausus* [92] and other charming features of the Purishkevich regime.

The Jews in the civilised world are not a nation, they have in the main become assimilated, say Karl Kautsky and Otto Bauer. The Jews in Galicia and in Russia are not a nation; unfortunately (through *no* fault of their own but through that of the Purishkeviches), they are still a *caste* here. Such is the incontrovertible judgement of people who are undoubtedly familiar with the history of Jewry and take the above-cited facts into consideration.

What do these facts prove? It is that only Jewish reactionary philistines, who want to turn back the wheel of history, and make it proceed, not from the conditions prevailing in Russia and Galicia to those prevailing in Paris and New York, but in the reverse direction — only they can clamour against "assimilation".

The best Jews, those who are celebrated in world history and have given the world foremost leaders of democracy and socialism, have never clamoured against assimilation. It is only those who contemplate the "rear aspect" of Jewry with reverential awe that clamour against assimilation.

A rough idea of the scale which the general process of assimilation of nations is assuming under the present conditions of advanced capitalism may be obtained, for example, from the immigration statistics of the United States of America. During the decade between 1891 and 1900, Europe sent 3,700,000 people there, and during the nine years between 1901 and 1909, 7,200,000. The 1900 census in the

United States recorded over 10,000,000 foreigners. New York State, in which, according to the same census, there were over 78,000 Austrians, 136,000 Englishmen, 20,000 Frenchmen, 480,000 Germans, 37,000 Hungarians, 425,000 Irish, 182,000 Italians, 70,000 Poles, 166,000 people from Russia (mostly Jews), 43,000 Swedes, etc., grinds down national distinctions. And what is taking place on a grand, international scale in New York is also to be seen in every big city and industrial township.

No one unobsessed by nationalist prejudices can fail to perceive that this process of assimilation of nations by capitalism means the greatest historical progress, the break-down of hidebound national conservatism in the various backwoods, especially in backward countries like Russia.

Take Russia and the attitude of Great Russians towards the Ukrainians. Naturally, every democrat, not to mention Marxists, will strongly oppose the incredible humiliation of Ukrainians, and demand complete equality for them. But it would be a downright betrayal of socialism and a silly policy even from the standpoint of the bourgeois "national aims" of the Ukrainians to weaken the ties and the alliance between the Ukrainian and Great-Russian proletariat that now exist within the confines of a single state.

Mr. Lev Yurkevich, who calls himself a "Marxist" (poor Marx!), is an example of that silly policy. In 1906, Sokolovsky (Basok) and Lukashevich (Tuchapsky) asserted, Mr. Yurkevich writes, that the Ukrainian proletariat had become completely Russified and needed no separate organisation. Without quoting a single fact bearing on the direct issue, Mr. Yurkevich falls upon both for saying this and cries out hysterically — quite in the spirit of the basest, most stupid and most reactionary nationalism — that this is "national passivity", "national renunciation", that these men have "split [!!] the Ukrainian Marxists", and so forth. Today, despite the "growth of Ukrainian national consciousness among the workers", the minority of the workers are "nationally conscious", while the majority, Mr. Yurkevich assures us, "are still under the influence of Russian culture". And it is our duty, this nationalist philistine exclaims, "not to follow the masses, but to lead them, to explain to them their national aims (natsionalna sprava)" (Dzvin,[93] p. 89).

This argument of Mr. Yurkevich's is wholly bourgeois-nationalistic. But even from the point of view of the bourgeois nationalists, some of whom stand for complete equality and autonomy for the Ukraine, while others stand for an independent Ukrainian state, this argument will not wash. The Ukrainians' striving for liberation is opposed by the Great-Russian and Polish landlord class and by the bourgeoisie of these two nations. What social force is capable of standing up to these classes? The first decade of the twentieth century provided an actual reply to this question: that force is none other than the working class, which rallies the democratic peasantry behind it. By striving to divide, and thereby weaken, the genuinely democratic force, whose victory would make national oppression impossible, Mr. Yurkevich is betraying, not only the interests of democracy in general, but also the interests of his own country, the Ukraine. Given united action by the Great-Russian and Ukrainian proletarians, a free Ukraine is *possible*; without such unity, it is out of the question.

But Marxists do not confine themselves to the bourgeois-national standpoint. For several decades a well-defined process of accelerated economic development has been going on in the South, i.e., the Ukraine, attracting hundreds of thousands of peasants and workers from Great Russia to the capitalist farms, mines, and cities. The "assimilation" — within these limits — of the Great-Russian and Ukrainian proletariat is an indisputable fact. *And this* fact is *undoubtedly* progressive. Capitalism is replacing the ignorant, conservative, settled muzhik of the Great-Russian or Ukrainian backwoods with a mobile proletarian whose conditions of life break down specifically national narrow-mindedness, both Great-Russian and Ukrainian. Even if we assume that, in time, there will be a state frontier between Great Russia and the Ukraine, the historically progressive nature of the "assimilation" of the Great-Russian and Ukrainian workers will be as undoubted as the progressive nature of the grinding down of nations in America. The freer the Ukraine and Great Russia become, the *more extensive and more rapid* will be the development of capitalism, which will still more powerfully attract the workers, the working masses of *all* nations from all regions of the state and from all the neighbouring states (should Russia become a neighbouring state in relation to the Ukraine) to the cities, the mines, and the factories.

Mr. Lev Yurkevich acts like a real bourgeois, and a short-sighted, narrow-minded, obtuse bourgeois at that, i.e., like a philistine, when he dismisses the benefits to be gained from the intercourse, amalgamation and assimilation of the *proletariat* of the two nations, for the sake of the momentary success of the Ukrainian national cause (*sprava*). The national cause comes first and the proletarian cause second, the bourgeois nationalists say, with the Yurkeviches, Dontsovs and similar would-be Marxists repeating it after them. The proletarian cause must come first, we say, because it not only protects the lasting and fundamental interests of labour and of humanity, but also those of democracy; and without democracy neither an autonomous nor an independent Ukraine is conceivable.

Another point to be noted in Mr. Yurkevich's argument, which is so extraordinarily rich in nationalist gems, is this: the minority of Ukrainian workers are nationally conscious, he says; "the majority are still under the influence of Russian culture" (*bilshist perebuvaye shche pid vplyvom rosiiskoi kultury*).

Contraposing Ukrainian culture as a whole to Great-Russian culture as a whole, when speaking of the proletariat, is a gross betrayal of the proletariat's interests for the benefit of bourgeois nationalism.

There are two nations in every modern nation — we say to all nationalist-socialists. There are two national cultures in every national culture. There is the Great-Russian culture of the Purishkeviches, Guchkovs and Struves — but there is also the Great-Russian culture typified in the names of Chernyshevsky and Plekhanov. There are *the same two* cultures in the Ukraine as there are in Germany, in France, in England, among the Jews, and so forth. If the majority of the Ukrainian workers are under the influence of Great-Russian culture, we also know definitely that the ideas of Great-Russian democracy and Social-Democracy operate parallel with the Great-Russian clerical and bourgeois culture. In fighting the latter kind of "culture", the Ukrainian *Marxist* will always bring the former into focus, and say to his workers: "We must snatch at, make use of, and develop to the utmost every opportunity for intercourse with the Great-Russian class-conscious workers, with their literature and with their range of ideas; the fundamental interests of *both* the Ukrainian and the Great-Russian working-class movements demand it."

If a Ukrainian Marxist allows himself to be swayed by his *quite legitimate and natural* hatred of the Great-Russian oppressors *to such a degree* that he transfers even a particle of this hatred, even if it be only estrangement, to the proletarian culture and proletarian cause of the Great-Russian workers, then such a Marxist will get bogged down in bourgeois nationalism. Similarly, the Great-Russian Marxists will be bogged down, not only in bourgeois, but also in Black-

Hundred nationalism, if he loses sight, even for a moment, of the demand for complete equality for the Ukrainians, or of their *right* to form an independent state.

The Great-Russian and Ukrainian workers must work together, and, as long as they live in a single state, act in the closest organisational unity and concert towards a common or international culture of the proletarian movement, displaying absolute tolerance in the question of the language in which propaganda is conducted, and in the purely local or purely national *details* of that propaganda. This is the imperative demand of Marxism. All advocacy of the segregation of the workers of one nation from those of another, all attacks upon Marxist "assimilation", or attempts, where the proletariat is concerned, to contrapose one national culture as a whole to another allegedly integral national culture, and so forth, is *bourgeois* nationalism, against which it is essential to wage a ruthless struggle.

Written in October-December 1913
Published in November-December
1913
in the journal *Prosveshcheniye*
Nos. 10, 11 and 12
Signed: *V. Ilyin*

Collected Works,
Vol. 20, pp. 20-33

Is a Compulsory Official Language Needed?

The liberals differ from the reactionaries in that they recognise the right to have instruction conducted in the native language, at least in the *elementary* schools. But they are completely at one with the reactionaries on the point that a compulsory official language is necessary.

What does a compulsory official language mean? In practice, it means that the language of the Great Russians, who are a *minority* of the population of Russia, is imposed upon all the rest of the population of Russia. In every school the teaching of the official language must be *obligatory*. All official correspondence must be conducted in the official language, not in the language of the local population.

On what grounds do the parties who advocate a compulsory official language justify its necessity?

The "arguments" of the Black Hundreds are curt, of course. They say: All non-Russians should be ruled with a rod of iron to keep them from "getting out of hand". Russia must be indivisible, and all the peoples must submit to Great-Russian rule, for it was the Great Russians who built up and united the land of Russia. Hence, the language of the ruling class must be the compulsory official language. The Purishkeviches would not mind having the "local lingoes" banned altogether, although they are spoken by about 60 per cent of Russia's total population.

The attitude of the liberals is much more "cultured" and "refined". They are for permitting the use of the native languages within certain limits (for example, in the elementary schools). At the same time they advocate an obligatory official language, which, they say, is necessary in the interests of "culture", in the interests of a "united" and "indivisible" Russia, and so forth.

"Statehood is the affirmation of cultural unity.... An official language is an essential constituent of state culture.... Statehood is based on unity of authority, the official language being an instrument of that unity. The official language possesses the same compulsory and universally coercive power as all other forms of statehood....
"If Russia is to remain united and indivisible, we must firmly insist on the political expediency of the Russian literary language."

This is the typical philosophy of a liberal on the necessity of an official language.

We have quoted the above passage from an article by Mr. S. Patrashkin in the liberal newspaper *Dyen*[94] (No. 7). For quite understandable reasons, the Black-Hundred *Novoye Vremya* rewarded the author of these ideas with a resounding kiss. Mr. Patrashkin expresses "very sound ideas", Menshikov's newspaper stated (No. 13588). Another paper the Black Hundreds are constantly praising for such very "sound" ideas is the national-liberal *Russkaya Mysl*. And how can they help praising them when the liberals, with the aid of "cultured" arguments, are advocating things that please the *Novoye Vremya* people so much?

Russian is a great and mighty language, the liberals tell us. Don't you want everybody who lives in the border regions of Russia to know this great and mighty language? Don't you see that the Russian language will enrich the literature of the non-Russians, put great treasures of culture within their reach, and so forth?

That is all true, gentlemen, we say in reply to the liberals. We know better than you do that the language of Turgenev, Tolstoy, Dobrolyubov and Chernyshevsky is a great and mighty one. We desire more than you do that the closest possible intercourse and fraternal unity should be established between the oppressed classes of all the nations that inhabit Russia, without any discrimination. And we, of course, are in favour of every inhabitant of Russia having the opportunity to learn the great Russian language.

What we do not want is the element of *coercion*. We do not want to have people driven into paradise with a cudgel; for no matter how many fine phrases about "culture" you may utter, a *compulsory* official language involves coercion, the use of the cudgel. We do not think that the great and mighty Russian language needs anyone having to study it by *sheer compulsion*. We are convinced that the development of capitalism in Russia, and the whole course of social life in general, are tending to bring all nations closer together. Hundreds of thousands of people are moving from one end of Russia to another; the different national populations are intermingling; exclusiveness and national conservatism must disappear. People whose conditions of life and work make it necessary for them to know the Russian language will learn it without being forced to do so. But coercion (the cudgel) will have only one result: it will hinder the great and mighty Russian language from spreading to other national groups, and, most important of all, it will sharpen antagonism, cause friction in a million new forms, increase resentment, mutual misunderstanding, and so on.

Who wants that sort of thing? Not the Russian people, not the Russian democrats. They do not recognise national oppression *in any form*, even in "the interests of Russian culture and statehood".

That is why Russian Marxists say that there must be *no* compulsory official language, that the population must be provided with schools where teaching will be carried on in all the local languages, that a fundamental law must be introduced in the constitution declaring invalid all privileges of any one nation and all violations of the rights of national minorities.

Proletarskaya Pravda No. 14 (32),   *Collected Works,*
January 18, 1914   Vol. 20, pp. 71-73

From the History
of the Workers' Press in Russia

(Excerpts)

The history of the workers' press in Russia is indissolubly linked up with the history of the democratic and socialist movement. Hence, only by knowing the chief stages of the movement for emancipation is it possible to understand why the preparation and rise of the workers' press proceeded in a certain way, and in no other.

The emancipation movement in Russia has passed through three main stages, corresponding to the three main classes of Russian society, which have left their impress on the movement: (1) the period of the nobility, roughly from 1825 to 1861; (2) the *raznochintsi* or bourgeois-democratic period, approximately from 1861 to 1895; and (3) the proletarian period, from 1895 to the present time.

The most outstanding figures of the nobility period were the Decembrists and Herzen. At that time, under the serf-owning system, there could be no question of differentiating a working *class* from among the general mass of serfs, the disfranchised "lower orders", "the ruck". In those days the illegal general democratic press, headed by Herzen's *Kolokol*,[95] was the forerunner of the workers' (proletarian-democratic or Social-Democratic) press.

Just as the Decembrists roused Herzen, so Herzen and his *Kolokol* helped to rouse the *raznochintsi*—the educated representatives of the liberal and democratic bourgeoisie who belonged, not to the nobility but to the civil servants, urban petty bourgeois, merchant and peasant classes. It was V. G. Belinsky who, even before the abolition of serfdom, was a forerunner of the *raznochintsi* who were to completely oust the nobility from our emancipation movement. The famous Letter to Gogol, which summed up Belinsky's literary activities, was one of the finest productions of the illegal democratic press, which has to this day lost none of its great and vital significance.

With the fall of the serf-owning system, the *raznochintsi* emerged as the chief actor from among the masses in the movement for emancipation in general, and in the democratic illegal press in particular. Narodism, which corresponded to the *raznochintsi* point of view, became the dominant trend. As a social trend, it never succeeded in dissociating itself from liberalism on the right and from anarchism on the left. But Chernyshevsky, who, after Herzen, developed the Narodnik views, made a great stride forward as compared with Herzen. Chernyshevsky was a far more consistent and militant democrat, his writings breathing the spirit of the class struggle. He resolutely pursued the line of exposing the treachery of liberalism, a line which to this day is hateful to the Cadets and liquidators. He was a remarkably profound critic of capitalism despite his utopian socialism.

The sixties and seventies saw quite a number of illegal publications, militant-democratic and utopian-socialist in content, which had started to circulate among the "masses". Very prominent among the personalities of that epoch were the workers Pyotr Alexeyev, Stepan Khalturin, and others. The proletarian-democratic current, however, was unable to free itself from the main stream of Narodism; this became possible only after Russian Marxism took ideological shape (the Emancipation of Labour group, 1883 [96]), and a steady workers' movement, linked with Social-Democracy, began (the St. Petersburg strikes of 1895-96).

Social-Democracy in Russia was founded by the Emancipation of Labour group, which was formed abroad in 1883. The writings of this group, which were printed abroad and uncensored, were the first systematically to expound and draw all the practical conclusions from the ideas of Marxism, which, as the experience of the entire world has shown, alone express the true essence of the working-class movement and its aims. For the twelve years between 1883 and 1895, practically the only attempt to establish a Social-Democratic workers' press in Russia was the publication in St. Petersburg in 1885 of the Social-Democratic newspaper *Rabochy*; it was of course illegal, but only two issues appeared. Owing to the absence of a mass working-class movement, there was no scope for the wide development of a workers' press.

The inception of a mass working-class movement, with the participation of Social-Democrats, dates from 1895-96, the time of the famous St. Petersburg strikes. It was then that a workers' press, in the real sense of the term, appeared in Russia.

All in all, the workers' leaflets and Social-Democratic newspapers of the time—i.e., twenty years ago—were the direct forerunners of the present-day working-class press: the same factory "exposures", the same reports on the "economic" struggle, the same treatment of the tasks of the working-class movement from the standpoint of Marxist principles and consistent democracy, and finally, *the same two main trends*—the Marxist and the opportunist—in the working-class press.

It is a remarkable fact, one that has not been duly appreciated to this day, that as soon as the *mass* working-class movement arose in Russia (1895-96), there at once appeared the division into Marxist and opportunist trends—a division which has changed in form and features, etc., but which has remained essentially the same from 1894 to 1914. Apparently, this particular kind of division and inner struggle among Social-Democrats has deep social and class roots.

The *Rabochaya Mysl*, mentioned above, represented the *opportunist* trend of the day, known as Economism.[97] This trend became apparent in the disputes among the local leaders of the working-class movement as early as 1894-95. And abroad, where the awakening of the Russian workers led to an efflorescence of Social-Democratic literature as early as 1896, the appearance and rallying of the Economists ended in a split in the spring of 1900 (that is, prior to the appearance of *Iskra*,[98] the first issue of which came off the press at the very end of 1900).

The history of the working-class press during the twenty years 1894-1914 is the history of the two trends in Russian Marxism and Russian (or rather all-Russia) Social-Democracy. To *understand* the history of the working-class press in Russia, one must know, not only and not so much the names of the various organs of the press—names which convey nothing to the present-day reader and simply confuse him—as the *content*, nature and ideological line of the different sections of Social-Democracy.

The chief organs of the Economists were *Rabochaya Mysl* (1897-1900) and *Rabocheye Dyelo* (1898-1901). *Rabocheye Dyelo* was edited by B. Krichevsky, who later went over to the syndicalists, A. Martynov, a prominent Menshevik and now a liquidator, and Akimov, now an "independent Social-Democrat" who in all essentials agrees with the liquidators. At first only Plekhanov and the whole Emancipation of Labour group (the journal *Rabotnik*,[99] etc.) fought the Economists, and then *Iskra* joined the fight (from 1900 to August 1903, up to the time of the Second Congress of the R.S.D.L.P.).

Iskra's complete victory over Economism, the victory of consistent proletarian tactics over opportunist-intellectualist tactics in 1903, still further stimulated the influx of "fellow-travellers" into the ranks of Social-Democracy; and opportunism revived *on the soil of Iskrism*, as part of it, in the form of "Menshevism".

Menshevism took shape at the Second Congress of the R.S.D.L.P. (August 1903), originating from the *minority* of the Iskrists (hence the name Menshevism *) *and from all the opportunist opponents of* "Iskra". The Mensheviks reverted to Economism in a slightly renovated form, of course; headed by A. Martynov, all the Economists who had remained in the movement flocked to the ranks of the Mensheviks.

The *new Iskra*, which from November 1903 appeared under a new editorial board, became the chief organ of Menshevism. "Between the old *Iskra* and the new lies a gulf," Trotsky, then an ardent Menshevik, frankly declared. *Vperyod*[100] and *Proletary*[101] (1905) were the chief Bolshevik newspapers, which upheld the tactics of consistent Marxism and remained faithful to the old *Iskra*.

From the point of view of real contact with the masses and as an expression of the tactics of the proletarian masses, 1905-07, the years of revolution, were a test of the two main trends in Social-Democracy and in the working-class press — the Menshevik and Bolshevik trends. A legal Social-Democratic press could not have appeared all at once in the autumn of 1905 had the way not been paved by the activities of the advanced workers, who were closely connected with the masses. The fact that the legal Social-Democratic press of 1905, 1906 and 1907 was a press of *two* trends, of two groups, can only be accounted

---

* The Russian word Menshevism is derived from *menshinstvo*, the English for which is minority.— *Ed.*

for by the different lines in the working-class movement at the time — the petty-bourgeois and the proletarian.

The workers' legal press appeared in all three periods of the upswing and of relative "freedom", namely, in the autumn of 1905 (the Bolsheviks' *Novaya Zhizn*, and the Mensheviks' *Nachalo*[102]— we name only the chief of the many publications); in the spring of 1906 (*Volna*,[103] *Ekho*,[104] etc., issued by the Bolsheviks, *Narodnaya Duma*[105] and others, issued by the Mensheviks); and in the spring of 1907.

The essence of the Menshevik tactics of the time was recently expressed by L. Martov in these words: "The Mensheviks saw no other way by which the proletariat could take a useful part in that crisis except by assisting the bourgeois-liberal democrats in their attempts to eject the reactionary section of the propertied classes from political power — but, while rendering this assistance, the proletariat was to maintain its complete political independence." (*Among Books* by Rubakin,[106] Vol. II, p. 772.) In practice, these tactics of "assisting" the liberals amounted to making the workers *dependent* on them; in practice they were liberal-labour tactics. The Bolsheviks' tactics, on the contrary, ensured the independence of the proletariat in the bourgeois crisis, by fighting to bring that crisis to a head, by exposing the treachery of liberalism, by enlightening and rallying the petty bourgeoisie (especially in the countryside) to counteract that treachery.

It is a fact — and the Mensheviks themselves, including the present-day liquidators, Koltsov, Levitsky, and others, have repeatedly admitted it — that in those years (1905-07) the masses of the workers followed the lead of the Bolsheviks. Bolshevism expressed the proletarian essence of the movement, Menshevism was its opportunist, petty-bourgeois intellectual wing.

We cannot here give a more detailed characterisation of the content and significance of the tactics of the two trends in the workers' press. We can do no more than accurately establish the main facts and define the main lines of historical development.

The working-class press in Russia has almost a century of history behind it; first, the pre-history, i.e., the history, *not* of the labour, *not* of the proletarian, but of the "general democratic", i.e., bourgeois-democratic movement for emancipation, followed by its own twenty-year history of the proletarian movement, proletarian democracy or Social-Democracy.

Nowhere in the world has the proletarian movement come into being, nor could it have come into being, "all at once", in a pure class form, ready-made, like Minerva from the head of Jupiter. Only through long struggle and hard work on the part of the most advanced workers, of all class-conscious workers, was it possible to build up and strengthen the class movement of the proletariat, ridding it of all petty-bourgeois admixtures, restrictions, narrowness and distortions. The working class lives side by side with the petty bourgeoisie, which, as it becomes ruined, provides increasing numbers of new recruits to the ranks of the proletariat. And Russia is the most petty-bourgeois, the most philistine of capitalist countries, which only now is passing through the period of bourgeois revolutions which Britain, for example, passed through in the seventeenth century, and France in the eighteenth and early nineteenth centuries.

The class-conscious workers, who are now tackling a job that is near and dear to them, that of running the working-class press, putting it on a sound basis and strengthening and developing it, will not forget the twenty-year history of Marxism and the Social-Democratic press in Russia.

A disservice is being done to the workers' movement by those of its weak-nerved friends among the intelligentsia who fight shy of the internal struggle among the Social-Democrats, and who fill the air with cries and calls to have nothing to do with it. They are well-meaning but futile people, and their outcries are futile.

Only by studying the history of Marxism's struggle against opportunism, only by making a thorough and detailed study of the manner in which independent proletarian democracy emerged from the petty-bourgeois hodge-podge can the advanced workers decisively strengthen their own class-consciousness and their workers' press.

Rabochy No. 1,
April 22, 1914

Collected Works,
Vol. 20, pp. 245-46, 247-48, 248-249, 250-253

To The Author
of *The Song of the Falcon*

Every class-conscious worker will feel a pang when he sees Gorky's signature alongside that of P. Struve under the chauvinistic-clerical protest against German barbarity.[107]

In a talk we once had about Chaliapin's genuflections, Gorky said: "You can't judge him too strictly; we artists have a different mentality." In other words, the artist frequently acts under the influence of his emotion, which attains such a force that it suppresses all other considerations.

Let that be so. Let us say that Chaliapin must not be strictly judged. He is an artist, and nothing more. He is a stranger to the cause of the proletariat: today, he is a friend of the workers, tomorrow, a reactionary, moved by his emotion.

But the workers have grown accustomed to regard Gorky as their own. They have always believed that his heart beats as warmly as theirs for the cause of the proletariat, and that he has dedicated his talent to the service of this cause.

That is why they keep sending messages of greetings to Gorky, and that is why his name is so dear to them. It is this trust on the part of the class-conscious workers that imposes on Gorky a certain *duty*— to cherish his good name and to refrain from putting his signature to all sorts of cheap chauvinist protests which could well confuse the workers who lack political consciousness. They are still unable to find their bearings in many situations, and could be led astray by Gorky's name. Struve's name will not confuse any worker, but Gorky's may.

Therefore, the class-conscious workers, who well realise the falsehood and the vulgarity of this hypocritical protest against the "German barbarians", must feel that they have to rebuke the author of *The Song of the Falcon*. They will tell him: "At this hard and responsible moment through which the proletariat of Russia is going, we expected you to go hand in hand with its leading fighters and not with Mr. Struve & Co.!"

Sotsial-Demokrat No. 34,
December 5, 1914

Collected Works,
Vol. 41, pp. 344-45

On the National Pride
of the Great Russians

What a lot of talk, argument and vociferation there is nowadays about nationality and the fatherland! Liberal and radical cabinet ministers in Britain, a host of "forward-looking" journalists in France (who have proved in full agreement with their reactionary colleagues), and a swarm of official, Cadet and progressive scribblers in Russia (including several Narodniks and "Marxists") — all have effusive praise for the liberty and independence of their respective countries, the grandeur of the principle of national independence. Here one cannot tell where the venal eulogist of the butcher Nicholas Romanov or of the brutal oppressors of Negroes and Indians ends, and where the common philistine begins, who from sheer stupidity or spinelessness drifts with the stream. Nor is that distinction important. We see before us an extensive and very deep ideological trend, whose origins are closely interwoven with the interests of the landowners and the capitalists of the dominant nations. Scores and hundreds of millions are being spent every year for the propaganda of ideas advantageous to those classes: it is a pretty big mill-race that takes its waters from all sources — from Menshikov, a chauvinist by conviction, to chauvinists for reason of opportunism or spinelessness, such as Plekhanov and Maslov, Rubanovich and Smirnov, Kropotkin and Burtsev.

Let us, Great-Russian Social-Democrats, also try to define our attitude to this ideological trend. It would be unseemly for us, representatives of a dominant nation in the far east of Europe and a goodly part of Asia, to forget the immense significance of the national question — especially in a country which has been rightly called the "prison of the peoples", and particularly at a time when, in the far east of Europe and in Asia, capitalism is awakening to life and self-consciousness a number of "new" nations, large and small; at a moment when the tsarist monarchy has called up millions of Great Russians and non-Russians, so as to "solve" a number of national problems in accordance with the interests of the Council of the

4–70

United Nobility[108] and of the Guchkovs, Krestovnikovs, Dolgorukovs, Kutlers and Rodichevs.

Is a sense of national pride alien to us, Great-Russian class-conscious proletarians? Certainly not! We love our language and our country, and we are doing our very utmost to raise *her* toiling masses (i.e., nine-tenths of *her* population) to the level of a democratic and socialist consciousness. To us it is most painful to see and feel the outrages, the oppression and the humiliation our fair country suffers at the hands of the tsar's butchers, the nobles and the capitalists. We take pride in the resistance to these outrages put up from our midst, from the Great Russians; in *that* midst having produced Radishchev, the Decembrists and the revolutionary commoners of the seventies; in the Great-Russian working class having created, in 1905, a mighty revolutionary party of the masses; and in the Great-Russian peasantry having begun to turn towards democracy and set about overthrowing the clergy and the landed proprietors.

We remember that Chernyshevsky, the Great-Russian democrat, who dedicated his life to the cause of revolution, said half a century ago: "A wretched nation, a nation of slaves, from top to bottom — all slaves."[109] The overt and covert Great-Russian slaves (slaves with regard to the tsarist monarchy) do not like to recall these words. Yet, in our opinion, these were words of genuine love for our country, a love distressed by the absence of a revolutionary spirit in the masses of the Great-Russian people. There was none of that spirit at the time. There is little of it now, but it already exists. We are full of national pride because the Great-Russian nation, *too*, has created a revolutionary class, because it, *too*, has proved capable of providing mankind with great models of the struggle for freedom and socialism, and not only with great pogroms, rows of gallows, dungeons, great famines and great servility to priests, tsars, landowners and capitalists.

We are full of a sense of national pride, and for that very reason we *particularly* hate *our* slavish past (when the landed nobility led the peasants into war to stifle the freedom of Hungary, Poland, Persia and China), and our slavish present, when these selfsame landed proprietors, aided by the capitalists, are leading us into a war in order to throttle Poland and the Ukraine, crush the democratic movement in Persia and China, and strengthen the gang of Romanovs, Bobrinskys and Purishkeviches, who are a disgrace to our Great-Russian national dignity. Nobody is to be blamed for being born a slave;

but a slave who not only eschews a striving for freedom but
justifies and eulogises his slavery (e.g., calls the throttling of
Poland and the Ukraine, etc., a "defence of the fatherland" of
the Great Russians)—such a slave is a lickspittle and a boor,
who arouses a legitimate feeling of indignation, contempt, and
loathing.

"No nation can be free if it oppresses other nations,"[110] said
Marx and Engels, the greatest representatives of consistent
nineteenth-century democracy, who became the teachers of
the revolutionary proletariat. And, full of a sense of national
pride, we Great-Russian workers want, come what may, a free
and independent, a democratic, republican and proud Great
Russia, one that will base its relations with its neighbours on the
human principle of equality, and not on the feudalist principle
of privilege, which is so degrading to a great nation. Just
because we want that, we say: it is impossible, in the twentieth
century and in Europe (even in the far east of Europe), to
"defend the fatherland" otherwise than by using every
revolutionary means to combat the monarchy, the landowners
and the capitalists of one's *own* fatherland, i.e., the *worst*
enemies of our country. We say that the Great Russians cannot
"defend the fatherland" otherwise than by desiring the defeat
of tsarism in any war, this as the lesser evil to nine-tenths of the
inhabitants of Great Russia. For tsarism not only oppresses
those nine-tenths economically and politically, but also de-
moralises, degrades, dishonours and prostitutes them by
teaching them to oppress other nations and to cover up this
shame with hypocritical and quasi-patriotic phrases.

The objection may be advanced that, besides tsarism and
under its wing, another historical force has arisen and become
strong, viz., Great-Russian capitalism, which is carrying on
progressive work by economically centralising and welding
together vast regions. This objection, however, does not
excuse, but on the contrary still more condemns our socialist-
chauvinists, who should be called tsarist-Purishkevich socialists
(just as Marx called the Lassalleans Royal-Prussian socialists).
Let us even assume that history will decide in favour of
Great-Russian dominant-nation capitalism, and against the
hundred and one small nations. That is not impossible, for the
entire history of capital is one of violence and plunder, blood
and corruption. We do not advocate preserving small nations
at all costs; *other conditions being equal*, we are decidedly for
centralisation and are opposed to the petty-bourgeois ideal of
federal relationships. Even if our assumption were true,

4*

however, it is, firstly, not our business, or that of democrats (let alone of socialists), to help Romanov-Bobrinsky-Purishkevich throttle the Ukraine, etc. In his own Junker fashion, Bismarck accomplished a progressive historical task, but he would be a fine "Marxist" indeed who, on such grounds, thought of justifying socialist support for Bismarck! Moreover, Bismarck promoted economic development by bringing together the disunited Germans, who were being oppressed by other nations. The economic prosperity and rapid development of Great Russia, however, require that the country be liberated from Great-Russian oppression of other nations—that is the difference that our admirers of the true-Russian would-be Bismarcks overlook.

Secondly, if history were to decide in favour of Great-Russian dominant-nation capitalism, it follows hence that the *socialist* role of the Great-Russian proletariat, as the principal driving force of the communist revolution engendered by capitalism, will be all the greater. The proletarian revolution calls for a prolonged education of the workers in the spirit of the *fullest* national equality and brotherhood. Consequently, the interests of the Great-Russian proletariat require that the masses be systematically educated to champion—most resolutely, consistently, boldly and in a revolutionary manner—complete equality and the right to self-determination for all the nations oppressed by the Great Russians. The interests of the Great Russians' national pride (understood not in the slavish sense) coincide with the *socialist* interests of the Great-Russian (and all other) proletarians. Our model will always be Marx, who, after living in Britain for decades and becoming half-English, demanded freedom and national independence for Ireland in the interests of the socialist movement of the British workers.

In the second hypothetical case we have considered, our home-grown socialist-chauvinists, Plekhanov, etc., etc., will prove traitors, not only to their own country—a free and democratic Great Russia, but also to the proletarian brotherhood of all the nations of Russia, i.e., to the cause of socialism.

Sotsial-Demokrat No. 35,   *Collected Works,*
December 12, 1914   Vol. 21, pp. 102-06

From British Pacifism and the British Dislike of Theory

With their dislike of abstract theory and their pride in their practicality, the British often pose political issues *more directly*, thus helping the socialists of other countries to discover the actual content *beneath* the husk of wording of every kind (including the "Marxist"). Instructive in this respect is the pamphlet *Socialism and War*,* published before the war by the jingoist paper, *The Clarion*. The pamphlet contains an anti-war "manifesto" by Upton Sinclair, the U.S. socialist, and also a reply to him from the jingoist Robert Blatchford, who has long adopted Hyndman's imperialist viewpoint.

Sinclair is a socialist of the emotions, without any theoretical training. He states the issue in "simple" fashion; incensed by the approach of war, he seeks salvation from it in socialism.

"We are told," Sinclair writes, "that the socialist movement is yet too weak so that we must wait for its evolution. But evolution is working in the hearts of men; we are its instruments, and if we do not struggle, there is no evolution. We are told that the movement [against war] would be crushed out; but I declare my faith that the crushing out of any rebellion which sought, from motive of sublime humanity, to prevent war, would be the greatest victory that socialism has ever gained—would shake the conscience of civilisation and rouse the workers of the world as nothing in all history has yet done. Let us not be too fearful for our movement, nor put too much stress upon numbers and the outward appearances of power. A thousand men aglow with faith and determination are stronger than a million grown cautious and respectable; and there is no danger to the socialist movement so great as the danger of becoming an established institution."

This, as can be seen, is a naïve, theoretically unreasoned, but profoundly correct warning against any vulgarising of socialism, and a call to revolutionary struggle.

What does Blatchford say in reply to Sinclair?

"It is capitalists and militarists who make wars. That is true," he says. Blatchford is as anxious for peace and for socialism

---

* *Socialism and War*. The Clarion Press, 44 Worship Street, London, E. C.

taking the place of capitalism as any socialist in the world. But Sinclair will not convince him, or do away with the facts with "rhetoric and fine phrases". "Facts, my dear Sinclair, are obstinate things, and the German danger is a fact." Neither the British nor the German socialists are strong enough to prevent war, and "Sinclair greatly exaggerates the power of British socialism. The British socialists ... are not united; they have no money, no arms, no discipline". The only thing they can do is *to help* the British Government build up the navy; there is not, nor can there be, any other guarantee of peace.

Neither before nor since the outbreak of the war have the chauvinists ever been so outspoken in Continental Europe. In Germany it is not frankness that is prevalent, but Kautsky's hypocrisy and playing at sophistry. The same is true of Plekhanov. That is why it is so instructive to cast a glance at the situation in a more advanced country, where nobody will be taken in with sophisms or a travesty of Marxism. Here issues are stated in a more straightforward and truthful manner. Let us learn from the "advanced" British.

Sinclair is naïve in his appeal, although fundamentally it is a very correct one; he is naïve because he ignores the development of mass socialism over the last fifty years and the struggle of trends within socialism; he ignores the conditions for the growth of revolutionary action when an objectively revolutionary situation and a revolutionary organisation exist. The "emotional" approach cannot make up for that. The intense and bitter struggle between powerful trends in socialism, between the opportunist and revolutionary trends, cannot be evaded by the use of rhetoric.

Blatchford speaks out undisguisedly, revealing the most covert argument of the Kautskyites and Co., who are afraid to tell the truth. We are still weak, that is all, says Blatchford; but his outspokenness at once lays bare his opportunism, his jingoism. It at once becomes obvious that he serves the bourgeoisie and the opportunists. By declaring that socialism is *"weak"* he *himself weakens* it by preaching an anti-socialist, bourgeois, policy.

Like Sinclair, but conversely, like a coward and not like a fighter, like a traitor and not like the recklessly brave, he, too, ignores the conditions making for a revolutionary situation.

Written in June 1915   *Collected Works,*
First published on July 27, 1924   Vol. 21, pp. 263-65
in *Pravda* No. 169

From Summing-Up Speech at the Third All-Russia Congress of Soviets of Workers', Soldiers' and Peasants' Deputies

January 18 (31), 1918

Of course, the working people had no experience in government but that does not scare us. The victorious proletariat looks out on a land that has now become a public good, and it will be quite able to organise the new production and consumption on socialist lines. In the old days, human genius, the brain of man, created only to give some the benefits of technology and culture, and to deprive others of the most essential — education and development. From now on all the marvels of science and the gains of culture belong to the nation as a whole, and never again will man's brain and human genius be used for oppression and exploitation. Of this we are sure, so shall we not dedicate ourselves and work with abandon to fulfil this greatest of all historical tasks? The working people will perform this titanic historical feat, for in them lie dormant the great forces of revolution, renascence and renovation.

Published in *Izvestia* No. 15,
January 20, 1918
and *Pravda* No. 15,
February 2 (January 20), 1918

Collected Works,
Vol. 26, pp. 481-82

The Character of Our Newspapers

Far too much space is being allotted to political agitation on outdated themes — to political ballyhoo — and far too little to the building of the new life, to the facts about it.

Why, instead of turning out 200-400 lines, don't we write twenty or even ten lines on such simple, generally known, clear topics with which the people are already fairly well acquainted, like the foul treachery of the Mensheviks — the lackeys of the bourgeoisie — the Anglo-Japanese invasion to restore the sacred rights of capital, the American multimillionaires baring their fangs against Germany, etc., etc.? We must write about these things and note every new fact in this sphere, but we need not write long articles and repeat old arguments; what is needed is to convey in just a few lines, "in telegraphic style", the latest manifestation of the old, known and already evaluated politics.

The bourgeois press in the "good old bourgeois times" never mentioned the "holy of holies"—the conditions in privately-owned factories, in the private enterprises. This custom fitted in with the interests of the bourgeoisie. We must radically break with it. We have *not* broken with it. So far our type of newspaper has *not* changed as it should in a society in transition from capitalism to socialism.

Less politics. Politics has been "elucidated" fully and reduced to a struggle between the two camps: the insurrectionary proletariat and the handful of capitalist slave-owners (with the whole gang, right down to the Mensheviks and others). We may, and, I repeat, we must, speak very briefly about these politics.

More economics. But not in the sense of "general" discussions, learned reviews, intellectual plans and similar piffle, for, I regret to say, they are all too often just piffle and nothing more. By economics we mean the gathering, *careful checking* and study of the facts of the actual organisation of the new life. Have *real* successes been achieved by big factories, agricultural communes, the Poor Peasants' Committees, and local Economic Councils in building up the new economy? What, precisely, are these successes? Have they been verified? Are they not fables, boasting, intellectual promises ("things are moving", "the plan has been drawn up", "we are getting under way", "we now vouch for", "there is undoubted improvement", and other charlatan phrases of which "we" are such masters)? How have the successes been achieved? What must be done to extend them?

Where is the black list with the names of the lagging factories which since nationalisation have remained models of disorder, disintegration, dirt, hooliganism and parasitism? Nowhere to be found. But there *are* such factories. We shall not be able to do our duty unless we wage *war* against these "guardians of capitalist traditions". We shall be jellyfish, not Communists, as long as we tolerate such factories. We have not learned to wage the class struggle in the newspapers as skilfully as the bourgeoisie did. Remember the skill with which it *hounded* its class enemies in the press, ridiculed them, disgraced them, and tried to sweep them away. And we? Doesn't the class struggle in the epoch of the transition from capitalism to socialism take the form of safeguarding the interests of the working *class* against the few, the groups and sections of workers who stubbornly cling to capitalist traditions and continue to regard the Soviet state in the old way: work as little and as badly as they can and grab as much money as possible from the state. Aren't there many such scoundrels, even among the compositors in Soviet printing works, among the Sormovo and Putilov workers, etc.? How many of them have we found, how many have we exposed and how many have we pilloried?

The press is silent. And if it mentions the subject at all it does so in a stereotyped, official way, not in the manner of a *revolutionary* press, not as an organ of the *dictatorship* of a class demonstrating that the resistance of the capitalists and of the parasites — the custodians of capitalist traditions — will be crushed with an iron hand.

The same with the war. Do we harass cowardly or inefficient officers? Have we denounced the really bad regiments to the whole of Russia? Have we "caught" enough of the bad types who should be removed from the army with the greatest publicity for unsuitability, carelessness, procrastination, etc.?

We are not yet waging an effective, ruthless and truly revolutionary *war* against the *specific* wrongdoers. We do very little to *educate the people* by living, concrete examples and models taken from all spheres of life, although that is the chief task of the press during the transition from capitalism to communism. We give little attention to that aspect of *everyday* life inside the factories, in the villages and in the regiments where, more than anywhere else, the new is being built, where attention, publicity, public criticism, condemnation of what is bad and appeals to learn from the good are needed most.

Less political ballyhoo. Fewer highbrow discussions. Closer to life. More attention to the way in which the workers and peasants are *actually* building the *new* in their everyday work, and more *verification* so as to ascertain the extent to which the new is *communistic*.

Pravda No. 202,
September 20, 1918
Signed: *N. Lenin*

Collected Works,
Vol. 28, pp. 96-98

A Little Picture
in Illustration of Big Problems

Comrade Sosnovsky, editor of *Bednota*,[111] has brought me a remarkable book. As many workers and peasants as possible should be made familiar with it. Most valuable lessons, splendidly illustrated by vivid examples, are to be drawn from it on some of the major problems of socialist construction. The book, by Comrade Alexander Todorsky, is called *A Year with Rifle and Plough* and was published in the little town of Vesyegonsk by the local uyezd Executive Committee to mark the anniversary of the October Revolution.

The author describes the year's experience of the men in charge of organising Soviet power in the Vesyegonsk Uyezd — first the Civil War, the revolt of the local kulaks and its suppression, and then "peaceful creative life". The author has succeeded in giving such a simple, and at the same time such a lively, account of the course of the revolution in this rural backwater, that to attempt to retell it could only weaken its effect. This book should be distributed as widely as possible, and it would be very good if many more of those who have been working among the people and with the people, in the very thick of life, sat down to describe their experiences. The publication of several hundred, or even several dozen, such descriptions, the best, most truthfully and plainly told and containing numerous valuable facts, would be infinitely more useful to the cause of socialism than many of the newspaper and magazine articles and books by professional journalists and writers who only too often cannot see real life for the paper they write on.

Let me give a brief example from Comrade Todorsky's narrative. It was suggested that "merchant hands" should not be allowed to go "unemployed", but should be encouraged to "set to work".

"...With this end in view, three young, energetic and very business-like manufacturers, E. Yefremov, A. Loginov and N. Kozlov, were summoned to the Executive Committee and ordered on pain of imprisonment and confiscation of all property to set up a sawmill and tannery. The work was started immediately.

"The Soviet authorities were not mistaken in their choice of men, and the manufacturers, to their credit, were among the first to realise that they were not dealing with 'casual and temporary guests', but with real masters who had taken power firmly into their hands.

"Having quite rightly realised this, they set to work energetically to carry out the orders of the Executive Committee, with the result that Vesyegonsk now has a sawmill going at full swing, covering the needs of the local population and filling orders for a new railway under construction.

"As to the tannery, the premises are now ready, and the engine, drums and other machinery, obtained from Moscow, are being installed, so that in a month and a half, or two at the most, Vesyegonsk will be getting fine leather of its own make.

"The building of two Soviet plants by 'non-Soviet' hands is a good example of how to fight a class which is hostile to us.

"To rap the exploiters over the knuckles, to render them harmless or 'finish them off', is only half the job. The whole job will be done only when we compel them to work, and with the fruits of their labour help to improve the new life and strengthen Soviet power."

These fine and absolutely true words should be carved in stone and prominently displayed in every Economic Council, food organisation, factory, land department and so on. For what has been understood by our comrades in remote Vesyegonsk is all too often stubbornly ignored by Soviet officials in the capitals. It is quite common to meet a Soviet intellectual or worker, a Communist, who turns his nose up at the mere mention of co-operative societies and declares with an air of profound importance — and with equally profound stupidity — that these are not Soviet hands, they are bourgeois people, shopkeepers, Mensheviks, that at such and such a time and place the co-operators used their financial manipulations to conceal aid given to whiteguards, and that in our Socialist Republic the supply and distribution apparatus must be built up by clean Soviet hands.

Such arguments are typical insofar as the truth is so mixed with falsehood that we consequently get a most dangerous distortion of the aims of communism that can do incalculable harm to our cause.

The co-operatives certainly are an apparatus of bourgeois society, an apparatus which grew up in an atmosphere of "shopkeeping" and which has trained its leaders in the spirit of bourgeois politics and in a bourgeois outlook, and has therefore been producing a large proportion of whiteguards or their accomplices. That is undeniable. But it is a bad thing when absurd conclusions are drawn from undeniable truths, by their oversimplification and slapdash application. We can only build communism out of the material created by capitalism, out of that refined apparatus which has been moulded under bourgeois conditions and which—as far as concerns the human material in the apparatus—is therefore inevitably imbued with the bourgeois mentality. That is what makes the building of communist society difficult, but it is also a guarantee that it can and will be built. In fact, what distinguishes Marxism from the old, utopian socialism is that the latter wanted to build the new society not from the mass human material produced by bloodstained, sordid, rapacious, shopkeeping capitalism, but from very virtuous men and women reared in special hothouses and cucumber frames. Everyone now sees that this absurd idea really is absurd and everyone has discarded it, but not everyone is willing or able to give thought to the opposite doctrine of Marxism and to think out how communism can (and should) be built from the mass human material which has been corrupted by hundreds and thousands of years of slavery, serfdom, capitalism, by small individual enterprise, and by the war of every man against his neighbour to obtain a place in the market, or a higher price for his product or his labour.

The co-operatives are a bourgeois apparatus. Hence they do not deserve to be trusted *politically*; but this does not mean we may turn our backs on the task of using them for administration and construction. Political distrust means we must not put non-Soviet people in *politically* responsible posts. It means the Cheka must keep a sharp eye on members of classes, sections or groups that have leanings towards the whiteguards. (Though, incidentally, one need not go to the same absurd lengths as Comrade Latsis, one of our finest, tried and tested Communists, did in his Kazan magazine, *Krasny Terror*. He wanted to say that Red terror meant the forcible suppression of exploiters who attempted to restore their rule, but instead, he put it this way, on page 2 of the first issue of his magazine: "Don't search [!!?] the records for evidence of whether his revolt against the Soviet was an armed or only a verbal one.")

Political distrust of the members of a bourgeois apparatus is legitimate and essential. But to refuse to use them in administration and construction would be the height of folly, fraught with untold harm to communism. If anybody tried to recommend a Menshevik as a socialist, or as a political leader, or even as a political adviser, he would be committing a great mistake, for the history of the revolution in Russia has definitely shown that the Mensheviks (and the Socialist-Revolutionaries [112]) are not socialists, but petty-bourgeois democrats who are capable of siding with the *bourgeoisie* every time the class struggle between the proletariat and the bourgeoisie becomes particularly acute. But petty-bourgeois democracy is not a chance political formation, not an exception, but a *necessary* product of capitalism. And it is not only the old, pre-capitalist, economically reactionary middle peasants who are the "purveyors" of this democracy. So, too, are the co-operative societies with their capitalist training that have sprung from the soil of large-scale capitalism, the intellectuals, etc. After all, even backward Russia produced, side by side with the Kolupayevs and Razuvayevs,[113] capitalists who knew to make use of the services of educated intellectuals, be they Menshevik, Socialist-Revolutionary or non-party. Are we to be more stupid than those capitalists and fail to use such "building material" in erecting a communist Russia?

Written at the end of 1918
or beginning of 1919
First published in *Pravda* No. 258,
November 7, 1926

Collected Works,
Vol. 28, pp. 386-89

From The Achievements and Difficulties of the Soviet Government

The old utopian socialists imagined that socialism could be built by men of a new type, that first they would train good, pure and splendidly educated people, and these would build socialism. We always laughed at this and said that this was playing with puppets, that it was socialism as an amusement for young ladies, but not serious politics.

We want to build socialism with the aid of those men and women who grew up under capitalism, were depraved and corrupted by capitalism, but steeled for the struggle by capitalism. There are proletarians who have been so hardened that they can stand a thousand times more hardship than any army. There are tens of millions of oppressed peasants, ignorant and scattered, but capable of uniting around the proletariat in the struggle, if the proletariat adopts skilful tactics. And there are scientific and technical experts all thoroughly imbued with the bourgeois world outlook, there are military experts who were trained under bourgeois conditions—if they were only bourgeois it would not be so bad, but there were also conditions of landed proprietorship, serfdom and the big stick. As far as concerns the economy, all the agronomists, engineers and school-teachers were recruited from the propertied class; they did not drop from the skies. Neither under the reign of Tsar Nicholas nor under the Republican President Wilson were the propertyless proletarians at the bench and the peasants at the plough able to get a university education. Science and technology exist only for the rich, for the propertied class; capitalism provides culture only for the minority. We must build socialism out of this culture, we have no other material. We want to start building socialism at once out of the material that capitalism left us yesterday to be used today, at this very moment, and not with people reared in hothouses, assuming that we were to take this fairy-tale seriously. We have bourgeois experts and nothing else. We have no other bricks with which to build. Socialism must triumph, and we socialists and Communists must prove by deeds that we are capable of building socialism with these bricks, with this material, that we are capable of building socialist society with the aid of proletarians who have enjoyed the fruits of culture only to an insignificant degree, and with the aid of bourgeois specialists.

If you do not build communist society with this material, you will prove that you are mere phrase-mongers and windbags.

This is how the question is presented by the historical legacy of world capitalism! This is the difficulty that confronted us concretely when we took power, when we set up the Soviet machinery of state!

This is only half the task, but it is the greater half. Soviet machinery of state means that the working people are united in such a way as to crush capitalism by the weight of their mass unity. The masses did this. But it is not enough to crush capitalism. We must take the entire culture that capitalism left behind and build socialism with it. We must take all its science, technology, knowledge and art. Without these we shall be unable to build communist society. But this science, technology and art are in the hands and in the heads of the experts.

This is the task that confronts us in all spheres. It is a task with inherent contradictions, like the inherent contradictions of capitalism as a whole. It is a most difficult task, but a practicable one. We cannot wait twenty years until we have trained pure, communist experts, until we have trained the first generation of Communists without blemish and without reproach. No, excuse me, but we must build now, in two months and not in twenty years' time, so as to be able to fight the bourgeoisie, to oppose the bourgeois science and technology of the whole world. Here we must achieve victory. It is difficult to make the bourgeois experts serve us by the weight of our masses, but it is possible, and if we do it, we shall triumph....

Naturally, on this path, which is a new and difficult one, we have made more than a few mistakes; on this path we have met with more than a few reverses. Everybody knows that a certain number of experts have systematically betrayed us. Among the experts in the factories, among the agronomists, and in the administration, we have seen and see today at every step a malicious attitude to work, malicious sabotage.

We know that all this presents tremendous difficulties and that we cannot achieve victory by violence alone.... We, of course, are not opposed to violence. We laugh at those who are opposed to the dictatorship of the proletariat, we laugh and say that they are fools who do not understand that there must be either the dictatorship of the proletariat or the dictatorship of the bourgeoisie. Those who think otherwise are either idiots, or are so politically ignorant that it would be a disgrace to allow them to come anywhere near a meeting, let alone on the platform. The only alternative is either violence against Liebknecht and Luxemburg, the murder of the best leaders of the workers, or the violent suppression of the exploiters; and whoever dreams of a middle course is our most harmful and dangerous enemy. That is how the matter stands at present. Hence, when we talk of utilising the services of the experts we must bear in mind the lesson taught by Soviet policy during the past year. During that year we have broken and defeated the exploiters and we must now solve the problem of using the bourgeois specialists. Here, I repeat, violence alone will get us nowhere. Here, in addition to violence, after successful violence, we need the organisation, discipline and moral weight of the victorious proletariat, which will subordinate all the bourgeois experts to its will and draw them into its work.

Some people may say that Lenin is recommending moral persuasion instead of violence! But it is foolish to imagine that we can solve the problem of organising a new science and technology for the development of communist society by violence alone. That is nonsense! We, as a Party, as people who have learned something during this year of Soviet activity, will not be so foolish as to think so, and we will warn the masses not to think so. The employment of all the institutions of bourgeois capitalist society requires not only the successful use of violence, but also organisation, discipline, comradely discipline among the masses, the organisation of proletarian influence over the rest of the population, the creation of a new, mass environment, which will convince the bourgeois specialists that they have no alternative, that there can be no return to the old society, and that they can do their work only in conjunction with the Communists who are working by their side, who are leading the masses, who enjoy the absolute confidence of the masses, and whose object is to ensure that the fruits of bourgeois science and technology, the fruits of thousands of years of the development of civilisation, shall be enjoyed not by a handful of people for the purpose of distinguishing themselves and amassing wealth, but by literally all the working people.

This is an immensely difficult task, the fulfilment of which will require decades! But to carry it out we must create a force, a discipline, comradely discipline, Soviet discipline, proletarian discipline, such as will not only physically crush the counter-revolutionary bourgeoisie, but also encompass them complete-ly, subordinate them to our will, compel them to proceed along our lines, to serve our cause.

I repeat that we come up against this problem every day in the work of organising our military forces, in the work of economic development, in the work of every economic council, in the work of every factory committee and of every nationalised factory. There was hardly a week during all past year that the Council of People's Commissars did not discuss and settle this question in one way or another. I am sure that there was not a single factory committee in Russia, not a single agricultural commune, not a single state farm, not a single uyezd land department which did not come up against this issue scores of times in the course of the past year's Soviet activity.

This is what makes this task so difficult, but it is also what makes it a really gratifying one. This is what we must do now, the day after the exploiters were crushed by the force of the proletarian insurrection. We suppressed their resistance — this had to be done. But this is not the only thing that has to be done. By the force of the new organisation, the comradely organisation of the working people, we must compel them to serve us. We must cure them of their old vices and prevent them from relapsing into their exploiting practices. They have remained bourgeois, and they occupy posts as commanders and staff officers in our army, as engineers and agronomists, and these old, bourgeois people call themselves Mensheviks and Socialist-Revolutionaries. It does not matter what they call themselves. They are bourgeois through and through, from head to foot, in their outlook and in their habits.

Well, what shall we do, throw them out? You cannot throw out hundreds of thousands! And if we did we should be harming only ourselves. We have no other material with which to build communism than that created by capitalism. We must not throw them out, but break their resistance, watch them at every step, make no political concessions to them, which spineless people are inclined to do every minute. Educated people yield to the policy and influence of the bourgeoisie because they acquired all their education in a bourgeois environment and from that environment. That is why they stumble at every step and make political concessions to the counter-revolutionary bourgeoisie.

A Communist who says that he must not get into a state where he will soil his hands, that he must have clean, communist hands, and that he will build communist society with clean communist hands and scorn the services of the contemptible, counter-revolutionary bourgeois co-operators, is a mere phrase-monger, because we cannot help resorting to their services.

The practical task that confronts us now is to enlist the services of all those whom capitalism has trained to oppose us, to watch them day after day, to place worker commissars over them in an environment of communist organisation, day after day to thwart their counter-revolutionary designs, and at the same time to learn from them.

The science which we, at best, possess, is the science of the agitator and propagandist, of the man who has been steeled by the hellishly hard lot of the factory worker, or starving peasant, a science which teaches us how to hold out for a long time and to persevere in the struggle, and this has saved us up to now. All this is necessary, but it is not enough. With this alone we cannot triumph. In order that our victory may be complete and final we must take all that is valuable from capitalism, take all its science and culture.

How can we take it? We must learn from them, from our enemies. Our advanced peasants, the class-conscious workers in their factories, our officials in the uyezd land departments must learn from the bourgeois agronomists, engineers, and others, so as to acquire the fruits of their culture.

In this respect, the struggle that flared up in our Party during the past year was extremely useful. It gave rise to numerous sharp collisions, but there are no struggles without sharp collisions. As a result, however, we gained practical experience in a matter that had never before confronted us, but without which it is impossible to achieve communism. I say again that the task of combining the victorious proletarian revolution with bourgeois culture, with bourgeois science and technology, which up to now has been available to few people, is a difficult one. Here, everything depends on the organisation and discipline of the advanced sections of the working people. If, in Russia, the millions of downtrodden and ignorant peasants who are totally incapable of independent development, who were oppressed by the landowners for centuries, did not have at their head, and by their side, an advanced section of the urban workers whom they understood, with whom they were intimate, who enjoyed their confidence, whom they believed as fellow-workers, if there were not this organisation which is capable of rallying the masses of the working people, of influencing them, of explaining to them and convincing them of the importance of the task of taking over the entire bourgeois culture, the cause of communism would be hopeless.

April 17, 1919

Published in pamphlet form in
1919 by the Petrograd Soviet of
Workers' and Red Army
Deputies

Collected Works,
Vol. 29, pp. 69-71,
71-75

Speech of Greeting at the First All-Russia Congress on Adult Education
May 6, 1919

Comrades, it gives me pleasure to greet the Congress on adult education. You do not, of course, expect me to deliver a speech that goes deeply into this subject, like that delivered by the preceding speaker, Comrade Lunacharsky, who is well-informed on the matter and has made a special study of it. Permit me to confine myself to a few words of greeting and to the observations I have made and thoughts that have occurred to me in the Council of People's Commissars when dealing more or less closely with your work. I am sure that there is not another sphere of Soviet activity in which such enormous progress has been made during the past eighteen months as in the sphere of adult education. Undoubtedly, it has been easier for us and for you to work in this sphere than in others. Here we had to cast aside the old obstacles and the old hindrances. Here it was much easier to do something to meet the tremendous demand for knowledge, for free education and free development, which was felt most among the masses of the workers and peasants; for while the mighty pressure of the masses made it easy for us to remove the external obstacles that stood in their path, to break up the historical bourgeois institutions which bound us to imperialist war and doomed Russia to bear the enormous burden that resulted from this war, we nevertheless felt acutely how heavy the task of re-educating the masses was, the task of organisation and instruction, spreading knowledge, combating that heritage of ignorance, primitiveness, barbarism and savagery that we took over. In this field the struggle had to be waged by entirely different methods; we could count only on the prolonged success and the persistent and systematic influence of the leading sections of the population, an influence which the masses willingly submit to, but often we are guilty of doing less than we could do. I think that in taking these first steps to spread adult education, education free from the old limits and conventionalities, which the adult population welcomes so much, we had at first to contend with two obstacles. Both these obstacles we inherited from the old capitalist society, which is clinging to us to this day, is dragging us down by thousands and millions of threads, ropes and chains.

The first was the plethora of bourgeois intellectuals, who very often regarded the new type of workers' and peasants' educational institution as the most convenient field for testing their individual theories in philosophy and culture, and in which, very often, the most absurd ideas were hailed as something new, and the supernatural and incongruous were offered as purely proletarian art and proletarian culture.[114] (*Applause.*) This was natural and, perhaps, pardonable in the early days, and the broad movement cannot be blamed for it. I hope that, in the long run, we shall try to get rid of all this and shall succeed.

The second was also inherited from capitalism. The broad masses of the petty-bourgeois working people who were thirsting for knowledge, broke down the old system, but could not propose anything of an organising or organised nature. I had opportunities to observe this in the Council of People's Commissars when the mobilisation of literate persons and the Library Department were discussed, and from these brief observations I realised the seriousness of the situation in this field. True, it is not quite customary to refer to something bad in a speech of greeting. I hope that you are free from these conventionalities, and will not be offended with me for telling you of my somewhat sad observations. When we raised the question of mobilising literate persons, the most striking thing was the brilliant victory achieved by our revolution without immediately emerging from the limits of the bourgeois revolution. It gave freedom for development to the available forces, but these available forces were petty-bourgeois and their watchword was the old one—each for himself and God for all—the very same accursed capitalist slogan which can never lead to anything but Kolchak and bourgeois restoration. If we review what we are doing to educate the illiterate, I think we shall have to draw the conclusion that we have done very little, and that our duty in this field is to realise that the organisation of proletarian elements is essential. It is not the ridiculous phrases which remain on paper that matter, but the introduction of measures which the people need urgently and which would compel every literate person to regard it his duty to instruct several illiterate persons. This is what our decree says[115]; but in this field hardly anything has been done.

When another question was dealt with in the Council of People's Commissars, that of the libraries, I said that the complaints we are constantly hearing about our industrial backwardness being to blame, about our having few books and being unable to produce enough—these complaints, I told myself, are justified. We have no fuel, of course, our factories are idle, we have little paper and we cannot produce books. All this is true, but it is also true that we cannot get at the books that are available. Here we continue to suffer from peasant simplicity and peasant helplessness; when the peasant ransacks the squire's library he runs home in the fear that somebody will take the books away from him, because he cannot conceive of just distribution, of state property that is not something hateful, but is the common property of the workers and of the working people generally. The ignorant masses of peasants are not to blame for this, and as far as the development of the revolution is concerned it is quite legitimate, it is an inevitable stage, and when the peasant took the library and kept it hidden, he could not do otherwise, for he did not know that all the libraries in Russia could be amalgamated and that there would be enough books to satisfy those who can read and to teach those who cannot. At present we must combat the survivals of disorganisation, chaos, and ridiculous departmental wrangling. This must be our main task. We must take up the simple and urgent matter of mobilising the literate to combat illiteracy. We must utilise the books that are available and set to work to organise a network of libraries which will help the people to gain access to every available book; there must be no parallel organisations, but a single, uniform planned organisation. This small matter reflects one of the fundamental tasks of our revolution. If it fails to carry out this task, if it fails to set about creating a really systematic and uniform organisation in place of our Russian chaos and inefficiency, then this revolution will remain a bourgeois revolution because the major specific feature of the proletarian revolution which is marching towards communism is this organisation—for all the bourgeoisie wanted was to break up the old system and allow freedom for the development of peasant farming, which revived the same capitalism as in all earlier revolutions.

Since we call ourselves the Communist Party, we must understand that only now that we have removed the external obstacles and have broken down the old institutions have we come face to face with the primary task of a genuine proletarian revolution in all its magnitude, namely, that of organising tens and hundreds of millions of people. After the eighteen months' experience that we all have acquired in this field, we must at last take the right road that will lead to victory over the lack of culture, and over the ignorance and barbarism from which we have suffered all this time. (*Stormy applause.*)

Published in *Pravda* No. 96,
May 7, 1919

Collected Works,
Vol. 29, pp. 335-38

From The Tasks of the Third International
Ramsay MacDonald on the Third International

As one of the particularly striking confirmations of the phenomenon observable everywhere, on a mass scale, namely, that of the growth of revolutionary consciousness among the masses, we may take the novels of Henri Barbusse, *Le feu* (Under Fire) and *Clarté* (Light). The former has already been translated into all languages, and in France 230,000 copies have been sold. The transformation of an absolutely ignorant rank-and-filer, utterly crushed by philistine ideas and prejudices, into a revolutionary under the influence of the war is depicted with extraordinary power, talent and truthfulness.

Published in August 1919
in the magazine
Kommunistichesky Internatsional
No. 4

Signed: *N. Lenin*

Collected Works,
Vol. 29, p. 509

Answers
to an American Journalist's Questions
(Excerpts)

We have made it possible, for instance, for the Bashkirian people to establish an autonomous republic within Russia, we are doing everything possible to help the independent, free development of every nationality, the growth and dissemination of literature in the native language of each of them, we are translating and propagandising our Soviet Constitution which has the misfortune to be more pleasing to more than a thousand million inhabitants of the earth who belong to colonial, dependent, oppressed, underprivileged nations than the constitutions of the West-European and American bourgeois-"democratic" states that perpetuate private property in land and capital, i.e., strengthen the oppression of the working people of their own countries and of hundreds of millions of people in the colonies of Asia, Africa, etc., by a small number of "civilised" capitalists.

The collapse of capitalism is inevitable. The revolutionary consciousness of the masses is everywhere growing; there are thousands of signs of this. One small sign, unimportant, but impressive to the man in the street, is the novels written by Henri Barbusse (*Le feu, Clarté*) who was a peaceful, modest, law-abiding petty bourgeois, a philistine, a man in the street, when he went to the war.

July 20, 1919

Pravda No. 162,
July 25, 1919

Collected Works,
Vol. 29, pp. 516, 518

Resolution of the C.C., R.C.P.(B.) on Soviet Rule in the Ukraine

On the question of the attitude towards the working people of the Ukraine now being liberated from the temporary occupation by Denikin bands the Central Committee of the R.C.P.(B.) resolves:

1. While steadfastly implementing the principle of national self-determination, the Central Committee deems it necessary to reaffirm that the R.C.P. adheres to the principle of recognition of the independence of the Ukrainian S.S.R.

2. Regarding it as beyond dispute for every Communist and for every politically-conscious worker that the closest alliance of all Soviet republics in their struggle against the menacing forces of world imperialism is essential, the R.C.P. maintains that the form of that alliance must be finally determined by the Ukrainian workers and labouring peasants themselves.

3. For the time being the relations between the Ukrainian S.S.R. and the R.S.F.S.R. are determined by the federative ties established by the decisions of the All-Russia Central Executive Committee of June 1, 1919 and the Ukrainian Central Executive Committee of May 18, 1919[116] (resolution attached).

4. In view of the fact that Ukrainian culture (language, school, etc.) has been suppressed for centuries by Russian tsarism and the exploiting classes, the C.C., R.C.P. makes it incumbent upon all Party members to use every means to help remove all barriers in the way of the free development of the Ukrainian language and culture. Since the many centuries of oppression have given rise to nationalist tendencies among the backward sections of the Ukrainian population, R.C.P. members must exercise the greatest tolerance and caution in respect of those tendencies and must oppose them with words of comradely explanation concerning the identity of interests of the working people of the Ukraine and Russia. R.C.P.

members on Ukrainian territory must put into practice the right of the working people to study in the Ukrainian language and to speak their native language in all Soviet institutions, opposing in every way the attempts to push the Ukrainian language into the background and taking steps to turn it into an instrument for the communist education of the working people. Steps must be taken immediately to ensure that in all Soviet institutions there are sufficient Ukrainian-speaking employees and that in future all employees are able to speak Ukrainian.

Bulletin of the C.C., R.C.P.(B.)
No. 8, December 2, 1919

Collected Works,
Fifth Russian
edition, Vol. 39,
pp. 334-35

Introduction to the Book by John Reed:
Ten Days that Shook the World

With the greatest interest and with never slackening attention I read John Reed's book, *Ten Days That Shook the World*. Unreservedly do I recommend it to the workers of the world. Here is a book which I should like to see published in millions of copies and translated into all languages. It gives a truthful and most vivid exposition of the events so significant to the comprehension of what really is the Proletarian Revolution and the Dictatorship of the Proletariat. These problems are widely discussed, but before one can accept or reject these ideas, he must understand the full significance of his decision. John Reed's book will undoubtedly help to clear this question, which is the fundamental problem of the international labor movement.

N. Lenin

Written at the end of 1919

First published in Russian in
1923 in the book: John Reed,
10 dnei, kotoriye potryasli mir,
Krasnaya Nov Publishers,
Moscow

Collected Works,
Vol. 36, p. 519

The Tasks of the Youth Leagues

Speech Delivered at the Third All-Russia Congress of the Russian Young Communist League October 2, 1920

(*The Congress greets Lenin with a tremendous ovation.*) Comrades, today I would like to talk on the fundamental tasks of the Young Communist League and, in this connection, on what the youth organisations in a socialist republic should be like in general.

It is all the more necessary to dwell on this question because in a certain sense it may be said that it is the youth that will be faced with the actual task of creating a communist society. For it is clear that the generation of working people brought up in capitalist society can, at best, accomplish the task of destroying the foundations of the old, the capitalist way of life, which was built on exploitation. At best it will be able to accomplish the tasks of creating a social system that will help the proletariat and the working classes retain power and lay a firm foundation, which can be built on only by a generation that is starting to work under the new conditions, in a situation in which relations based on the exploitation of man by man no longer exist.

And so, in dealing from this angle with the tasks confronting the youth, I must say that the tasks of the youth in general, and of the Young Communist Leagues and all other organisations in particular, might be summed up in a single word: learn.

Of course, this is only a "single word". It does not reply to the principal and most essential questions: what to learn, and how to learn? And the whole point here is that, with the transformation of the old, capitalist society, the upbringing, training and education of the new generations that will create the communist society cannot be conducted on the old lines. The teaching, training and education of the youth must proceed from the material that has been left to us by the old society. We can build communism only on the basis of the totality of knowledge, organisations and institutions, only by using the stock of human forces and means that have been left to us by the old society. Only by radically remoulding the teaching, organisation and training of the youth shall we be able to ensure that the efforts of the younger generation will result in the creation of a society that will be unlike the old society, i.e., in the creation of a communist society. That is why we must deal in detail with the question of what we should teach the youth and how the youth should learn if it really wants to justify the name of communist youth, and how it should be trained so as to be able to complete and consummate what we have started.

I must say that the first and most natural reply would seem to be that the Youth League, and the youth in general, who want to advance to communism, should learn communism.

But this reply — "learn communism" — is too general. What do we need in order to learn communism? What must be singled out from the sum of general knowledge so as to acquire a knowledge of communism? Here a number of dangers arise, which very often manifest themselves whenever the task of learning communism is presented incorrectly, or when it is interpreted in too one-sided a manner.

Naturally, the first thought that enters one's mind is that learning communism means assimilating the sum of knowledge that is contained in communist manuals, pamphlets and books. But such a definition of the study of communism would be too crude and inadequate. If the study of communism consisted solely in assimilating what is contained in communist books and pamphlets, we might all too easily obtain communist text-jugglers or braggarts, and this would very often do us harm, because such people, after learning by rote what is set forth in communist books and pamphlets, would prove incapable of combining the various branches of knowledge, and would be unable to act in the way communism really demands.

One of the greatest evils and misfortunes left to us by the old, capitalist society is the complete rift between books and practical life; we have had books explaining everything in the best possible manner, yet in most cases these books contained the most pernicious and hypocritical lies, a false description of capitalist society.

That is why it would be most mistaken merely to assimilate book knowledge about communism. No longer do our speeches and articles merely reiterate what used to be said

about communism, because our speeches and articles are
connected with our daily work in all fields. Without work and
without struggle, book knowledge of communism obtained
from communist pamphlets and works is absolutely worthless,
for it would continue the old separation of theory and practice,
the old rift which was the most pernicious feature of the old,
bourgeois society.

It would be still more dangerous to set about assimilating
only communist slogans. Had we not realised this danger in
time, and had we not directed all our efforts to averting this
danger, the half million or million young men and women who
would have called themselves Communists after studying
communism in this way would only greatly prejudice the cause
of communism.

The question arises: how is all this to be blended for the
study of communism? What must we take from the old schools,
from the old kind of science? It was the declared aim of the old
type of school to produce men with an all-round education, to
teach the sciences in general. We know that this was utterly
false, since the whole of society was based and maintained on
the division of people into classes, into exploiters and
oppressed. Since they were thoroughly imbued with the class
spirit, the old schools naturally gave knowledge only to the
children of the bourgeoisie. Every word was falsified in the
interests of the bourgeoisie. In these schools the younger
generation of workers and peasants were not so much
educated as drilled in the interests of that bourgeoisie. They
were trained in such a way as to be useful servants of the
bourgeoisie, able to create profits for it without disturbing its
peace and leisure. That is why, while rejecting the old type of
schools, we have made it our task to take from it only what we
require for genuine communist education.

This brings me to the reproaches and accusations which we
constantly hear levelled at the old schools, and which often lead
to wholly wrong conclusions. It is said that the old school was a
school of purely book knowledge, of ceaseless drilling and
grinding. That is true, but we must distinguish between what
was bad in the old schools and what is useful to us, and we must
be able to select from it what is necessary for communism.

The old schools provided purely book knowledge; they
compelled their pupils to assimilate a mass of useless,
superfluous and barren knowledge, which cluttered up the
brain and turned the younger generation into bureaucrats
regimented according to a single pattern. But it would mean

Lenin delivers a speech at the unveiling of a temporary
monument to Marx and Engels on Revolution Square.
Photo, November 7, 1918

falling into a grave error for you to try to draw the conclusion that one can become a Communist without assimilating the wealth of knowledge amassed by mankind. It would be mistaken to think it sufficient to learn communist slogans and the conclusions of communist science, without acquiring that sum of knowledge of which communism itself is a result. Marxism is an example which shows how communism arose out of the sum of human knowledge.

You have read and heard that communist theory—the science of communism created in the main by Marx, this doctrine of Marxism—has ceased to be the work of a single socialist of the nineteenth century, even though he was a genius, and that it has become the doctrine of millions and tens of millions of proletarians all over the world, who are applying it in their struggle against capitalism. If you were to ask why the teachings of Marx have been able to win the hearts and minds of millions and tens of millions of the most revolutionary class, you would receive only one answer: it was because Marx based his work on the firm foundation of the human knowledge acquired under capitalism. After making a study of the laws governing the development of human society, Marx realised the inevitability of capitalism developing towards communism. What is most important is that he proved this on the sole basis of a most precise, detailed and profound study of this capitalist society, by fully assimilating all that earlier science had produced. He critically reshaped everything that had been created by human society, without ignoring a single detail. He reconsidered, subjected to criticism, and verified on the working-class movement everything that human thinking had created, and therefrom formulated conclusions which people hemmed in by bourgeois limitations or bound by bourgeois prejudices could not draw.

We must bear this in mind when, for example, we talk about proletarian culture. We shall be unable to solve this problem unless we clearly realise that only a precise knowledge and transformation of the culture created by the entire development of mankind will enable us to create a proletarian culture. The latter is not clutched out of thin air; it is not an invention of those who call themselves experts in proletarian culture. That is all nonsense. Proletarian culture must be the logical development of the store of knowledge mankind has accumulated under the yoke of capitalist, landowner and bureaucratic society. All these roads have been leading, and will continue to lead up to proletarian culture, in the same way as political economy, as reshaped by Marx, has shown us what human society must arrive at, shown us the passage to the class struggle, to the beginning of the proletarian revolution.

When we so often hear representatives of the youth, as well as certain advocates of a new system of education, attacking the old schools, claiming that they used the system of cramming, we say to them that we must take what was good in the old schools. We must not borrow the system of encumbering young people's minds with an immense amount of knowledge, nine-tenths of which was useless and one-tenth distorted. This, however, does not mean that we can restrict ourselves to communist conclusions and learn only communist slogans. You will not create communism that way. You can become a Communist only when you enrich your mind with a knowledge of all the treasures created by mankind.

We have no need of cramming, but we do need to develop and perfect the mind of every student with a knowledge of fundamental facts. Communism will become an empty word, a mere signboard, and a Communist a mere boaster, if all the knowledge he has acquired is not digested in his mind. You should not merely assimilate this knowledge, but assimilate it critically, so as not to cram your mind with useless lumber, but enrich it with all those facts that are indispensable to the well-educated man of today. If a Communist took it into his head to boast about his communism because of the cut-and-dried conclusions he had acquired, without putting in a great deal of serious and hard work and without understanding facts he should examine critically, he would be a deplorable Communist indeed. Such superficiality would be decidedly fatal. If I know that I know little, I shall strive to learn more; but if a man says that he is a Communist and that he need not know anything thoroughly, he will never become anything like a Communist.

The old schools produced servants needed by the capitalists; the old schools turned men of science into men who had to write and say whatever pleased the capitalists. We must therefore abolish them. But does the fact that we must abolish them, destroy them, mean that we should not take from them everything mankind has accumulated that is essential to man? Does it mean that we do not have to distinguish between what was necessary to capitalism and what is necessary to communism?

We are replacing the old drill-sergeant methods practised in bourgeois society, against the will of the majority, with the class-conscious discipline of the workers and peasants, who combine hatred of the old society with a determination, ability and readiness to unite and organise their forces for this struggle so as to forge the wills of millions and hundreds of millions of people — disunited, and scattered over the territory of a huge country — into a single will, without which defeat is inevitable. Without this solidarity, without this conscious discipline of the workers and peasants, our cause is hopeless. Without this, we shall be unable to vanquish the capitalists and landowners of the whole world. We shall not even consolidate the foundation, let alone build a new, communist society on that foundation. Likewise, while condemning the old schools, while harbouring an absolutely justified and necessary hatred for the old schools, and appreciating the readiness to destroy them, we must realise that we must replace the old system of instruction, the old cramming and the old drill, with an ability to acquire the sum total of human knowledge, and to acquire it in such a way that communism shall not be something to be learned by rote, but something that you yourselves have thought over, something that will embody conclusions inevitable from the standpoint of present-day education.

That is the way the main tasks should be presented when we speak of the aim: learn communism.

I shall take a practical example to make this clear to you, and to demonstrate the approach to the problem of how you must learn. You all know that, following the military problems, those of defending the republic, we are now confronted with economic tasks. Communist society, as we know, cannot be built unless we restore industry and agriculture, and that, not in the old way. They must be re-established on a modern basis, in accordance with the last word in science. You know that electricity is that basis, and that only after electrification of the entire country, of all branches of industry and agriculture, only when you have achieved that aim, will you be able to build for yourselves the communist society which the older generation will not be able to build. Confronting you is the task of economically reviving the whole country, of reorganising and restoring both agriculture and industry on modern technical lines, based on modern science and technology, on electricity. You realise perfectly well that illiterate people cannot tackle electrification, and that elementary literacy is not enough either. It is insufficient to understand what electricity is; what is needed is the knowledge of how to apply it technically in industry and agriculture, and in the individual branches of

5*

industry and agriculture. This has to be learnt for oneself, and it must be taught to the entire rising generation of working people. That is the task confronting every class-conscious Communist, every young person who regards himself a Communist and who clearly understands that, by joining the Young Communist League, he has pledged himself to help the Party build communism and to help the whole younger generation create a communist society. He must realise that he can create it only on the basis of modern education, and if he does not acquire this education communism will remain merely a pious wish.

It was the task of the older generation to overthrow the bourgeoisie. The main task then was to criticise the bourgeoisie, arouse hatred of the bourgeoisie among the masses, and foster class-consciousness and the ability to unite their forces. The new generation is confronted with a far more complex task. Your duty does not lie only in assembling your forces so as to uphold the workers' and peasants' government against an invasion instigated by the capitalists. Of course, you must do that; that is something you clearly realise, and is distinctly seen by the Communist. However, that is not enough. You have to build up a communist society. In many respects half of the work has been done. The old order has been destroyed, just as it deserved, it has been turned into a heap of ruins, just as it deserved. The ground has been cleared, and on this ground the younger communist generation must build a communist society. You are faced with the task of construction, and you can accomplish that task only by assimilating all modern knowledge, only if you are able to transform communism from cut-and-dried and memorised formulas, counsels, recipes, prescriptions and programmes into that living reality which gives unity to your immediate work, and only if you are able to make communism a guide in all your practical work.

That is the task you should pursue in educating, training and rousing the entire younger generation. You must be foremost among the millions of builders of a communist society in whose ranks every young man and young woman should be. You will not build a communist society unless you enlist the mass of young workers and peasants in the work of building communism.

This naturally brings me to the question of how we should teach communism and what the specific features of our methods should be.

I first of all shall deal here with the question of communist ethics.

You must train yourselves to be Communists. It is the task of the Youth League to organise its practical activities in such a way that, by learning, organising, uniting and fighting, its members shall train both themselves and all those who look to it for leadership; it should train Communists. The entire purpose of training, educating and teaching the youth of today should be to imbue them with communist ethics.

But is there such a thing as communist ethics? Is there such a thing as communist morality? Of course, there is. It is often suggested that we have no ethics of our own; very often the bourgeoisie accuse us Communists of rejecting all morality. This is a method of confusing the issue, of throwing dust in the eyes of the workers and peasants.

In what sense do we reject ethics, reject morality?

In the sense given to it by the bourgeoisie, who based ethics on God's commandments. On this point we, of course, say that we do not believe in God, and that we know perfectly well that the clergy, the landowners and the bourgeoisie invoked the name of God so as to further their own interests as exploiters. Or, instead of basing ethics on the commandments of morality, on the commandments of God, they based it on idealist or semi-idealist phrases, which always amounted to something very similar to God's commandments.

We reject any morality based on extra-human and extra-class concepts. We say that this is deception, dupery, stultification of the workers and peasants in the interests of the landowners and capitalists.

We say that our morality is entirely subordinated to the interests of the proletariat's class struggle. Our morality stems from the interests of the class struggle of the proletariat.

The old society was based on the oppression of all the workers and peasants by the landowners and capitalists. We had to destroy all that, and overthrow them but to do that we had to create unity. That is something that God cannot create.

This unity could be provided only by the factories, only by a proletariat trained and roused from its long slumber. Only when that class was formed did a mass movement arise which has led to what we have now—the victory of the proletarian revolution in one of the weakest of countries, which for three years has been repelling the onslaught of the bourgeoisie of the whole world. We can see how the proletarian revolution is developing all over the world. On the basis of experience, we now say that only the proletariat could have created the solid force which the disunited and scattered peasantry are following and which has withstood all onslaughts by the exploiters. Only this class can help the working masses unite, rally their ranks and conclusively defend, conclusively consolidate and conclusively build up a communist society.

That is why we say that to us there is no such thing as a morality that stands outside human society; that is a fraud. To us morality is subordinated to the interests of the proletariat's class struggle.

What does that class struggle consist in? It consists in overthrowing the tsar, overthrowing the capitalists, and abolishing the capitalist class.

What are classes in general? Classes are that which permits one section of society to appropriate the labour of another section. If one section of society appropriates all the land, we have a landowner class and a peasant class. If one section of society owns the factories, shares and capital, while another section works in these factories, we have a capitalist class and a proletarian class.

It was not difficult to drive out the tsar — that required only a few days. It was not very difficult to drive out the landowners — that was done in a few months. Nor was it very difficult to drive out the capitalists. But it is incomparably more difficult to abolish classes; we still have the division into workers and peasants. If the peasant is installed on his plot of land and appropriates his surplus grain, that is, grain that he does not need for himself or for his cattle, while the rest of the people have to go without bread, then the peasant becomes an exploiter. The more grain he clings to, the more profitable he finds it; as for the rest, let them starve: "The more they starve, the dearer I can sell this grain." All should work according to a single common plan, on common land, in common factories and in accordance with a common system. Is that easy to attain? You see that it is not as easy as driving out the tsar, the landowners and the capitalists. What is required is that the proletariat re-educate a section of the peasantry; it must win over the working peasants in order to crush the resistance of those peasants who are rich and are profiting from the poverty and want of the rest. Hence the task of the proletarian struggle is not quite completed after we have overthrown the tsar and driven out the landowners and capitalists; to accomplish that is the task of the system we call the dictatorship of the proletariat.

The class struggle is continuing; it has merely changed its

forms. It is the class struggle of the proletariat to prevent the return of the old exploiters, to unite in a single union the scattered masses of unenlightened peasants. The class struggle is continuing and it is our task to subordinate all interests to that struggle. Our communist morality is also subordinated to that task. We say: morality is what serves to destroy the old exploiting society and to unite all the working people around the proletariat, which is building up a new, a communist society.

Communist morality is that which serves this struggle and unites the working people against all exploitation, against all petty private property; for petty property puts into the hands of one person that which has been created by the labour of the whole of society. In our country the land is common property.

But suppose I take a piece of this common property and grow on it twice as much grain as I need, and profiteer on the surplus? Suppose I argue that the more starving people there are, the more they will pay? Would I then be behaving like a Communist? No, I would be behaving like an exploiter, like a proprietor. That must be combated. If that is allowed to go on, things will revert to the rule of the capitalists, to the rule of the bourgeoisie, as has more than once happened in previous revolutions. To prevent the restoration of the rule of the capitalists and the bourgeoisie, we must not allow profiteering; we must not allow individuals to enrich themselves at the expense of the rest; the working people must unite with the proletariat and form a communist society. This is the principal feature of the fundamental task of the League and the organisation of the communist youth.

The old society was based on the principle: rob or be robbed; work for others or make others work for you; be a slave-owner or a slave. Naturally, people brought up in such a society assimilate with their mother's milk, one might say, the psychology, the habit, the concept which says: you are either a slave-owner or a slave, or else, a small owner, a petty employee, a petty official, or an intellectual — in short, a man who is concerned only with himself, and does not care a rap for anybody else.

If I work this plot of land, I do not care a rap for anybody else; if others starve, all the better, I shall get the more for my grain. If I have a job as a doctor, engineer, teacher, or clerk, I do not care a rap for anybody else. If I toady to and please the powers that be, I may be able to keep my job, and even get on in life and become a bourgeois. A Communist cannot harbour such a psychology and such sentiments. When the workers and

peasants proved that they were able, by their own efforts, to
defend themselves and create a new society—that was the
beginning of the new, communist education, education in the
struggle against the exploiters, education in alliance with the
proletariat against the self-seekers and petty proprietors,
against the psychology and habits which say: I seek my own
profit and don't care a rap for anything else.

That is the reply to the question of how the young and rising
generation should learn communism.

It can learn communism only by linking up every step in its
studies, training and education with the continuous struggle
the proletarians and the working people are waging against the
old society of exploiters. When people tell us about morality,
we say: to a Communist all morality lies in this united discipline
and conscious mass struggle against the exploiters. We do not
believe in an eternal morality, and we expose the falseness of
all the fables about morality. Morality serves the purpose of
helping human society rise to a higher level and rid itself of the
exploitation of labour.

To achieve this we need that generation of young people
who began to reach political maturity in the midst of a
disciplined and desperate struggle against the bourgeoisie. In
this struggle that generation is training genuine Communists;
it must subordinate to this struggle, and link up with it, each
step in its studies, education and training. The education of the
communist youth must consist, not in giving them suave talks
and moral precepts. This is not what education consists in.
When people have seen the way in which their fathers and
mothers lived under the yoke of the landowners and
capitalists; when they have themselves experienced the suffer-
ings of those who began the struggle against the exploiters;
when they have seen the sacrifices made to keep what has been
won, and seen what deadly enemies the landowners and capitalists are—they are taught by these conditions to become
Communists. Communist morality is based on the struggle for
the consolidation and completion of communism. That is also
the basis of communist training, education, and teaching. That
is the reply to the question of how communism should be
learnt.

We could not believe in teaching, training and education if
they were restricted only to the schoolroom and divorced from
the ferment of life. As long as the workers and peasants are
oppressed by the landowners and capitalists, and as long as the
schools are controlled by the landowners and capitalists, the
young generation will remain blind and ignorant. Our schools

must provide the youth with the fundamentals of knowledge, the ability to evolve communist views independently; they must make educated people of the youth. While they are attending school, they must learn to become participants in the struggle for emancipation from the exploiters. The Young Communist League will justify its name as the League of the young communist generation only when every step in its teaching, training and education is linked up with participation in the common struggle of all working people against the exploiters. You are well aware that, as long as Russia remains the only workers' republic and the old, bourgeois system exists in the rest of the world, we shall be weaker than they are, and be constantly threatened with a new attack; and that only if we learn to be solidly united shall we win in the further struggle and — having gained strength — become really invincible. Thus, to be a Communist means that you must organise and unite the entire young generation and set an example of training and discipline in this struggle. Then you will be able to start building the edifice of communist society and bring it to completion.

To make this clearer to you, I shall quote an example. We call ourselves Communists. What is a Communist? Communist is a Latin word. *Communis* is the Latin for "common". Communist society is a society in which all things — the land, the factories — are owned in common and the people work in common. That is communism.

Is it possible to work in common if each one works separately on his own plot of land? Work in common cannot be brought about all at once. That is impossible. It does not drop from the skies. It comes through toil and suffering; it is created in the course of struggle. The old books are of no use here; no one will believe them. One's own experience of life is needed. When Kolchak and Denikin were advancing from Siberia and the South, the peasants were on their side. They did not like Bolshevism because the Bolsheviks took their grain at a fixed price. But when the peasants in Siberia and the Ukraine experienced the rule of Kolchak and Denikin, they realised that they had only one alternative: either to go to the capitalists, who would at once hand them over into slavery under the landowners; or to follow the workers, who, it is true, did not promise a land flowing with milk and honey, and demanded iron discipline and firmness in an arduous struggle, but would lead them out of enslavement by the capitalists and landowners. When even the ignorant peasants saw and realised this from their own experience, they became conscious adherents of communism, who had gone through a severe school. It is such experience that must form the basis of all the activities of the Young Communist League.

I have replied to the questions of what we must learn, what we must take from the old schools and from the old science. I shall now try to answer the question of how this must be learnt. The answer is: only by inseparably linking each step in the activities of the schools, each step in training, education and teaching, with the struggle of all the working people against the exploiters.

I shall quote a few examples from the experience of the work of some of the youth organisations so as to illustrate how this training in communism should proceed. Everybody is talking about abolishing illiteracy. You know that a communist society cannot be built in an illiterate country. It is not enough for the Soviet government to issue an order, or for the Party to issue a particular slogan, or to assign a certain number of the best workers to this task. The young generation itself must take up this work. Communism means that the youth, the young men and women who belong to the Youth League, should say: this is our job; we shall unite and go into the rural districts to abolish illiteracy, so that there shall be no illiterates among our young people. We are trying to get the rising generation to devote their activities to this work. You know that we cannot rapidly transform an ignorant and illiterate Russia into a literate country. But if the Youth League sets to work on the job, and if all young people work for the benefit of all, the League, with a membership of 400,000 young men and women, will be entitled to call itself a Young Communist League. It is also a task of the League, not only to acquire knowledge itself, but to help those young people who are unable to extricate themselves by their own efforts from the toils of illiteracy. Being a member of the Youth League means devoting one's labour and efforts to the common cause. That is what a communist education means. Only in the course of such work do young men and women become real Communists. Only if they achieve practical results in this work will they become Communists.

Take, for example, work in the suburban vegetable gardens. Is that not a real job of work? It is one of the tasks of the Young Communist League. People are starving; there is hunger in the factories. To save ourselves from starvation, vegetable gardens must be developed. But farming is being carried on in the old way. Therefore, more class-conscious elements should engage in this work, and then you will find that the number of vegetable gardens will increase, their acreage will grow, and the results will improve. The Young Communist League must take an active part in this work. Every League and League branch should regard this as its duty.

The Young Communist League must be a shock force, helping in every job and displaying initiative and enterprise. The League should be an organisation enabling any worker to see that it consists of people whose teachings he perhaps does not understand, and whose teachings he may not immediately believe, but from whose practical work and activity he can see that they are really people who are showing him the right road.

If the Young Communist League fails to organise its work in this way in all fields, it will mean that it is reverting to the old bourgeois path. We must combine our education with the struggle of the working people against the exploiters, so as to help the former accomplish the tasks set by the teachings of communism.

The members of the League should use every spare hour to improve the vegetable gardens, or to organise the education of young people at some factory, and so on. We want to transform Russia from a poverty-stricken and wretched country into one that is wealthy. The Young Communist League must combine its education, learning and training with the labour of the workers and peasants, so as not to confine itself to schools or to reading communist books and pamphlets. Only by working side by side with the workers and peasants can one become a genuine Communist. It has to be generally realised that all members of the Youth League are literate people and at the same time are keen at their jobs. When everyone sees that we have ousted the old drill-ground methods from the old schools and have replaced them with conscious discipline, that all young men and women take part in subbotniks, and utilise every suburban farm to help the population — people will cease to regard labour in the old way.

It is the task of the Young Communist League to organise assistance everywhere, in village or city block, in such matters as — and I shall take a small example — public hygiene or the distribution of food. How was this done in the old, capitalist society? Everybody worked only for himself and nobody cared a straw for the aged and the sick, or whether housework was the concern only of the women, who, in consequence, were in a condition of oppression and servitude. Whose business is it to combat this? It is the business of the Youth Leagues, which must say: we shall change all this; we shall organise detachments of young people who will help to assure public hygiene or distribute food, who will conduct systematic house-to-house inspections, and work in an organised way for the benefit of the whole of society, distributing their forces properly and demonstrating that labour must be organised.

The generation of people who are now at the age of fifty cannot expect to see a communist society. This generation will be gone before then. But the generation of those who are now fifteen will see a communist society, and will itself build this society. This generation should know that the entire purpose of their lives is to build a communist society. In the old society, each family worked separately and labour was not organised by anybody except the landowners and capitalists, who oppressed the masses of the people. We must organise all labour, no matter how toilsome or messy it may be, in such a way that every worker and peasant will be able to say: I am part of the great army of free labour, and shall be able to build up my life without the landowners and capitalists, able to help establish a communist system. The Young Communist League should teach all young people to engage in conscious and disciplined labour from an early age. In this way we can be confident that the problems now confronting us will be solved. We must assume that no less than ten years will be required for the electrification of the country, so that our impoverished land may profit from the latest achievements of technology. And so, the generation of those who are now fifteen years old, and will be living in a communist society in ten or twenty years' time, should tackle all its educational tasks in such a way that every day, in every village and city, the young people shall engage in the practical solution of some problem of labour in common, even though the smallest or the simplest. The success of communist construction will be assured when this is done in every village, as communist emulation develops, and the youth prove that they can unite their labour. Only by regarding your every step from the standpoint of the success of that construction, and only by asking ourselves whether we have done all we can to be united and politically-conscious working people will the Young Communist League succeed in uniting its half a million members into a single army of labour and win universal respect. (*Stormy applause.*)

Pravda Nos. 221, 222 and 223,
October 5, 6 and 7, 1920

Collected Works,
Vol. 31, pp. 283-99

On Proletarian Culture

We see from *Izvestia* of October 8 that, in his address to the Proletcult Congress, Comrade Lunacharsky said things that were *diametrically opposite* to what he and I had agreed upon yesterday.

It is necessary that a draft resolution (of the Proletcult Congress) should be drawn up with the utmost urgency, and that it should be endorsed by the Central Committee, in time to have it put to the vote *at this very* session of the Proletcult. On behalf of the Central Committee it should be submitted not later than today, for endorsement both by the Collegium of the People's Commissariat for Education and by the Proletcult Congress, because the Congress is closing today.

Draft Resolution

1) All educational work in the Soviet Republic of workers and peasants, in the field of political education in general and in the field of art in particular, should be imbued with the spirit of the class struggle being waged by the proletariat for the successful achievement of the aims of its dictatorship, i.e., the overthrow of the bourgeoisie, the abolition of classes, and the elimination of all forms of exploitation of man by man.

2) Hence, the proletariat, both through its vanguard — the Communist Party — and through the many types of proletarian organisations in general, should display the utmost activity and play the leading part in all the work of public education.

3) All the experience of modern history and, particularly, the more than half-century-old revolutionary struggle of the proletariat of all countries since the appearance of the *Communist Manifesto* has unquestionably demonstrated that the Marxist world outlook is the only true expression of the

interests, the viewpoint, and the culture of the revolutionary proletariat.

4) Marxism has won its historic significance as the ideology of the revolutionary proletariat because, far from rejecting the most valuable achievements of the bourgeois epoch, it has, on the contrary, assimilated and refashioned everything of value in the more than two thousand years of the development of human thought and culture. Only further work on this basis and in this direction, inspired by the practical experience of the proletarian dictatorship as the final stage in the struggle against every form of exploitation, can be recognised as the development of a genuine proletarian culture.

5) Adhering unswervingly to this stand of principle, the All-Russia Proletcult Congress rejects in the most resolute manner, as theoretically unsound and practically harmful, all attempts to invent one's own particular brand of culture, to remain isolated in self-contained organisations, to draw a line dividing the field of work of the People's Commissariat for Education and the Proletcult, or to set up a Proletcult "autonomy" within establishments under the People's Commissariat for Education and so forth. On the contrary, the Congress enjoins all Proletcult organisations to fully consider themselves in duty bound to act as auxiliary bodies of the network of establishments under the People's Commissariat of Education, and to accomplish their tasks under the general guidance of the Soviet authorities (specifically, of the People's Commissariat of Education) and of the Russian Communist Party, as part of the tasks of the proletarian dictatorship.

* * *

Comrade Lunacharsky says that his words have been distorted. In that case this resolution is needed *all the more* urgently.

Written on October 8, 1920

First published in 1926
in the magazine *Krasnaya Nov*
No. 3

Collected Works,
Vol. 31, pp. 316-17

A Capably Written Little Book

A Dozen Knives in the Back of the Revolution, Paris, 1921. This small volume of stories was written by the whiteguard Arkady Averchenko, whose rage rises to the pitch of frenzy. It is interesting to note how his burning hatred brings out the remarkably strong and also the remarkably weak points of this extremely capably written book. When the author takes for his stories subjects he is unfamiliar with, they are inartistic. An example is the story showing the home life of Lenin and Trotsky. There is much malice, but little truth in it, my dear Citizen Averchenko! I assure you that Lenin and Trotsky have many faults in all respects, including their home life. But to describe them skilfully one must know what they are. This you do not know.

But most of the stories in the book deal with subjects Arkady Averchenko is very familiar with, has experienced, given thought to and felt. He depicts with amazing skill the impressions and moods of the representative of the old, rich, gorging and guzzling Russia of the landowners and capitalists. That is exactly what the revolution must look like to the representatives of the ruling classes. Averchenko's burning hatred makes some — in fact most — of his stories amazingly vivid. There are some really magnificent stories, as, for example, "Grass Trampled by Jackboots", which deals with the psychology of children who have lived and are living through the Civil War.

But the author shows real depth of feeling only when he talks about food; when he relates how the rich people fed in old Russia, how they had snacks in Petrograd — no, not in Petrograd, in St. Petersburg — costing fourteen and a half rubles, fifty rubles, etc. He describes all this in really voluptuous terms. These things he knows well; these things he has experienced; here he makes no mistakes. His knowledge of the subject and his sincerity are most extraordinary.

In his last story, "Fragments of the Shattered", he describes an ex-Senator in the Crimea, in Sevastopol, who was "rich, generous and well-connected", but who is "now a day labourer at the artillery dumps, unloading and sorting shells", and an ex-director of a "vast steel plant which was considered to be the largest works in Vyborg District. Now he is a salesman at a shop which sells second-hand goods on commission, and has lately even acquired a certain amount of experience in fixing the price of ladies' second-hand robes and plush teddy-bears that people bring to be sold on commission."

The two old fogies recall the old days, the St. Petersburg sunsets, the streets, the theatres and, of course, the meals at the "Medved", "Vienna", "Maly Yaroslavets", and similar restaurants. And they interrupt their reminiscences to exclaim: "What have we done to deserve this? Now did we get in anyone's way? Who did we interfere with?... Why did they treat Russia so?" ...

Arkady Averchenko is not the one to understand why. The workers and peasants, however, seem to understand quite easily and need no explanations.

In my opinion some of these stories are worth reprinting. Talent should be encouraged.

Pravda No. 263,   Collected Works,
November 22, 1921   Vol. 33, pp. 125-26
Signed: N. Lenin

The International and Domestic Situation of the Soviet Republic

From the Speech Delivered to a Meeting of the Communist Group at the All-Russia Congress of Metalworkers, March 6, 1922

... Yesterday I happened to read in *Izvestia* a political poem by Mayakovsky.[117] I am not an admirer of his poetical talent, although I admit that I am not a competent judge. But I have not for a long time read anything on politics and administration with so much pleasure as I read this. In his poem he derides this meeting habit, and taunts the Communists with incessantly sitting at meetings. I am not sure about the poetry; but as for the politics, I vouch for their absolute correctness. We are indeed in the position, and it must be said that it is a very absurd position, of people sitting endlessly at meetings, setting up commissions and drawing up plans without end. There was a character who typified Russian life — Oblomov. He was always lolling on his bed and mentally drawing up schemes. That was a long time ago. Russia has experienced three revolutions, but the Oblomovs have survived, for there were Oblomovs not only among the landowners but also among the peasants; not only among the peasants, but among the intellectuals too; and not only among the intellectuals, but also among the workers and Communists. It is enough to watch us at our meetings, at our work on commissions, to be able to say that *old Oblomov still lives; and it will be necessary to give him a good washing and cleaning, a good rubbing and scouring to make a man of him.* In this respect we must have no illusions about our position. We have not imitated any of those who write the word "revolution" with a capital R, as the Socialist-Revolutionaries do. But we can quote the words of Marx that many foolish things are done during a revolution, perhaps more than at any other time.[118] We revolutionaries must learn to regard these foolish acts dispassionately and fearlessly.

Pravda No. 54,
March 8, 1922

Collected Works,
Vol. 33, pp. 223-24

From On the Significance
of Militant Materialism

Engels long ago advised the contemporary leaders of the proletariat to translate the militant atheist literature of the late eighteenth century [119] for mass distribution among the people. We have not done this up to the present, to our shame be it said (this is one of the numerous proofs that it is much easier to seize power in a revolutionary epoch than to know how to use this power properly). Our apathy, inactivity and incompetence are sometimes excused on all sorts of "lofty" grounds, as, for example, that the old atheist literature of the eighteenth century is antiquated, unscientific, naïve, etc. There is nothing worse than such pseudo-scientific sophistry, which serves as a screen either for pedantry or for a complete misunderstanding of Marxism. There is, of course, much that is unscientific and naïve in the atheist writings of the eighteenth-century re-volutionaries. But nobody prevents the publishers of these writings from abridging them and providing them with brief postscripts pointing out the progress made by mankind in the scientific criticism of religions since the end of the eighteenth century, mentioning the latest writings on the subject, and so forth. It would be the biggest and most grievous mistake a Marxist could make to think that the millions of the people (especially the peasants and artisans), who have been con-demned by all modern society to darkness, ignorance and superstition, can extricate themselves from this darkness only along the straight line of a purely Marxist education. These masses should be supplied with the most varied atheist propaganda material, they should be made familiar with facts from the most diverse spheres of life, they should be approached in every possible way, so as to interest them, rouse them from their religious torpor, stir them from the most varied angles and by the most varied methods, and so forth.

The keen, vivacious and talented writings of the old eighteenth-century atheists wittily and openly attacked the prevailing clericalism and will very often prove a thousand times more suitable for arousing people from their religious torpor than the dull and dry paraphrases of Marxism, almost completely unillustrated by skilfully selected facts, which predominate in our literature and which (it is no use hiding the fact) frequently distort Marxism. We have translations of all the major works of Marx and Engels. There are absolutely no grounds for fearing that the old atheism and old materialism will remain unsupplemented by the corrections introduced by Marx and Engels. The most important thing — and it is this that is most frequently overlooked by those of our Communists who are supposedly Marxists, but who in fact mutilate Marxism — is to know how to awaken in the still undeveloped masses an intelligent attitude towards religious questions and an intelligent criticism of religions.

On the other hand, take a glance at modern scientific critics of religions. These educated bourgeois writers almost invariably "supplement" their own refutations of religious superstitions with arguments which immediately expose them as ideological slaves of the bourgeoisie, as "graduated flunkeys of clericalism".

Two examples. Professor R. Y. Wipper published in 1918 a little book entitled *Vozniknoveniye Khristianstva* (The Origin of Christianity — Pharos Publishing House, Moscow). In his account of the principal results of modern science, the author not only refrains from combating the superstitions and deception which are the weapons of the church as a political organisation, not only evades these questions, but makes the simply ridiculous and most reactionary claim that he is above both "extremes" — the idealist and the materialist. This is toadying to the ruling bourgeoisie, which all over the world devotes to the support of religion hundreds of millions of rubles from the profits squeezed out of the working people.

The well-known German scientist, Arthùr Drews, while refuting religious superstitions and fables in his book, *Die Christusmythe* (The Christ Myth), and while showing that Christ never existed, at the end of the book declares in favour of religion, albeit a renovated, purified and more subtle religion, one that would be capable of withstanding "the daily growing naturalist torrent" (fourth German edition,1910, p. 238). Here we have an outspoken and deliberate reactionary, who is openly helping the exploiters to replace the old, decayed religious superstitions by new, more odious and vile superstitions.

This does not mean that Drews should not be translated. It means that while in a certain measure effecting an alliance with the progressive section of the bourgeoisie, Communists and all consistent materialists should unflinchingly expose that section when it is guilty of reaction. It means that to shun an alliance with the representatives of the bourgeoisie of the eighteenth century, i.e., the period when it was revolutionary, would be to betray Marxism and materialism; for an "alliance" with the Drewses, in one form or another and in one degree or another, is essential for our struggle against the predominating religious obscurantists.

Pod Znamenem Marksizma, [120] which sets out to be an organ of militant materialism, should devote much of its space to atheist propaganda, to reviews of the literature on the subject and to correcting the immense shortcomings of our governmental work in this field. It is particularly important to utilise books and pamphlets which contain many concrete facts and comparisons showing how the class interests and class organisations of the modern bourgeoisie are connected with the organisations of religious institutions and religious propaganda. [121]

All material relating to the United States of America, where the official, state connection between religion and capital is less manifest, is extremely important. But, on the other hand, it becomes all the clearer to us that so-called modern democracy (which the Mensheviks, the Socialist-Revolutionaries, partly also the anarchists, etc., so unreasonably worship) is nothing but the freedom to preach whatever is to the advantage of the bourgeoisie, to preach, namely, the most reactionary ideas, religion, obscurantism, defence of the exploiters, etc.

One would like to hope that a journal which sets out to be a militant materialist organ will provide our reading public with reviews of atheist literature, showing for which circle of readers any particular writing might be suitable and in what respect, and mentioning what literature has been published in our country (only decent translations should be given notice, and they are not so many), and what is still to be published.

Pod Znamenem Marksizma   *Collected Works*,
No. 3, March 1922   Vol. 33, pp. 229-32
Signed: *N. Lenin*

Our Revolution

(Apropos of N. Sukhanov's Notes)

I

I have lately been glancing through Sukhanov's notes on the revolution. What strikes one most is the pedantry of all our petty-bourgeois democrats and of all the heroes of the Second International. [122] Apart from the fact that they are all extremely faint-hearted, that when it comes to the minutest deviation from the German model even the best of them fortify themselves with reservations — apart from this characteristic, which is common to all petty-bourgeois democrats and has been abund antly manifested by them throughout the revolution, what strikes one is their slavish imitation of the past.

They all call themselves Marxists, but their conception of Marxism is impossibly pedantic. They have completely failed to understand what is decisive in Marxism, namely, its revolutionary dialectics. They have even absolutely failed to understand Marx's plain statements that in times of revolution the utmost flexibility [123] is demanded, and have even failed to notice, for instance, the statements Marx made in his letters — I think it was in 1856 — expressing the hope of combining a peasant war in Germany, which might create a revolutionary situation, with the working-class movement [124] — they avoid even this plain statement and walk round and about it like a cat around a bowl of hot porridge.

Their conduct betrays them as cowardly reformists who are afraid to deviate from the bourgeoisie, let alone break with it, and at the same time they disguise their cowardice with the wildest rhetoric and braggartry. But what strikes one in all of them even from the purely theoretical point of view is their utter inability to grasp the following Marxist considerations: up to now they have seen capitalism and bourgeois democracy in Western Europe follow a definite path of development, and cannot conceive that this path can be taken as a model only *mutatis mutandis*, only with certain amendments (quite insignificant from the standpoint of the general development of world history).

First— the revolution connected with the first imperialist world war. Such a revolution was bound to reveal new features, or variations, resulting from the war itself, for the world has never seen such a war in such a situation. We find that since the war the bourgeoisie of the wealthiest countries have to this day been unable to restore "normal" bourgeois relations. Yet our reformists — petty bourgeois who make a show of being revolutionaries — believed, and still believe, that normal bourgeois relations are the limit (thus far shalt thou go and no farther). And even their conception of "normal" is extremely stereotyped and narrow.

Secondly, they are complete strangers to the idea that while the development of world history as a whole follows general laws it is by no means precluded, but, on the contrary, presumed, that certain periods of development may display peculiarities in either the form or the sequence of this development. For instance, it does not even occur to them that because Russia stands on the border-line between the civilised countries and the countries which this war has for the first time definitely brought into the orbit of civilisation — all the Oriental, non-European countries — she could and was, indeed, bound to reveal certain distinguishing features; although these, of course, are in keeping with the general line of world development, they distinguish her revolution from those which took place in the West-European countries and introduce certain partial innovations as the revolution moves on to the countries of the East.

Infinitely stereotyped, for instance, is the argument they learned by rote during the development of West-European Social-Democracy, namely, that we are not yet ripe for socialism, that, as certain "learned" gentlemen among them put it, the objective economic premises for socialism do not exist in our country. It does not occur to any of them to ask: but what about a people that found itself in a revolutionary situation such as that created during the first imperialist war? Might it not, influenced by the hopelessness of its situation, fling itself into a struggle that would offer it at least some chance of securing conditions for the further development of civilisation that were somewhat unusual?

"The development of the productive forces of Russia has not

attained the level that makes socialism possible." All the heroes
of the Second International, including, of course, Sukhanov,
beat the drums about this proposition. They keep harping on
this incontrovertible proposition in a thousand different keys,
and think that it is the decisive criterion of our revolution.

But what if the situation, which drew Russia into the
imperialist world war that involved every more or less
influential West-European country and made her a witness of
the eve of the revolutions maturing or partly already begun in
the East, gave rise to circumstances that put Russia and her
development in a position which enabled us to achieve
precisely that combination of a "peasant war" with the
working-class movement suggested in 1856 by no less a Marxist
than Marx himself as a possible prospect for Prussia?

What if the complete hopelessness of the situation, by
stimulating the efforts of the workers and peasants tenfold,
offered us the opportunity to create the fundamental requisites of civilisation in a different way from that of the
West-European countries? Has that altered the general line of
development of world history? Has that altered the basic
relations between the basic classes of all the countries that are
being, or have been, drawn into the general course of world
history?

If a definite level of culture is required for the building of
socialism (although nobody can say just what that definite
"level of culture" is, for it differs in every West-European
country), why cannot we begin by first achieving the prerequisites for that definite level of culture in a revolutionary way, and
then, with the aid of the workers' and peasants' government
and the Soviet system, proceed to overtake the other nations?

January 16, 1923.

II

You say that civilisation is necessary for the building of
socialism. Very good. But why could we not first create such
prerequisites of civilisation in our country as the expulsion of
the landowners and the Russian capitalists, and then start
moving towards socialism? Where, in what books, have you
read that such variations of the customary historical sequence
of events are impermissible or impossible?

Napoleon, I think, wrote: "*On s'engage et puis ... on voit.*"
Rendered freely this means: "First engage in a serious battle

and then see what happens." Well, we did first engage in a serious battle in October 1917, and then saw such details of development (from the standpoint of world history they were certainly details) as the Brest peace, [125] the New Economic Policy, [126] and so forth. And now there can be no doubt that in the main we have been victorious.

Our Sukhanovs, not to mention Social-Democrats still farther to the right, never even dream that revolutions cannot be made in any other way. Our European philistines never even dream that the subsequent revolutions in Oriental countries, which possess much vaster populations and a much vaster diversity of social conditions, will undoubtedly display even greater distinctions than the Russian revolution.

It need hardly be said that a textbook written on Kautskian lines was a very useful thing in its day. But it is time, for all that, to abandon the idea that it foresaw all the forms of development of subsequent world history. It would be timely to say that those who think so are simply fools.

January 17, 1923

Published in *Pravda* No. 117,
May 30, 1923
Signed: *Lenin*

Collected Works,
Vol. 33, pp. 476-80

Letters

From A Letter to Maxim Gorky

February 2, 1908

...All three of us have come together here now, having been sent from Russia to establish *Proletary*[127] (Bogdanov, I and one "Praktik" [128]). Everything is in running order, in a day or two we shall publish an announcement. You are on our list of contributors. Drop us a line as to whether you could give us something for the first issues (something after the manner of your *"notes on philistinism"*[129] in *Novaya Zhizn,* or fragments from a story you are writing,[130] etc.).

All the very best. Best regards to M. F.! Yours,

V. Ulyanov

Sent from Geneva to
Capri (Italy)
First published in 1924
in *Lenin Miscellany I*

Collected Works,
Vol. 34, pp. 377-78

To Maxim Gorky

February 7, 1908

Dear A. M.,

I shall consult A. A. about your statement; since you did not know him personally I think it is not worth while publishing it.[131]

To what Bolshevik symposium have you sent the article on cynicism?[132] I am puzzled, because people write to me a good deal about Bolshevik symposia, but I have never heard of this one. I hope it is to the St. Petersburg one. Send me a copy of your letter to Sienkiewicz,[133] if you have one (indicating *when* it was sent) — but Sienkiewicz will no doubt publish it since it is an opinion poll.

Your plans are very interesting and I should like to come. But, you will agree, I cannot very well throw up the Party job, which needs organising immediately. It is difficult to get a new job going. I can't throw it up. We shall have it going in about a couple of months or so, and then I shall be free to tear myself away for a week or two.

I agree with you a thousand times about the need for *systematically* combating political decadence, apostasy, whining, and so forth. I do not think that there would be any disagreement between us about "society" and the "youth". The significance of the intellectuals in our Party is declining; news comes from all sides that the intelligentsia is *fleeing* the Party. And a good riddance to these scoundrels. The Party is purging itself from petty-bourgeois dross. The workers are having a bigger say in things. The role of the worker-professionals is increasing. All this is wonderful, and I am sure that your "kicks" must be understood in the same sense.

Now — how are we to exert influence, what exactly should our literature be? Symposia *or Proletary?* Of course, the easier thing is to reply: not *or*, but *and* — the reply will be irreproachable but of little practical value. We must have legal symposia, of course; our comrades in St. Petersburg are working on them by the sweat of the brow, and I, too, have been working on them after London, while sitting in Kwakalla.[134] If possible, *all* efforts should be made to support them and continue these symposia.

But my experience from London up to November 1907 (half a year!) has convinced me that no *systematic* legal literature can now be produced. I am convinced that what the *Party* now needs is a regular political organ, consistently and vigorously pursuing a policy of struggle against disintegration and despondency—a *Party* organ, a political newspaper. Many people in Russia do not believe in a foreign-based organ. But this is an error, and our collegium knew what it was doing when it decided to transfer *Proletary* here. That it is difficult to organise, set it up and run it—goes without saying. But it *has* to be done and it will be done.

Why shouldn't literary criticism be included in it? Too little space? I don't know, of course, your system of working. Unfortunately, when we have met, we spent more time chattering than talking business. If you don't like writing small, short, periodical (weekly or fortnightly) articles, if you prefer to work on *big* things—then, of course, I would not advise you to interrupt it. It will be of greater benefit!

If, however, you are inclined towards joint work in a political newspaper—why not continue and make a regular feature of the genre which you began with "Notes on Philistinism" in *Novaya Zhizn*, and began very well, in my opinion? I wrote to you about this "with an ulterior motive" in one of the first letters, thinking: if it appeals to him, he will seize on the idea. And it seems to me that in your last letter you are seizing on it after a fashion. Or am I mistaken? How great would be the gain, both for Party work through the newspaper, which would not be so one-sided as it previously was, and for literary work, which would be more closely linked with Party work, with systematic, continuous influence on the Party! There should be not "forays", but a solid onslaught all along the line, without stops or gaps; Bolshevik Social-Democrats should not only attack all kinds of duffers piecemeal, but should conquer all and everything as the Japanese conquered Manchuria from the Russians.

Of the three subjects that you mention for the symposia (philosophy, literary criticism, and current tactics) one-and-a-half would go into the political newspaper, into *Proletary*, viz.:

current tactics and a good half of the literary criticism. Ah, there is nothing good about all those special, long articles of literary criticism scattered through various semi-Party and non-Party periodicals! We should try to take a step away from this old, intellectualist, stuffed-shirt manner, that is, we should link literary criticism, too, *more closely* with Party work, with Party leadership. That is what the adult Social-Democratic parties in Europe are doing. That is what we should do, too, without being afraid of the difficulties of the first steps of collective newspaper activity in this field.

Large works of literary criticism — in books, partially in periodicals.

Systematic, periodic articles, in the concert of a political newspaper, linked with Party work, in the spirit of what was begun by *Novaya Zhizn* — tell me, have you any inclination towards this, or not?

The third subject is philosophy. I am fully aware of my unpreparedness in this sphere, which prevents me from speaking about it in public. But, as a rank-and-file Marxist, I read attentively our Party philosophers, I read attentively the empirio-monist Bogdanov and the empirio-critics Bazarov, Lunacharsky, etc.— and *they* drive me to give *all* my sympathy *to Plekhanov!* It takes physical strength to keep oneself from being carried away by the mood, as Plekhanov does! His tactics are the height of ineptitude and baseness. In philosophy, however, he upholds the right cause. I am for materialism against "empirio-", etc.

Can, and should, philosophy be linked with the trend of Party work? With Bolshevism? I think this should not be done at the present time. Let our Party philosophers put in some more work on theory for a while, let them dispute and ... *seek a meeting of minds.* For the time being, I would stand for *such* philosophical disputes as those between materialists and "empirios" being separated from integral Party work.

I look forward to your reply, meanwhile I must conclude.

Yours,

Lenin

Sent from Geneva to   *Collected Works,*
Capri (Italy)   Vol. 34, pp. 379-82
First published in 1934
in *Lenin Miscellany XXVI*

To A. V. Lunacharsky

To Anat. Vas.

February 13, 1908

Dear An. Vas.,

Yesterday I sent you a short note about Bringmann. I hasten to reply to your letter of February 11.

I don't quite understand why you should feel hurt by my letter. Not on account of philosophy, surely! Your plan for a section of *belles-lettres* in *Proletary* and for having A. M. run it is an excellent one, and pleases me exceedingly. I have in fact been dreaming of making the *literature and criticism* section a permanent feature in *Proletary* and having A. M. to run it. But I was *afraid*, terribly afraid of making the proposal outright, as I *do not know* the nature of A. M.'s work (and his work-bent). If a man is busy with an important work, and if this work would suffer from him being torn away for minor things, such as a newspaper, and journalism, then it would be foolish and criminal to disturb and interrupt him! That is something I very well understand and feel.

Being on the spot, you will know best, dear An. Vas. *If you consider* that A. M.'s work *will not suffer* by his being harnessed to regular Party work (and the Party work will gain a great deal from this!), then try to arrange it.

Proletary No. 21 will come out on February 13 (26). So there is still time. It is desirable to have the manuscripts by *Friday*, which will give us plenty of time to put them in the issue which comes out on Wednesday. If it's something urgent we could manage it even if the copy arrives on Sunday (to avoid delay, write and send it directly to my address), or even (in an extreme case!) on Monday.

You, too, must write without fail. Won't you send us for No. 21 either a political article on Russian affairs (10,000-16,000 characters) or an article on Ferri's resignation [135] (8,000-10,000

characters)? Better still, not "either ... or", but "both ... and".
I send you my best regards and ask you to reply whether A.
M.'s contribution to *Proletary* is being arranged. If it is, let him
begin at once, *without waiting* for the "meeting" [136] and an
agreement.

Sent from Geneva to
Capri (Italy)   *Collected Works,*
First published in 1924   Vol. 34, pp. 383-84
in *Lenin Miscellany I*

To Maxim Gorky

February 13, 1908

Dear Al. M.,

I think that some of the questions you raise about our differences of opinion are a sheer misunderstanding. Never, of course, have I thought of "chasing away the intelligentsia", as the silly syndicalists do, or of denying its necessity for the workers' movement. There *can be no* divergence between us on any of *these* questions; of that I am quite sure, and since we cannot get together at the moment, we must start work together at once. At work we shall best of all find a common language.

I am very, very pleased with your plan of writing short paragraphs for *Proletary* (the announcement has been sent to you). Naturally, if you are working on something big, *do not break it off*.

Regarding Trotsky, I wanted to reply last time, but I forgot. We (i.e., the editorial board of *Proletary*, Al. Al., myself and "Inok"[137] — a very good colleague from the home Bolsheviks) decided straight away to invite him on to *Proletary*. We wrote him a letter, proposing and outlining a theme. *By general agreement* we signed it the "Editorial Board of *Proletary*", so as to put the matter on a more collegial footing (I personally, for example, had had a big fight with Trotsky, a regular fierce battle in 1903-05 when he was a Menshevik). Whether there was something in the form of our letter that offended Trotsky, I do not know, but he sent us a letter, not written by him: "On Comrade Trotsky's instructions" the editorial board of *Proletary* was informed that he refused to write, he was too busy.

In my opinion, this is mere posturing. At the London Congress, too, he acted the *poseur*. I don't know really whether he will go with the Bolsheviks....

The Mensheviks here have issued an announcement about the monthly *Golos Sotsial-Demokrata*[138] over the signatures of Plekhanov, Axelrod, Dan, Martov and Martynov. I shall get it and send it to you. The struggle may become sharper. But Trotsky wants to stand "above the contending factions"....

It is in regard to materialism as a world outlook that I think I disagree with you in substance. Not the "materialist conception of history" (our "empirios" do not deny that), but philosophical materialism. That the Anglo-Saxons and Germans owed their philistinism to "materialism", and the Romance people their anarchism, is something I emphatically dispute. Materialism, as a philosophy, was *everywhere pushed into the background* by them. *Neue Zeit,*[139] that most sober and well-informed organ, is indifferent to philosophy, was never a zealous supporter of philosophical materialism, and of late has been publishing the empirio-critics without a single reservation. It is wrong, absolutely wrong to think that dead philistinism could be deduced from the materialism which Marx and Engels taught! All the philistine trends in Social-Democracy are most of all at war with philosophical materialism, they lean towards Kant, neo-Kantianism,[140] the critical philosophy. No, the philosophy which Engels substantiated in *Anti-Dühring* keeps philistinism at arm's length. Plekhanov does harm to this philosophy by linking the struggle *here* with the factional struggle, but after all no Russian Social-Democrat ought to confuse the present Plekhanov with the old Plekhanov.

Al. Al. has just now left me. I shall communicate with him again about the "meeting". If you insist — it could be arranged for a couple of days and very soon at that.

All the best,
Lenin

Sent from Geneva to
Capri (Italy)
First published in 1924   *Collected Works,*
in *Lenin Miscellany I*   Vol. 34, pp. 385-86

To Maxim Gorky

February 25, 1908

Dear A. M.,

I did not answer your letter immediately because, strange as it may seem at first glance, we had quite a serious fight on the editorial board with Al. Al. over your article,[141] or rather in a certain connection with it. Ahem, ahem.... I spoke *not in that place* and not on that subject which you thought!

It happened like this.

The book, *Studies in the Philosophy of Marxism*,[142] has considerably sharpened the old differences among the Bolsheviks on questions of philosophy. I do not consider myself sufficiently competent on these questions to rush into print. But I have always followed our *Party* debates on philosophy very closely, beginning with Plekhanov's struggle against Mikhailovsky and Co. in the late eighties and up to 1895, then his struggle against the Kantians from 1898 onwards (here I not only followed it, but participated in it to some extent, as a member of the *Zarya*[143] editorial board since 1900), and, finally, his struggle against the empirio-critics and Co.

I have been following Bogdanov's writings on philosophy since his energeticist book, *The Historical View of Nature*, which I studied during my stay in Siberia. For Bogdanov, this position was merely a transition to other philosophical views. I became personally acquainted with him in 1904, when we immediately gave each other presents — I, my *Steps*,[144] he, one of his *current* philosophical works.[145] And I at once (in the spring or the early summer of 1904) wrote him in Paris from Geneva that his writings strongly convinced me that his views were wrong and as strongly convinced me that those of Plekhanov were correct.

When we worked together, Plekhanov and I often discussed Bogdanov. Plekhanov explained the fallacy of Bogdanov's views to me, but he did not think the deviation a terribly

6—70

serious one. I remember perfectly well that in the summer of
1903 Plekhanov and I, as representatives of the *Zarya* editorial
board, had a conversation in Geneva with a delegate from the
editors of the symposium *Outlines of a Realistic World
Outlook,* [146] at which we *agreed* to contribute — I, on the agrarian
question, Plekhanov *on anti-Machist philosophy.* Plekhanov made
it *a condition* of his collaboration that he would write against
Mach, a condition that the symposium delegate readily
accepted. Plekhanov at that time regarded Bogdanov as an ally
in the fight against revisionism, but an ally who erred in
following Ostwald and, later on, Mach.

In the summer and autumn of 1904, Bogdanov and I
reached a complete agreement, as *Bolsheviks,* and formed the
tacit bloc, which tacitly ruled out philosophy as a neutral field,
that existed all through the revolution and enabled us in that
revolution to carry out together the tactics of revolutionary
Social-Democracy (= Bolshevism), which, I am profoundly
convinced, were the only correct tactics.

There was little opportunity to engage in philosophy in the
heat of the revolution. Bogdanov wrote another piece in prison
at the beginning of 1906 — the third issue of *Empirio-monism,* I
believe. He presented it to me in the summer of 1906, and I sat
down to study it. After reading it I was furious. It became
clearer to me than ever that he was on an absolutely wrong
track, not the Marxist track. I thereupon wrote him a
"declaration of love", a letter on philosophy taking up three
notebooks. I explained to him that I was just *an ordinary Marxist*
in philosophy, but that it was precisely his lucid, popular, and
splendidly written works that had finally convinced me that he
was essentially wrong and that Plekhanov was right. I showed
these notebooks to some friends (including Lunacharsky) and
thought of publishing them under the title "Notes of an
Ordinary Marxist on Philosophy", but I never got round to it. I
am sorry now that I did not have them published at the
moment. I wrote to St. Petersburg the other day to have these
notebooks hunted out and forwarded to me. [147]

Now the *Studies in the Philosophy of Marxism* have appeared. I
have read all the articles except Suvorov's (I am reading it
now), and every article made me furiously indignant. No, no,
this is not Marxism! Our empirio-critics, empirio-monists, and
empirio-symbolists are floundering in a bog. To try to
persuade the reader that "belief" in the reality of the external
world is "mysticism" (Bazarov); to confuse in the most
disgraceful manner materialism with Kantianism (Bazarov and

TO MAXIM GORKY. FEBRUARY 25, 1908

Bogdanov); to preach a variety of agnosticism (empirio-criticism) and idealism (empirio-monism); to teach the workers "religious atheism" and "worship" of the higher human potentialities (Lunacharsky); to declare Engels's teaching on dialectics to be mysticism (Berman); to draw from the stinking well of some French "positivists" or other, of agnostics or metaphysicians, the devil take them, with their "symbolic theory of cognition" (Yushkevich)! No, really, it's too much. To be sure, we ordinary Marxists are not well up in philosophy, but why insult us by serving this stuff up to us as the philosophy of Marxism! I would rather let myself be drawn and quartered than consent to collaborate in an organ or body that preaches such things.

I felt a renewed interest in my "Notes of an Ordinary Marxist on Philosophy" and I began to write them, [148] but to Al. Al., in the process of reading the *Studies*, I gave my impressions bluntly and sharply, of course.

But what has your article got to do with it, you will ask? It has this to do with it: just at a time when these differences of opinion among the Bolsheviks threaten to become particularly acute, you are obviously beginning to expound the views of one trend in your article for *Proletary*. I do not know, of course, what you would have made of it, taken as a whole. Besides, I believe that an artist can glean much that is useful to him from philosophy of all kinds. Finally, I absolutely agree with the view that in matters that concern the art of writing you are the best judge, and that in deriving *this* kind of views both from your artistic experience *and from philosophy, even if idealistic philosophy*, you can arrive at conclusions that will be of tremendous benefit to the workers' party. All that is true; nevertheless *Proletary* must remain absolutely neutral towards all our divergencies in philosophy and not give the reader *the slightest grounds* for associating the Bolsheviks, as a trend, as a tactical line of the revolutionary wing of the Russian Social-Democrats, with empirio-criticism or empirio-monism.

When, after reading and re-reading your article, I told A. A. that I was against its publication, he grew as black as a thundercloud. The threat of a split was in the air. Yesterday our editorial trio held a special meeting to discuss the matter. A stupid trick on the part of *Neue Zeit* came unexpectedly to our rescue. In its issue No. 20, an unknown translator published Bogdanov's article on Mach, and blurted out in a foreword that the differences between Plekhanov and Bogdanov had a tendency, among Russian Social-Democracy, to become a

6*

factional disagreement between the Bolsheviks and the Mensheviks. The fool, whether man or woman, who wrote this foreword succeeded in uniting us. We agreed at once that an announcement of our neutrality was now essential in the very next issue of *Proletary*. This was perfectly in keeping with my own frame of mind after the appearance of the *Studies*. A statement was drawn up, unanimously endorsed, and tomorrow it will appear in issue No. 21 of *Proletary*, which will be forwarded to you.

As regards your article, it was decided to postpone the matter, explain the situation to you in letters from each of *Proletary's* three editors, and hasten my and Bogdanov's trip to see you.

And so you will be receiving a letter also from Al. Al. and from the third editor, about whom I wrote you previously.

I consider it necessary to give you my opinion quite frankly. Some sort of fight among the Bolsheviks on the question of philosophy I regard now as quite unavoidable. It would be stupid, however, to split on this. We formed a bloc in order to secure the adoption of definite tactics in the workers' party. We have been pursuing these tactics up to now *without disagreement* (the only difference of opinion was on the boycott of the Third Duma, but that, first, was never so sharp among us as to lead to even a hint of a split, and, secondly, it never corresponded to the disagreement between the materialists and the Machists, for the Machist Bazarov, for example, was with me in opposing the boycott and wrote a long article on this in *Proletary*).

To hinder the application of the tactics of revolutionary Social-Democracy in the workers' party for the sake of disputes on the question of materialism or Machism, would be, in my opinion, unpardonable folly. We ought to fight over philosophy in such a way that *Proletary* and the Bolsheviks, as a faction of the *party, would not be affected by it*. And that is quite possible.

And you, I think, ought to help in this. You can help by contributing to *Proletary* on neutral questions (that is, unconnected with philosophy) of literary criticism, publicism, *belles-lettres*, and so on. As for your article, if you wish to prevent a split and help to localise the new fight—you should rewrite it, and everything that even indirectly bears on Bogdanov's philosophy should be placed somewhere else. You have other mediums, thank God, besides *Proletary*. Everything that is not connected with Bogdanov's philosophy—and the *bulk* of your article is not connected with it—you could set out in a series of articles for *Proletary*. Any other attitude on your part, that is, a refusal to rewrite the article or to collaborate with *Proletary* would, in my opinion, unavoidably tend to aggravate the conflict among the Bolsheviks, make it difficult to localise the new fight, and weaken the vital cause, so essential practically and politically, of revolutionary Social-Democracy in Russia.

That is my opinion. I have told you all my thoughts and am now looking forward to your reply.

We intended to go to you today, but find that we have to postpone our visit for not less than a week, perhaps two or three weeks.

With very best regards,

Yours,
N. Lenin

Sent from Geneva to
Capri (Italy)

First published in 1924   *Collected Works,*
in *Lenin Miscellany I*   Vol. 13, pp. 448-54

To Maxim Gorky

November 16, 1909

Dear Alexei Maximovich,

I have been fully convinced all the time that you and Comrade Mikhail were the most hardened factionalists of the new faction, with whom it would be silly of me to try and talk in a friendly way. Today for the first time I met Comrade Mikhail, and had a heart-to-heart chat with him both about affairs and about you, and I perceived that I had been cruelly mistaken. Believe me, the philosopher Hegel was right: life proceeds by contradictions, and living contradictions are so much richer, more varied and deeper in content than they may seem at first sight to a man's mind. I regarded the school as *merely* the centre of a new faction. [149] This has turned out to be wrong — not in the sense that it was not the centre of a new faction (the school was this centre and is so at the present time), but in the sense that this was incomplete, not the whole truth. Subjectively, certain people made such a centre out of the school, objectively, it was such, but in addition the school drew to it real front-rank workers from real working-class life. What happened was that, besides the contradiction between the old and the new faction, a contradiction developed on Capri, between some of the Social-Democratic intellectuals and the workers from Russia, who will bring Social-Democracy on to the true path *at all costs* and whatever happens, and who will do so despite all the squabbling and dissension abroad, despite the "incidents", and so on and so forth. People like Mikhail are a guarantee of it. Moreover, it turned out that a contradiction developed in the school between elements of the Capri Social-Democratic intelligentsia.

I gathered from Mikhail that you are taking things hard, dear A. M. You have seen the working-class and Social-Democratic movement from an aspect and in forms and manifestations which already more than once in the history of Russia and Western Europe have led intellectuals of little faith to despair of the workers' movement and Social-Democracy. I am confident that this will not happen in your case, and after my talk with Mikhail I want to shake your hand heartily. With your gifts as an artist you have rendered such a tremendous service to the working-class movement of Russia — and indeed not only of Russia — and will render a still greater service yet, that it is on no account permissible for you to fall a prey to moods of depression evoked by episodes of the struggle abroad. Conditions occur when the course of the working-class movement inevitably gives rise to this struggle abroad, and to splits, dissension and the quarrelling among the circles — but this is not because of the workers' movement being intrinsically weak or Social-Democracy intrinsically erroneous, but because the elements out of which the working class has to forge its Party are too heterogeneous and diverse in calibre. The working class will forge it in any case, it will forge an excellent revolutionary Social-Democratic Party in Russia, and it will do so more speedily than sometimes seems likely from the standpoint of the thrice-accursed emigrant position; it will forge it more surely than might be imagined if one were to judge by some external manifestations and individual episodes. People like Mikhail are a guarantee of that.

All the very best to you and to Maria Fyodorovna. I am now hopeful that we shall meet again and not as enemies.

Yours,
Lenin

Wl. Oulianoff,
4, Rue Marie Rose, 4,
Paris, XIV

Sent to Capri (Italy)

First published in
Krasnaya Gazeta No. 236,
October 15, 1924

Collected Works,
Vol. 34, pp. 403-04

To Maxim Gorky

November 22, 1910

Dear A. M.,

I wrote you a few days ago when sending *Rabochaya Gazeta,*[150] and asked what had come of the journal we talked about in the summer and about which you promised to write to me.

I see in *Rech* today a notice about *Sovremennik,*[151] published "with the closest and *exclusive* [that is what is printed! illiterately, but so much the more pretentiously and significantly] participation of Amfiteatrov" and with you as a regular contributor.

What is this? How does it happen? A "large monthly" journal, with sections on "politics, science, history, social life" — why, this is something quite different from symposia aiming at a concentration of the best forces of *belles-lettres.* Such a journal should either have a perfectly definite, serious and consistent *trend,* or it will inevitably disgrace itself and those taking part in it. *Vestnik Yevropy*[152] has a trend — a poor, watery, worthless trend — but one which serves a definite element, certain sections of the bourgeoisie, and which also unites definite circles of the professorate and officialdom, and the so-called intelligentsia from among the "respectable" (or rather, would-be respectable) liberals. *Russkaya Mysl*[153] has a trend, an odious trend, but one which performs a very good service for the counter-revolutionary liberal bourgeoisie. *Russkoye Bogatstvo*[154] has a trend — a Narodnik, Narodnik-Cadet trend — but one which has kept its line for scores of years, and which serves definite sections of the population. *Sovremenny Mir*[155] has a trend — often a Menshevik-Cadet trend (at present with a leaning towards pro-Party Menshevism) — but a trend. A journal without a trend is an absurdity, a ridiculous, scandalous and harmful thing. And what sort of trend can there be with the "exclusive participation" of Amfiteatrov? One cannot expect G. Lopatin to provide a trend, and if the talk (said also to have got into the newspapers) is true about Kachorovsky's participation, then that is a "trend", but a trend of the blockheads, an S.R. trend.

During our talk in the summer when I told you that I had all but written you a disappointed letter about *Confessions* but did not send it because of the split with the Machists which had begun at that time, you replied: "*it's a pity* you did not send it." Then you went on to reproach me for not going to the Capri school, and you said that, if matters had taken a different course, the breakaway of the Machists and otzovists might have cost you less nervous strain, less waste of energy. Recalling these talks, I have now decided to write to you without putting it off and without waiting for any verification, while the impression the news has made is still fresh.

I think that a political and economic monthly with the exclusive participation of Amfiteatrov is something many times worse than a special Machist-Otzovist faction. What was and still is bad about this faction is that the *ideological* trend deviated and still deviates from Marxism, from Social-Democracy, without, however, going so far as a break with Marxism, and only creating confusion.

Amfiteatrov's journal (his *Krasnoye Znamya* [156] did well to die when it did!) is a political act, a political enterprise in which there is not even a realisation that a general "leftism" is not enough for a policy, that after 1905 to talk seriously about politics without making clear one's attitude towards Marxism and Social-Democracy is out of the question, impossible, inconceivable.

Things are turning out bad. It's saddening.

Yours,
Lenin

To M. F.— *salut et fraternité!*

Sent from Paris to'
Capri (Italy)

First published in 1924   *Collected Works,*
in *Lenin Miscellany I*   Vol. 34, pp. 434-35

To Maxim Gorky

Dear A. M.,

I am very glad you have agreed to try and write a May Day leaflet.

I enclose the Conference resolutions.

I have seen *Zhivoye Dyelo*.[157] A rotten little liquidationist rag with an "approach". Liberal propaganda. They are glad that the police prevent the question of the Party being openly discussed.

Zvezda[158] will continue, either as a weekly *or as a kopek daily*. You helped *Zvezda* very, very much with your splendid *Tales*, and that made me extremely joyful, so that the joy — if I am to talk straight — outweighed my sadness at yor "affair" with the Chernovs and Amfiteatrovs.... Brr! I am glad, I must confess, that they are "going up the spout".

But as for your having nothing to live on and not being able to get printed anywhere, that's bad. You ought to have got rid of that leech Pyatnitsky long ago and appointed an honest agent, an agent pure and simple, to deal with Znaniye (perhaps it's already too late, I don't know)!!! If only.... It would have been a gold mine....

I see Rozhkov's *Irkutskoye Slovo*[159] very rarely. The man's become a liquidator. And Chuzhak is an old ass, hardened and pretentious.

Yours,
Lenin

Thank M. F. for her letter to Moscow, and a thousand greetings!

Written in February-March 1912

Sent from Paris to Capri (Italy)

First published
in *Bakinsky Rabochy* No. 17,
January 21, 1927

Collected Works,
Vol. 35, p. 24

From A Letter to the Editor of *Pravda*

...I take advantage of this opportunity to congratulate Comrade Vitimsky (I hope it will not be difficult for you to pass this letter on to him) on the remarkably fine article in *Pravda* (No. 98)[160] which I received today. The subject chosen was extremely topical, and was splendidly worked out in a brief but clear form. In general it would be useful from time to time to recall, quote and explain in *Pravda* Shchedrin and other writers of the "old" Narodnik democratic movement. For the readers of *Pravda*—for the 25,000—this would be appropriate and interesting, and also it would throw light on present-day questions of working-class democracy from another point of view, and in other words.

Written on September 8, 1912

Sent from Cracow to
St. Petersburg

First published in 1923
in the book *Iz epokhi "Zvezdy"*
i *"Pravdy" (1911-14)*, Part III

Collected Works,
Vol. 35, p. 57

Dear A. M.,

Now, sir, what's the meaning of this bad behaviour of yours? You're overworked, tired, your nerves are out of order. This is all wrong. On Capri of all places, and in the winter when there are probably less "visitors", you ought to have a regular way of life. You have no one to look after you, is that why you have let yourself slide like this? Honestly, it's no good. Pull yourself together and give yourself a stricter régime, really! Falling ill in times like these just isn't allowed. Have you begun working at night? Why, when I was on Capri, I was told that it was only with my coming that things had got out of hand, while before me everyone went to bed at the right time. You must rest and establish a régime, without fail.

I will write to Troyanovsky and his wife about your wish to meet them. This would be a really good thing. They are good people. We haven't seen much of them at work yet, but everything we have heard up to now speaks in their favour. They also have money. They might get into their stride and do a great deal for the journal. Troyanovskaya is going to Russia soon.

It is a great joy to me, and to all of us, that you are *taking up Prosveshcheniye.* I confess that I did have the thought: now as soon as I write about our little journal, A. M. will lose his enthusiasm. I repent, I repent of such thoughts.

Now it really will be splendid if little by little we draw in fiction writers and set *Prosveshcheniye* going! Excellent! The reader is new, proletarian; we shall make the journal cheap; you will let in only democratic fiction, without moaning, without renegade stuff. We shall consolidate the workers. And the workers now are fine. Our six deputies in the Duma from the worker curia have now begun to work *outside the Duma* so energetically that it is a joy to see. This is where people will build up a real workers'party! We were never able to bring this off in the Third Duma. Have you seen the letter in *Luch* [161] (No. 24) from the four deputies about their resignation? A good letter, wasn't it?

And have you seen in *Pravda* how mildly Alexinsky is writing, and so far not making a row? Wonderful! He sent one "Manifesto" (why he entered *Pravda*). They didn't print it. And still, *so far,* he is not making a row. Won-der-ful! But Bogdanov is making a row: a piece of exceptional stupidity in *Pravda* No. 24. No, we shall never get anywhere with him! I have read his *Engineer Mannie.* It's the same old Machism-idealism, so concealed that neither the workers nor the stupid editors of *Pravda* understood it. No, this Machist is as hopeless as Lunacharsky (thanks for his article). If only Lunacharsky could be separated from Bogdanov in aesthetics, as Alexinsky has begun to draw apart from him in politics ... if only....

As regards the theory of matter and its structure, I am fully in agreement with you that one should write about it, and that it is a good remedy against "the poison which the shapeless Russian soul is sucking". Only you are wrong to call this poison 'metaphysics". It ought to be called *idealism* and agnosticism.

For the Machists call materialism metaphysics! And it so happens that a *host* of the most prominent present-day physicists, *on the occasion* of the "wonders" of radium, electrons, etc., are smuggling in the *God business*—both the crudest and the most subtle—in the shape of philosophical idealism.

Written between February 15
and 25, 1913
Sent from Cracow to
Capri (Italy)

First published in 1924
in *Lenin Miscellany I*

Collected Works,
Vol. 35, pp. 83-84

**From A Letter to the Editorial Board
of *Pravda***

As regards Demyan Bedny, I continue *to be for*. Don't find fault, friends, with human failings! Talent is rare. It should be systematically and carefully supported. It will be a sin on your conscience, a great sin (a hundred times bigger than various personal "sins", if such occur...) against the democratic working-class movement, if you don't draw in this talented contributor and *don't help* him. The disputes were petty, the cause is a serious one. Think over this! [162]

Written not earlier than
May 25, 1913

Sent to St. Petersburg

First published in 1933
in *Lenin Miscellany XXV*

Collected Works,
Vol. 35, pp. 99-100

To Maxim Gorky

Dear A. M.,

Whatever are you doing? This is simply terrible, it really is! Yesterday I read your reply in *Rech* to the "howling" over Dostoyevsky,[163] and was preparing to rejoice, but today the liquidators' paper arrives, and *in it there is a paragraph of your article* which was not in *Rech.*

This paragraph runs as follows:

"And 'god-seeking' should be *for the time being*" (only for the time being?) "put aside — it is a useless occupation: it's no use seeking where there is nothing to be found. Unless you sow, you cannot reap. You have no God, you have not *yet*" (yet!) "created him. Gods are not sought — *they are created*; people do not invent life, they create it."

So it turns out that you are against "god-seeking" only "for the time being"!! It turns out that you are against god-seeking *only* in order to replace it by god-building!!

Well, isn't it horrible that such a thing should *appear* in your article?

God-seeking differs from god-building or god-creating or god-making, etc., no more than a yellow devil differs from a blue devil. To talk about god-seeking, not in order to declare against *all* devils and gods, against every ideological necrophily (all worship of a divinity is necrophily — be it the cleanest, most ideal, not sought-out but built-up divinity, it's all the same), but to prefer a blue devil to a yellow one is a hundred times worse than not saying anything about it at all.

In the freest countries, in countries where it is *quite* out of place to appeal "to democracy, to the people, to public opinion and science", in such countries (America, Switzerland and so forth) particular zeal is applied to render the people and the workers obtuse with just this very idea of a clean, spiritual, built-up god. Just because any religious idea, any idea of any god at all, any flirtation even with a god, is the most inexpressible foulness, particularly tolerantly (and often even favourably) accepted by the *democratic* bourgeoisie — for that very reason it is the most dangerous foulness, the most shameful "infection". A million *physical* sins, dirty tricks, acts of violence and infections are much more easily discovered by the crowd, and therefore are much less dangerous, than the *subtle*, spiritual idea of god, dressed up in the most attractive "ideological" costumes. The Catholic priest corrupting young girls (about whom I have just read by chance in a German newspaper) is *much less* dangerous, precisely to "democracy", than a priest without his robes, a priest without crude religion, an ideologically equipped and democratic priest preaching the creation and the invention of a god. For it is *easy* to expose, condemn and expel the first priest, while the second *cannot* be expelled so simply; to expose the latter is 1,000 times more difficult, and not a single "frail and pitifully wavering" philistine will agree to "condemn" him.

And you, knowing the "frailty and pitiful wavering" of the (Russian: why Russian? Is the Italian any better??) *philistine* soul, confuse that soul with the sweetest of poisons, most effectively disguised in lollipops and all kinds of gaily-coloured wrappings!!

Really, it is terrible.

"Enough of self-humiliation, which is our substitute for self-criticism."

And isn't god-building the *worst* form of self-humiliation?? Everyone who sets about building up a *God*, or who even merely tolerates such activity, *humiliates* himself in the worst possible way, because instead of "deeds" he is *actually* engaged in self-contemplation, self-admiration and, moreover, such a man "contemplates" the dirtiest, most stupid, most slavish features or traits of his "ego", deified by god-building.

From the point of view, not of the individual, but of society, *all* god-building is precisely the *fond self-contemplation* of the thick-witted philistine, the frail man in the street, the dreamy "self-humiliation" of the vulgar petty bourgeois, "exhausted and in despair" (as you condescended to say very truly about the *soul*: only you should have said, not "the Russian", but the *petty-bourgeois*, for the Jewish, the Italian, the English varieties are all *one and the same devil*; stinking philistinism everywhere is equally disgusting—but "democratic philistinism", occupied in ideological necrophily, is particularly disgusting).

Reading your article over and over again, and *trying to discover* where this *slip* of your tongue could come from, I am at a loss. What does it mean? A relic of the "Confession", which *you yourself* did not approve?? Or its echo??

Or something different: for example, an unsuccessful

attempt to *bend back* to the viewpoint of *democracy in general,* instead of the viewpoint of the *proletariat?* Perhaps it was in order to talk with "democracy in general" that you decided (excuse the expression) to indulge in baby-talk? Perhaps it was "for a popular exposition" to the *philistines* that you decided to accept for a moment *their,* the philistines', prejudices??

But then that is a *wrong* approach, in all senses and in all respects!

I wrote above that in *democratic* countries it would be *quite* out of place for a proletarian writer to appeal "to democracy, to the people, to public opinion and science". Well, but what about us in Russia?? Such an appeal is *not quite* appropriate, because it also in some ways flatters the prejudices of the philistines. A kind of general appeal, general to the point of vagueness — even Izgoyev of *Russkaya Mysl* will sign it with *both hands.* Why then select watchwords which *you* distinguish perfectly well from those of Izgoyev, but which the *reader* will not be able to distinguish?? Why throw a democratic veil over the question for the reader, instead of *clearly* distinguishing the *petty bourgeois* (frail, pitifully wavering, exhausted, despairing, self-contemplating, god-contemplating, god-building, god-indulging, self-humiliating, *uncomprehendingly anarchistic* — wonderful word!! — et cetera, et cetera) — from the *proletarians* (who know how to be of good cheer not only in words, and who are able to distinguish the "science and public opinion" of the *bourgeoisie* from their own, bourgeois democracy from proletarian democracy)?

Why do you do this?

It's damnably disappointing.

Yours,

V. I.

P.S. We sent you the novel by registered book post. Did you receive it?

P.P.S. Get as good *medical* treatment as you can, please, so that you can travel in the winter, *without colds* (it's dangerous in the winter).

Yours,

V. Ulyanov

Written on November 13 or
14, 1913
Sent from Cracow to
Capri (Italy)
First published in *Pravda* No. 51,
March 2, 1924

Collected Works,
Vol. 35, pp. 121-24

To Inessa Armand

I have just read, my dear friend,* Vinnichenko's new novel which you sent me.[164] There's balderdash and stupidity! To combine together as much as possible of every kind of "horror", to collect in one story "vice" and "syphilis" and romantic crime, with extortion of money by means of blackmail (with the sister of the blackmailed person turned into a mistress), and the trial of the doctor! All this with hysterical outbursts, eccentricities, claims of having one's "own" theory of organising prostitutes. This organisation represents nothing bad in itself; but it is the *author*, Vinnichenko himself, who makes nonsense of it, *smacks his lips* over it, makes it his "hobby horse".

The review in *Rech* says that it is an imitation of Dostoyevsky and that there are good parts in it. There is an imitation, in my opinion, and a supremely bad imitation of the supremely bad in Dostoyevsky. Of course, in real life there are individual cases of all the "horrors" which Vinnichenko describes. But to lump them all together, and in *such* a way, means laying on the horrors *with a trowel*, frightening both one's own imagination and the reader's, "stunning" both oneself and the reader.

Once I had to spend a night with a sick comrade (delirium tremens), and once I had to "talk round" a comrade who had attempted suicide (after the attempt), and who some years later did commit suicide. Both recollections à la Vinnichenko. But in both cases these were small fragments of the lives of both comrades. But this pretentious, crass idiot Vinnichenko, in self-admiration, has from such things compiled a collection that is nothing but horrors — a kind of "twopenny dreadful". Brrr.... Muck, nonsense, pity I spent so much time reading it.

Yours,

V. I.

Written earlier than June 5, 1914
Sent from Poronin to Lovran
(Austria-Hungary, now
Yugoslavia)
Published for the first time
in the Fourth (Russian) Edition
of the *Collected Works*

Collected Works,
Vol. 35, pp. 144-45

---

* The words "my dear friend" were written by Lenin in English.— *Ed.*

To Inessa Armand

Dear Friend,

I very much advise you to write the plan of the pamphlet in as much detail as possible.[165] Otherwise too much is unclear.

One opinion I must express here and now:

I advise you to throw out altogether § 3 — the "demand (women's) for freedom of love".

That is not really a proletarian but a bourgeois demand.

After all, what do you understand by that phrase? What *can* be understood by it?

1. Freedom *from* material (financial) calculations in affairs of love?

2. The same, *from* material worries?

3. From religious prejudices?

4. From prohibitions by Papa, etc.?

5. From the prejudices of "society"?

6. From the narrow circumstances of one's environment (peasant or petty-bourgeois or bourgeois intellectual)?

7. From the fetters of the law, the courts and the police?

8. From the serious element in love?

9. From child-birth?

10. Freedom of adultery? Etc.

I have enumerated many shades (not all, of course). You have in mind, of course, not Nos. 8-10, but either Nos. 1-7 or something *similar* to Nos. 1-7.

But then for Nos. 1-7 you must choose a different wording, because freedom of love does not express this idea exactly.

And the public, the readers of the pamphlet, will *inevitably* understand by "freedom of love", in general, something like Nos. 8-10, even *without your wishing it.*

Just because in modern society the most talkative, noisy and "top-prominent" classes understand by "freedom of love"

Nos. 8-10, just for that very reason this is not a proletarian but a bourgeois demand.

For the proletariat Nos. 1-2 are the most important, and then Nos. 1-7, and those, in fact, are not "freedom of love".

The thing is not what you *subjectively* "mean" by this. The thing is the *objective logic* of class relations in affairs of love.

Friendly shake hands! *

W. I.

Written on January 17, 1915

Sent from Berne

First published in 1939
in the magazine *Bolshevik*
No. 13

Collected Works,
Vol. 35, pp. 180-81

---

* These words, like "Dear Friend" at the beginning, were written by Lenin in English.— *Ed.*

To Inessa Armand

Dear Friend,

I apologise for my delay in replying: I wanted to do it yesterday, but was prevented, and I had no time to sit down and write.

As regards your plan for the pamphlet, my opinion was that "the demand for freedom of love" was unclear and — independently of your will and your wish (I emphasised this when I said that what mattered was the objective, class relations, and not your subjective wishes) — would, in present social conditions, turn out to be a bourgeois, not a proletarian demand.

You do not agree.

Very well. Let us look at the thing again.

In order to make the unclear clear, I enumerated approximately ten *possible* (and, in conditions of class discord, inevitable) different interpretations, and in doing so remarked that interpretations 1-7, in my opinion, would be typical or characteristic of proletarian women, and 8-10 of bourgeois women.

If you are to refute this, you have to show (1) that these interpretations are wrong (and then replace them by others, or indicate which are wrong), or (2) incomplete (then you should add those which are missing), or (3) are not divided into proletarian and bourgeois in that way.

You don't do either one, or the other, or the third.

You don't touch on points 1-7 at all. Does this mean that you admit them to be true (on the whole)? (What you write about the prostitution of proletarian women and their dependence: "impossibility of saying no" fully comes under points 1-7. No difference at all can be detected between us here.)

Nor do you deny that this is a *proletarian* interpretation.

There remain points 8-10.

These you "don't quite understand" and "object" to: "I don't understand how it is *possible*" (that is what you have written!) "to *identify*" (!!??) "freedom of love with" point 10....

So it appears that *I* am "identifying", while you have undertaken to refute and demolish *me?*

How so?

Bourgeois women understand by freedom of love points 8-10—that is my thesis.

Do you deny this? Will you say what *bourgeois* ladies understand by freedom of love?

You don't say that. Do not literature and life really *prove* that that is just how bourgeois women understand it? They prove it completely! You tacitly admit this.

And if that is so, the point is their class position, and it is hardly possible and almost naïve to "refute" *them.*

What you must do is *separate* from them clearly, *contrast* with them, the proletarian point of view. One must take into account the objective fact that otherwise *they* will snatch the appropriate passages from your pamphlet, interpret them in their own way, make your pamphlet into water pouring on their mill, distort your ideas in the workers' eyes, "*confuse*" the workers (sowing in their minds the fear that *you* may be bringing them *alien* ideas). And in their hands are a host of newspapers, etc.

While you, completely forgetting the objective and class point of view, go over to the "offensive" against *me*, as though I am "identifying" freedom of love with points 8-10.... Marvellous, really marvellous....

"Even a fleeting passion and intimacy" are "more poetic and cleaner" than "kisses without love" of a (vulgar and shallow) married couple. That is what you write. And that is what you intend to write in your pamphlet. Very good.

Is the contrast logical? Kisses without love between a vulgar couple are *dirty.* I agree. To them one should contrast... what?... One would think: kisses *with* love? While you contrast them with "fleeting" (why fleeting?) "passion" (why not love?)—so, logically, it turns out that kisses without love (fleeting) are contrasted with kisses without love by married people.... Strange. For a popular pamphlet, would it not be better to contrast philistine-intellectual-peasant (I think they're in my point *6* or point *5*) vulgar and dirty marriage without love to proletarian civil marriage with love (adding, *if you absolutely insist*, that fleeting intimacy and passion, too, may be dirty and may be clean). What you have arrived at is, not the contrast of class *types*, but something like an "incident", which of course is possible. But is it a question of particular incidents? If you take the theme of an incident, an individual case of dirty kisses in marriage and pure ones in a fleeting intimacy, that is a theme to be worked out in a novel (because there the whole *essence* is in the *individual* circumstances, the analysis of the *characters* and psychology of *particular* types). But in a pamphlet?

You understood my idea very well about the unsuitable quotation from Key, when you said it is "stupid" to appear in the role of "professors of love". Quite so. Well, and what about the role of professors of fleeting, etc.?

Really, I don't want to engage in polemics at all. I would willingly throw aside this letter and postpone matters until we can talk about it. But I want the pamphlet to be a good one, so that *no* one *could* tear out of it phrases which would cause you unpleasantness (sometimes *one single* phrase is enough to be the spoonful of tar in a barrel of honey), *could misinterpret you.* I am sure that here, too, you wrote "without wishing it", and the only reason why I am sending you this letter is that you may examine the plan in greater detail as a result of the letters than you would after a talk — and the plan, you know, is a very important thing.

Have you not some French socialist friend? Translate my points 1-10 to her (as though it were from English), together with your remarks about "fleeting", etc., and watch her, listen to her as attentively as possible: a little experiment as to what *outside* people will say, what their impressions will be, what they will expect of the pamphlet.

I shake you by the hand, and wish you fewer headaches and to get better soon.

V. U.

P.S. About Baugy [166] I don't know.... Possibly my friend * promised too much.... But what? I don't know. The thing has been postponed, i.e., the conflict has been postponed, *not* eliminated. We shall have to fight and fight!! Shall we succeed in dissuading them? What is your opinion?

Written on January 24, 1915

Sent from Berne
First published in 1939
in *Bolshevik* No. 13

Collected Works,
Vol. 35, pp. 182-85

---

* These two words were written by Lenin in English.— *Ed.*

To the Commissariats for Education and Properties of the Republic

You are directed to submit information without delay as to what exactly has been done to implement the decree of 13. IV. 1918, particularly in regard to 1) the removal of old monuments, 2) their replacement by new monuments, at least temporary ones, and 3) the replacement of old inscriptions on public buildings by new ones (§ 5 of the decree).

The two months' procrastination in carrying out the decree—important both as propaganda and as providing work to the unemployed—is unpardonable.

Chairman, C.P.C.*

Written on June 15, 1918
First published in 1933
in *Lenin Miscellany XXI*

Collected Works,
Vol. 44, p. 105

----

* There is a typewritten text of this document on C.P.C. note-paper, signed by Lenin, which was sent to the People's Commissariat for Education.— *Ed.*

Telegram to A. V. Lunacharsky

September 18, 1918

People's Commissar Lunacharsky
Petrograd
Copy to Pokrovsky, 53 Ostozhenka, Moscow

I have heard today Vinogradov's report on the busts and monuments, and am utterly outraged; nothing has been done for months; to this day there is not a single bust, the disappearance of the bust of Radishchev is a farce. There is no bust of Marx on public display, nothing has been done in the way of propaganda by putting up inscriptions in the streets. I reprimand you for this criminal and lackadaisical attitude, and demand that the names of all responsible persons should be sent me for prosecution. Shame on the saboteurs and thoughtless loafers.

Lenin
Chairman, Council of People's Commissars

First published in 1933
in *Lenin Miscellany XXI*

Collected Works,
Vol. 35, p. 360

To Maxim Gorky

July 31, 1919

Dear Alexei Maximych,

The more I read over your letter, and the more I think of the connection between its conclusions and what it sets forth (and what you described at our meetings), the more I arrive at the conviction that the letter, and your conclusions, and all your impressions, are quite sick.

Petrograd has been one of the sickest places in recent times. This is quite understandable, since its population has suffered most of all, the workers have given up more of their best forces than anyone else, the food shortage is grave, and the military danger too. Obviously your nerves can't stand it. That is not surprising. Yet you won't listen when you are told that you ought to change your abode, because to let oneself flog the nerves to a state of sickness is very unwise, unwise even from the plain common-sense point of view, not to speak of other points of view.

Just as in your conversations, there is in your letter a sum of sick impressions, leading you to sick conclusions.

You begin with dysentery and cholera, and immediately a kind of sick resentment comes over you: "fraternity, equality". Unconscious, but the result is something like communism being responsible for the privations, poverty and diseases of a besieged city!!

Then follow some bitter witticisms, which I don't understand, against "hoarding" literature (which? why connected with Kalinin?). And the conclusion that a "wretched remainder of the intelligent workers" say that they have been "betrayed" into "captivity to the muzhik".

That, now, has no sense in it at all. Is it Kalinin who is being accused of betraying the workers to the muzhik? That is what it amounts to.

This might be invented by workers who are either quite green, stupid, with a "Left" phrase instead of a brain, or else by those who are overwrought, exhausted, hungry, sick, or else by the "remainder of the aristocracy" who have a splendid ability to distort everything, a splendid gift for picking on every trifle to vent their frenzied hatred of Soviet power. You yourself mention this remainder at the same point in your letter. Their state of mind is having an unhealthy influence on you.

You write that you see "people of the most varied sections of society". It's one thing to see them, another thing to feel daily contact with them, in all aspects of one's life. What you mainly experience is from the "remainder"—if only by virtue of your profession, which obliges you to "receive" dozens of embittered bourgeois intellectuals, and also by virtue of your general circumstances.

As though the "remainder" cherish "something bordering on sympathy for Soviet power", while "the majority of the workers" produce thieves, "Communists" who have jumped on the band-waggon, etc.! And you talk yourself into the "conclusion" that a revolution cannot be made with the help of thieves, cannot be made without the intelligentsia.

This is a completely sick psychology, acutely aggravated in the environment of embittered bourgeois intellectuals.

Everything is being done to draw the intelligentsia (the non-whiteguard intelligentsia) into the struggle against the thieves. And *month by month* the Soviet Republic acquires a *growing* percentage of bourgeois intellectuals who are *sincerely* helping the workers and peasants, not merely grumbling and spitting fury. This cannot be "seen" in Petrograd, because Petrograd is a city with an exceptionally large number of bourgeois people (and "intelligentsia") who have lost their place in life (and their heads), but for all Russia this is an unquestionable fact.

In Petrograd, or from Petrograd, one can only become convinced of this if one is exceptionally well informed *politically* and has a specially wide political experience. This you haven't got. And you are engaged, not in politics and not in observing the *work* of political construction, but in particular profession, which surrounds you with embittered bourgeois intellectuals, who have understood nothing, forgotten nothing, learned nothing and *at best*—a very rare best—have lost their bearings, are in despair, moaning, repeating old prejudices, have been frightened to death or are frightening themselves to death.

If you want to *observe,* you must observe from below, where it
is possible to *survey* the work of building a new life, in a
workers' settlement in the provinces or in the countryside.
There one does not have to make a political summing-up of
extremely complex data, there one need only observe. Instead
of this, you have put yourself in the position of a professional
editor of translations, etc., a position in which it is impossible to
observe the new building of a new life, a position in which all
your strength is frittered away on the sick grumbling of a sick
intelligentsia, on observing the "former" capital * in conditions
of desperate military peril and fierce privations.

You have put yourself in a position in which you *cannot*
directly observe the new features in the life of the workers and
peasants, i.e., nine-tenths of the population of Russia; in which
you are compelled to observe the fragments of life of a former
capital, from where the flower of the workers has gone to the
fronts and to the countryside, and where there remain a
disproportionately large number of intellectuals without a
place in life and without jobs, who *specially "besiege"* you.
Counsels to go away you stubbornly reject.

Quite understandably, you have reduced yourself to a
condition of sickness: you write that you find life not only
hard, but also "extremely revolting"!!! I should say so! At such
a time to chain oneself to the sickest of places as an editor of
translated literature (the most suitable occupation for observing people, for an artist!). As an artist, you *cannot* see and study
anything there that is new — in the army, in the countryside, in
the factory. You have deprived yourself of any opportunity of
doing what would satisfy the artist: in Petrograd a politician
can work, but you are not a politician. Today it's windows being
broken for no reason at all, tomorrow it's shots and screams
from prison, then snatches of oratory by the most weary of the
non-workers who have remained in Petrograd, then millions of
impressions from the intelligentsia, the intelligentsia of a
capital which is no longer a capital, then hundreds of
complaints from those who have been wronged, *inability* to see
any building of the new life in the time you have left after
editing (the building goes on in a particular way, and least of all
in Petrograd) — how could you fail to reduce yourself to a
point when it is extremely revolting to go on living?

The country is living in a feverish struggle against the
bourgeoisie of the whole world, which is taking a frenzied

---

* Petrograd. In March 1918 the capital was transferred to Moscow.— *Ed.*

revenge for its overthrow. Naturally. For the first Soviet Republic, the first blows *from everywhere*. Naturally. Here one must live either as an active politician or (if one's heart does not draw one to politics), as an artist, observe how people are building life anew somewhere that is not, as the capital is, the centre of furious attack, of a furious struggle against conspiracies, of the furious anger of the capital's intelligentsia — somewhere in the countryside, or in a provincial factory (or at the front). There it is easy, merely by observing, to distinguish the decomposition of the old from the first shoots of the new.

Life has become revolting, the "divergence" from communism "is deepening". Where the divergence lies, it is impossible to tell. Not a shadow of an indication of a divergence in politics or in ideas. There is a divergence of *mood*—between people who are engaged in politics or are absorbed in a struggle of the most furious kind, and the mood of a man who has artificially driven himself into a situation where he can't observe the new life, while his impressions of the decay of a vast bourgeois capital are getting the better of him.

I have expressed my thoughts to you frankly on the subject of your letter. From my conversations (with you) I have long been approaching the same ideas, but your letter gave shape and conclusion, it rounded off the sum total of the impressions I have gained from these conversations. I don't want to thrust my advice on you, but I cannot help saying: change your circumstances radically, your environment, your abode, your occupation — otherwise life may disgust you for good.

All the best.

Yours,
Lenin

Sent to Petrograd

First published in 1925   *Collected Works,*
in *Krasnaya Letopis* No. 1   Vol. 35, pp. 410-14

To A. M. Gorky

September 15

Dear Alexei Maximych,

I received Tonkov, and even before that and before receiving your letter we had decided in the Central Committee to appoint Kamenev and Bukharin to check on the arrests of bourgeois intellectuals of the near-Cadet type and to release whoever possible. For it is clear to us that there have been mistakes here, too.

It is also clear that in general the measure of arrest applied to Cadet (and near-Cadet) people has been necessary and correct.

Reading your frank opinion on this matter, I recall a remark of yours, which sank into my mind during our talks (in London, on Capri, and afterwards):

"We artists are irresponsible people."

Exactly! You utter incredibly angry words about what? About a few dozen (or perhaps even a few hundred) Cadet and near-Cadet gentry spending a few days in jail *in order to prevent plots like that of the surrender of Krasnaya Gorka,*[167] plots which threaten the lives of *tens* of thousands of workers and peasants.

A calamity, indeed! What injustice! A few days, or even weeks, in jail for intellectuals in order to prevent the massacre of tens of thousands of workers and peasants!

"Artists are irresponsible people."

It is wrong to confuse the "intellectual forces" of the people with the "forces" of bourgeois intellectuals. As a sample of the latter I take Korolenko: I recently read the pamphlet *War, the Fatherland and Mankind,* which he wrote in August 1917. Mind you, Korolenko is the best of the "near-Cadets", almost a Menshevik. But what a disgusting, base, vile defence of imperialist war, concealed behind honeyed phrases! A wretched philistine in thrall to bourgeois prejudices! For such gentlemen 10,000,000 killed in an imperialist war is a deed worthy of support (by *deeds,* accompanied by honeyed phrases "against" war), but the death of hundreds of thousands in a *just* civil war against the landowners and capitalists evokes ahs and ohs, sighs and hysterics.

No. There is no harm in such "talents" being made to spend some weeks or so in prison, if this *has* to be done to *prevent* plots (like Krasnaya Gorka) and the death of tens of thousands. But we exposed these plots of the Cadets and "near-Cadets". And we *know* that the near-Cadet professors quite often *help* the plotters. That's a fact.

The intellectual forces of the workers and peasants are growing and gaining strength in the struggle to overthrow the bourgeoisie and its henchmen, the intellectual lackeys of capital, who imagine they are the brains of the nation. Actually, they are not the brains, but sh...

To the "intellectual forces" who want to bring science to the people (and not to act as servants to capital), we pay a salary *above the average*. That is a fact. We take care of them. That is a fact. Tens of thousands of officers are serving in the Red Army with us and are winning victory, despite the hundreds of traitors. That is a fact.

As for your moods, I can "understand" them all right (since you raise the question whether I shall be able to understand you). Often, both on Capri and afterwards, I told you: You allow yourself to be surrounded by the very worst elements of the bourgeois intelligentsia and succumb to their whining. You hear and listen to the howl of hundreds of intellectuals over the "terrible" arrest for a few weeks, but the voice of the masses, the millions, the workers and peasants, whom Denikin, Kolchak, Lianozov, Rodzyanko, the Krasnaya Gorka (and other *Cadet*) plotters are threatening — this voice you do not hear and do not listen to. I quite understand, I quite fully understand, that in this way one can write oneself not only into saying that "the Reds are just as much enemies of the people as the Whites" (the fighters for the overthrow of the capitalists and landowners are just as much enemies of the people as the landowners and capitalists), but also into a belief in the merciful God or our Father the Tsar. I fully understand.

            ×

No really, you will go under unless you tear yourself out of this environment of bourgeois intellectuals! With all my heart I wish that you do this quickly.

All the best,
Yours,
Lenin

×For you are not writing anything! And for an artist to waste oneself on the whining of rotting intellectuals and not to write — is this not ruin, is it not shameful?

Written on September 15, 1919

Sent to Petrograd

First published in 1965 in
Collected Works,
Fifth Russian Ed., Vol. 51

Collected Works,
Vol. 44, pp. 283-84

To A. V. Lunacharsky

January 18, 1920

Comrade Lunacharsky,

Recently I had occasion — to my regret and shame, for the first time — to look through the famous Dahl dictionary.[168]

It's a magnificent thing, but then it's a dictionary of *regional* terms, and out of date. Is it not time to produce a dictionary of the *real* Russian language, a dictionary, say, of words used *nowadays* and by the *classics*, from Pushkin to Gorky?.

What if 30 scholars were set to work at this, and provided with Red Army rations?

What would be your attitude to this idea?

A dictionary of the classical Russian language?

Without making a noise about it, have a talk with people who know the subject, if it's not too much trouble, and let me know your opinion.

Yours,

Lenin

First published in *Pravda* No. 21,
January 21, 1940

Collected Works,
Vol. 35, p. 434

Lenin in conversation with Herbert G. Wells at the Kremlin.
Photo, October 1920

To A. S. Serafimovich

May 21, 1920

To Comrade Serafimovich

Dear Comrade,

My sister has just told me of the terrible misfortune which has overtaken you.[169] Allow me to give you the very warmest handshake, and to wish you courage and firmness of spirit. I very much regret that I have not been able to fulfil my desire to see you more often and to become better acquainted. But your books, and what my sister has often told me, have aroused a profound affection for you in me, and I very much want to say to you how *necessary* your work is for the workers and for all of us, and how essential it is now for you to be firm, in order to overcome your grief and *force* yourself to return to work. Forgive me for writing in a hurry. Once again, I shake you very warmly by the hand.

Yours,
Lenin

First published in 1924
in the book: V. Veshnev,
*A. Serafimovich kak khudozhnik
slova*

Collected Works,
Vol. 35, p. 448

Telegram to the Crimean Revolutionary Committee

Sevastopol

February 26, 1921

Take resolute measures for the effective protection of art treasures, paintings, porcelain, bronze and marble articles, etc., in the Yalta palaces and private residences, now set aside for sanatoria of the People's Commissariat for Health, which according to the information available to us are being removed. Pending the arrival of a special commission from Moscow to examine and arrange for the protection of the said articles you will be held responsible for their preservation.

Lenin
Chairman, Council of Labour and Defence

Written on February 26, 1921
First published in 1945
in *Lenin Miscellany XXXV*

Collected Works,
Fifth Russian
Ed, Vol. 52,
pp. 309-10

To A. V. Lunacharsky

Aren't you ashamed to vote for printing 5,000 copies of Mayakovsky's "150,000,000"?
It is nonsense, stupidity, double-dyed stupidity and affectation.[170]
I believe such things should be published one in ten and *not more than 1,500 copies*, copies for libraries and cranks.
As for Lunacharsky, he should be flogged for his futurism.

Lenin

Written on May 6, 1921
First published in 1957
in the magazine
Kommunist No. 18

Collected Works,
Vol. 45, pp. 138-39

7*

To G. Myasnikov

August 5, 1921

Comrade Myasnikov,

I have only just managed to read *both* your articles. I am unaware of the nature of the speeches you made in the Perm (I think it was Perm) organisation and of your conflict with it. I can say nothing about that; it will be dealt with by the Organisation Bureau, which, I hear, has appointed a special commission.

My object is a different one: it is to appraise your articles as literary and political documents.

They are interesting documents.

Your main mistake is, I think, most clearly revealed in the article "Vexed Questions". And I consider it my duty to do all I can to try to convince you.

At the beginning of the article you make a correct application of dialectics. Indeed, whoever fails to understand the substitution of the slogan of "civil peace" for the slogan of "civil war" lays himself open to ridicule, if nothing worse. In this, you are right.

But precisely because you are right on this point, I am surprised that in drawing your conclusions, you should have forgotten the dialectics which you yourself had properly applied.

"Freedom of the press, from the monarchists to the anarchists, inclusively".... Very good! But just a minute: every Marxist and every worker who ponders over the four years' experience of our revolution will say, "Let's look into this — *what sort* of freedom of the press? What *for*? For *which class?*"

We do not believe in "absolutes". We laugh at "pure democracy".

The "freedom of the press" slogan became a great world

slogan at the close of the Middle Ages and remained so up to the nineteenth century. Why? Because it expressed the ideas of the progressive bourgeoisie, i. e., its struggle against kings and priests, feudal lords and landowners.

No country in the world has done as much to liberate the masses from the influence of *priests* and *landowners* as the R.S.F.S.R. has done, and is doing. We have been performing *this* function of "freedom of the press" *better than anyone else* in the world.

All over the world, wherever there are capitalists, freedom of the press means freedom to *buy up* newspapers, to *buy* writers, to *bribe*, buy and fake "public opinion" for the *benefit of the bourgeoisie.*

This is a fact.

No one will ever be able to refute it.

And what about us?

Can anyone deny that the bourgeoisie in this country has been defeated, *but not destroyed?* That it *has gone into hiding?* Nobody can deny it.

Freedom of the press in the R.S.F.S.R., which is surrounded by the bourgeois enemies of the whole world, means freedom of *political organisation* for the bourgeoisie and its most loyal servants, the Mensheviks and Socialist-Revolutionaries.

This is an irrefutable fact.

The bourgeoisie (all over the world) is still very much stronger than we are. To place in its hands yet *another* weapon like freedom of political organisation (=freedom of the press, for the press is the core and foundation of political organisation) means facilitating the enemy's task, means helping the class enemy.

We have no wish to commit suicide, and therefore, we will not do this.

We clearly see this *fact:* "freedom of the press" means *in practice* that the international bourgeoisie will immediately buy up hundreds and thousands of Cadet, Socialist-Revolutionary and Menshevik writers, and will organise their propaganda and fight against us.

That is a fact. "They" are richer than we are and will buy a "force" ten times larger than we have, to fight us.

No, we will not do it; we will not help the international bourgeoisie.

How could you *descend* from a class appraisal—from the appraisal of the relations between *all* classes—to the sentimental, philistine appraisal? This is a mystery to me.

On the question: "civil peace or civil war", on the question of how *we* have won over, and *will continue* to "win over", the peasantry (to the side of the proletariat), on these two key world questions (=questions that affect the very *substance* of world politics), on these questions (which are dealt with in *both* your articles), you *were able* to take the Marxist standpoint, instead of the philistine, sentimental standpoint. You *did take account* of the relationships of *all* classes in a *practical,* sober way.

And suddenly you slide down into the abyss of sentimentalism!

"Outrage and abuses are rife in this country: freedom of the press will expose them."

That, as far as I can judge from your two articles, is where you slipped up. You have allowed yourself to *be depressed* by certain sad and deplorable *facts,* and lost the ability *soberly* to appraise the forces.

Freedom of the press will help *the force* of the world bourgeoisie. That is a fact. "Freedom of the press" *will not help to purge the Communist Party* in Russia of a number of its weaknesses, mistakes, misfortunes and maladies (it cannot be denied that there is a spate of these maladies), because this is *not* what the world bourgeoisie wants. But freedom of the press will be a weapon in the hands of *this world bourgeoisie.* It is not dead; it is alive. It is lurking nearby and watching. It has already *hired* Milyukov, to whom Chernov and Martov (partly because of their stupidity, and partly because of factional spleen against us; but mainly because of the objective logic of their petty-bourgeois-democratic position) are giving "faithful and loyal" service.

You took the wrong fork in the road.

You wanted to *cure* the Communist Party of its maladies and have snatched at *a drug* that will cause certain death — not at your hands, of course, but at the hands of the world bourgeoisie (+Milyukov+Chernov+Martov).

You forgot a minor point, a very tiny point, namely: the world bourgeoisie and its "freedom" to buy up *for itself* newspapers, and *centres of political ogranisation.*

No, we will not take this course. *Nine hundred* out of every thousand *politically* conscious workers will refuse to take this course.

We have many maladies. Mistakes (our *common* mistakes, all of us have made mistakes, the *Council of Labour and Defence,* the

Council of People's Commissars and the Central Committee) like those we made in distributing fuel and *food* in the autumn and winter of 1920 (those were enormous mistakes!) have greatly aggravated the maladies springing from our situation. Want and calamity abound.

They have been terribly *intensified* by the famine of 1921.

It will cost us a supreme effort to extricate ourselves, but we will get out, and have already begun to do so.

We will extricate ourselves, for, in the main, our policy is a correct one, and takes into account *all* the class forces on an *international* scale. We will extricate ourselves because we do not try to make our position look better than it is. We realise all the difficulties. We see *all* the maladies, and are taking measures to cure them methodically, with perseverance, and without giving way to panic.

You have allowed panic to get the better of you; panic is a slope — once you stepped on it you slid down into a position that looks very much as if you are forming a new party, or are about to commit suicide.

You must not give way to panic.

Is there any isolation of the Communist Party cells from the Party? There is. It is an evil, a misfortune, a malaise.

It is there. It is a severe ailment.

We can see it.

It must be cured by proletarian and Party measures and not by means of "freedom" (*for the bourgeoisie*).

Much of what you say about reviving the country's economy, about mechanical ploughs, etc., about fighting for "influence" over the peasantry, etc., is true and useful.

Why not *bring this out* separately? We shall get together and work harmoniously in one party. The benefits will be great; *they will not come all at once,* but *very* slowly.

Revive the Soviets; secure the co-operation of non-Party people; let *non-Party* people verify the work of Party members: this is absolutely right. *No end* of work there, and it has hardly been started.

Why not amplify *this* in a *practical* way? In a pamphlet for the Congress?

Why not take that up?

Why be afraid of *spade* work (*denounce* abuses through the Central Control Commission,[171] or the Party press, *Pravda*)? Misgivings about slow, difficult and arduous spade work cause people to give way to panic and to seek an "easy" way out: "freedom of the press" (*for the bourgeoisie*).

Why should you persist in your mistake—an obvious mistake—in your non-Party, *anti-proletarian* slogan of "freedom of the press"? Why not take up the less "brilliant" (scintillating with bourgeois brilliance) spade work of driving out abuses, combating them, and *helping* non-Party people in a practical and business-like way?

Have you ever brought up any *particular* abuse to the notice of the C.C., and suggested a definite *means* of eradicating it?

No, you have not.

Not a single time.

You saw a spate of misfortunes and maladies, gave way to despair and rushed into the arms of the enemy, the bourgeoisie ("freedom of the press" *for the bourgeoisie*). My advice is: do not give way to despair and panic.

We, and those who sympathise with us, the workers and peasants, still have an immense reservoir of strength. We still have plenty of health and vigour.

We are not doing enough to cure our ailments.

We are not doing a good job of practising the slogan: promote non-Party people, let non-Party people verify the work of Party members.

But we can, and will, do a hundred times more in this field than we are doing.

I hope that after thinking this over carefully you will not, out of false pride, persist in an obvious political mistake ("freedom of the press"), but, pulling yourself together and overcoming the panic, will get down to practical work: help to establish *ties* with non-Party people, and help non-Party people to *verify* the work of Party members.

There is no end of work in this field. Doing this work you can (and should) help to *cure* the disease, slowly but surely, instead of chasing after will-o'-the-wisps like "freedom of the press".

With communist greetings,

Lenin

Published in 1921   *Collected Works,*
                                           Vol. 32, pp. 504-09

To the *Clarté* Group [172]

November 15, 1922

Dear Friends,

I take this opportunity to send you best greetings. I have been seriously ill, and for over a year I have not been able to see a single one of the productions of your group. I hope that your organisation "*des anciens combattants*"* still exists and is growing stronger not only numerically, but also spiritually, in the sense of intensifying and spreading the struggle against imperialist war. It is worth devoting one's whole life to the struggle against this kind of war; it is a struggle in which one must be ruthless and chase to the furthermost corners of the earth all the sophistry that is uttered in its defence.

Best greetings.

Yours,

Lenin

First published in 1925
in French in *Clarté* No. 71

First published in Russian
in 1930

Collected Works,
Vol. 33, p. 434

---

* Ex-servicemen.— *Ed.*

Decrees and Decisions
Signed by Lenin

*On the Protection of the Objects
of Antiquity and Works of Art Belonging
to the Polish People

Considering that there are objects of great artistic or historical value to the Polish people in Western and North-Western gubernias of the Russian Republic and in many towns and estates belonging to people of Polish extraction, most of which objects were taken out of Poland during the retreat of the Russian troops or still earlier, and with a view to returning these objects in good repair to the Polish people, the Council of People's Commissars resolves and decrees the following principles of action for the appropriate revolutionary authorities:

1. Objects of antiquity and works of art, libraries, archives, paintings and museum exhibits, irrespective of their whereabouts, are to be placed as the property of the Polish people under the protection of the Workers' and Peasants' Government, as represented by the Commissariat for Polish Affairs and the Society for the Protection of Objects of Antiquity pending their transfer to Polish national museums.

2. Deeds are to be drawn up for all objects and the deeds concerning the voluntary transfer of the objects on the Polish estates are to be signed by the estate owner or a person authorised by him. The deed is to be drawn up in two copies, one of them to be kept by the Commissariat for Polish Affairs under the auspices of the Council of People's Commissars and the other by the Petrograd branch of the Polish Society for the Protection of Objects of Antiquity (the official representation of Polish art and historical societies in Russia).

3. Besides the deeds, an exact inventory of all transferred objects is to be made in four copies, one for the owner, the

---

second for the Commissariat for Polish Affairs, the third for the particular district Commissariat charged with protection of objects of antiquity or the Bureau of the nearest Executive Committee of the Union of Polish Servicemen and the fourth for the Board of the Society for the Protection of Objects of Antiquity in Petrograd.

4. The Commissariat for Polish Affairs shall appoint district commissars vested with powers equivalent to those of the commissars of the Workers' and Peasants' Government who will be charged with the drawing up of deeds and inventories and with the implementing of the present decree.

5. All the afore-mentioned organisations and persons shall work in conjunction with local revolutionary authorities as represented by the local Soviets of Soldiers', Workers' and Peasants' Deputies, whose duty it will be to render full assistance to them in protecting and transporting the Polish cultural treasures.

January 12 (25), 1918   *Decrees of the Soviet Power,*
                                                      Vol. I, 1957, pp. 343-44

*On the Monuments of the Republic

To commemorate the great revolution which has transformed Russia the Council of People's Commissars resolves:

1. The monuments erected in honour of tsars and their minions and which have no historical or artistic value are to be removed from the squares and streets and stored up or used for utilitarian purposes.

2. A special commission made up of the People's Commissars for Education and Property of the Republic and the chief of the Fine Arts Department of the Commissariat for Education is instructed to determine through agreement with the Art Collegium of Moscow and Petrograd which monuments shall be·pulled down.

3. The said commission is instructed to mobilise the artists and organise a broad competition in designing monuments to commemorate the great days of the Russian Socialist Revolution.

4. The Council of People's Commissars wishes that by May the First some of the most monstrous idols be removed and that models of new monuments be put in their place for the public to judge.

5. The said commission is instructed to prepare at short notice May Day decorations for the city and to change the old inscriptions, emblems, names of streets, coats of arms, etc., to new ones reflecting the ideas and sentiments of the revolutionary working population of Russia.

6. The regional and gubernia Soviets shall take the same steps only by agreement with the above-mentioned commission.

7. The necessary sums shall be allocated after estimates have been submitted and the usefulness of such projects has been verified.

April 12, 1918

Decrees of the Soviet Power,
Vol. II, 1959, pp. 95-96

*On the Nationalisation of the Tretyakov Gallery

With regard to the fact that the Moscow City Art Gallery named after P. and S. M. Tretyakov due to its cultural and artistic significance represents an institution fulfilling national educational functions and that the interests of the working class require that the Tretyakov Gallery should form part of the network of national museums, the activities of which are directed by the People's Commissariat for Education, the Council of People's Commissars resolves:

1. To proclaim the Moscow City Art Gallery bearing the name of P. and S. M. Tretyakov the state property of the Russian Federative Soviet Republic and place it under the control of the People's Commissariat for Education on the same basis as the other state museums.

2. The Collegium for Museum Affairs and the Protection of Monuments of Art and Antiquities under the auspices of the People's Commissariat for Education is instructed to draft and enact at short notice new regulations on the running of the gallery and its work adapted to the present-day requirements of the museums and the tasks of democratising the artistic and educational institutions of the Russian Soviet Republic.

June 3 (May 21), 1918

Decrees of the Soviet Power,
Vol. II, 1959, pp. 389-90

The List

of Persons Monuments to Whom Are to Be Erected
in Moscow and Other Towns of the Russian Socialist
Federative Soviet Republic, Submitted to the Council
of People's Commissars by the Fine Arts Department
of the People's Commissariat for Education

I. *Revolutionaries and Public Figures*

1. Spartacus. 2. Tiberius Gracchus. 3. Brutus. 4. Babeuf.
5. Marx. 6. Engels. 7. Bebel. 8. Lassalle. 9. Jaurès.
10. Lafargue. 11. Vaillant. 12. Marat. 13. Robespierre.
14. Danton. 15. Garibaldi. 16. Stepan Razin. 17. Pestel.
18. Ryleyev. 19. Herzen. 20. Bakunin. 21. Lavrov. 22. Khalturin. 23. Plekhanov. 24. Kalayev. 25. Volodarsky.
26. Fourier. 27. Saint-Simon. 28. Robert Owen.
29. Zhelyabov. 30. Sofia Perovskaya. 31. Kibalchich.

II. *Writers and Poets*

1. Tolstoy. 2. Dostoyevsky. 3. Lermontov. 4. Pushkin.
5. Gogol. 6. Radishchev. 7. Belinsky. 8. Ogaryov. 9. Chernyshevsky. 10. Mikhailovsky. 11. Dobrolyubov. 12. Pisarev.
13. Gleb Uspensky. 14. Saltykov-Shchedrin. 15. Nekrasov.
16. Shevchenko. 17. Tyutchev. 18. Nikitin. 19. Novikov.
20. Koltsov.

III. *Philosophers and Scientists*

1. Skovoroda. 2. Lomonosov. 3. Mendeleyev.

IV. *Artists*

1. Rublyov. 2. Kiprensky. 3. Alexander Ivanov. 4. Vrubel.
5. Shubin. 6. Kozlovsky. 7. Kazakov.

V. *Composers*

1. Moussorgsky. 2. Scriabin. 3. Chopin.

VI. *Actors*

1. Komissarzhevskaya. 2. Mochalov.

Izvestia VTsIK No. 163,
August 2, 1918

*On Prohibiting the Export
of the Objects of Art and Antiquity

For the purpose of putting a stop to the export of objects possessing a special artistic and historical value, which could lead to the loss of the people's cultural treasures the Council of People's Commissars resolves:

1. To prohibit the export from all parts of the Republic and the sale by all persons of objects of artistic and historical value without permits issued by the Collegium for Museum Affairs and the Protection of Monuments of Art and Antiquities in Petrograd and Moscow under the auspices of the People's Commissariat for Education by the bodies authorised to do so by the Collegium. The Commissariat for Foreign Trade can issue permits for the export of antiquities and objects of art only after preliminary consultation with and permission from the People's Commissariat for Education.

2. All shops, commissioners' offices and individuals, who trade in works of art and antiques, or their intermediaries, as well as persons who undertake paid evaluation or expertise of objects of art and antiques, must register within three days after the promulgation of the decree with the Collegium for the Protection of Monuments of Art and Antiquities in Petrograd and Moscow under the auspices of the People's Commissariat for Education or with the bodies authorised by the Collegium and in localities with the Education Department of gubernia Soviets of Workers' and Peasants' Deputies.

3. Those who fail to abide by the decree shall be subject to the full severity of the revolutionary legislation and liable to confiscation of all their property and imprisonment.

4. The decree becomes effective on the day of its publication.

September 19, 1918

Collection of the Laws and Directives of the Workers' and Peasants' Government No. 69, September 25, 1918, pp. 853-54

On the Nationalisation of Art Collections

The Council of People's Commissars resolves:
To proclaim the art collections of A. I. Morozov, I. S. Ostroukhov and V. A. Morozov state property of the Russian

Socialist Federative Soviet Republic and place them under the control of the People's Commissariat for Education which shall be directed to draw up and implement at short notice Regulations as to the use of the collections in keeping with the current needs and the tasks connected with the democratising of the artistic and educational institutions of the Russian Socialist Federative Soviet Republic.

December 19,1918

Collection of the Laws and Directives of the Workers' and Peasants' Government No. 99, December 30, 1918, p. 1272

*On the Nationalisation of Leo Tolstoy's House in Moscow

With a view to preserving the house where L. N. Tolstoy lived and worked, the Council of People's Commissars resolves:

Leo Tolstoy's house, 21 Khamovnichesky Pereulok, Moscow, complete with the adjoining land, buildings and all its contents is proclaimed state property of the Russian Socialist Federative Soviet Republic and placed under the control of the People's Commissariat for Education.

April 6, 1920

Collection of the Laws and Directives of the Workers' and Peasants' Government No. 26, April 20, 1920, p. 125

RECOLLECTIONS OF V. I. LENIN

DMITRY ULYANOV

His Love of Music

Vladimir Ilyich learned to play the piano when he was still a boy. Mother used to say that he had a fine ear and an aptitude for music. At the age of eight he could play children's tunes well on the piano and often sat down to play a duet with some older person. However, when he entered the gymnasium he gave up music — not because it interfered with his studies, for he had great natural ability and found it easy to study. Most likely he did so because in those days piano playing was considered rather an unsuitable occupation for boys. All his life, however, Vladimir Ilyich loved music and always appreciated its finer points.

I have a vivid recollection of going with him to the opera when we lived in Kazan during the winter of 1888. Our seats were high up in the gallery and afterwards we walked home to have our supper of bread and milk. Vladimir Ilyich was still under the spell of the music, and quietly, because the household was asleep, he hummed the arias that had made the greatest impression on him. He was in a cheerful mood, for, from the god-forsaken village of Kokushkino where he had been under police surveillance, he had gone-straight to the opera....

Mother was very fond of the piano. She played and sang many of the old airs and love songs and had a particular liking for selections from the opera *Askold's Grave*. She had some old, faded copies of the music and we liked to listen to her playing and singing some parts of the opera; Volodya would often hum the melodies from the opera.

During those years, 1888-90, Volodya sang very often with Olya as his accompanist. Very little is known about Olya: she was Volodya's best and closest companion in childhood and youth. She was younger than her brother, but not behind him in accomplishment. When she was eighteen years of age she could speak four foreign languages — German, French, English and Swedish. It was said of her that the only time she was not working was when she was asleep. She died in May 1891 of typhoid fever.

Vladimir Ilyich had always admired her talents and industry. They used to sing a duet — a song by Yazykov — *The Swimmer* (*Our Sea Is Friendless*). I was particularly impressed with the last couplet:

> *But the billows carry over*
> *Only those whose hearts are strong!*
> *Courage, brothers,*
> *Let the tempest*
> *Swifter bear our boat along.*

Volodya liked to sing *The Wedding Song* by Dargomyzhsky.

> *Not in church were we married,*
> *Not with candles and singing,*
> *No priest gave his blessing,*
> *And no bells were there ringing.*

He knew one of Heine's lyrics containing the line: "I feel your eyes will kill me, my darling", which had to be taken on a very high note. After taking it Volodya would laugh and say, "They've killed me, they really have!"

I hardly remember a time when Vladimir Ilyich, as a young man, was ever in low spirits. He always radiated confidence, daring and buoyancy of spirit.

Another favourite song of his was Valentine's aria from *Faust*. He sang "God Almighty, god of love" because the words were part of the song and could hardly be left out, but the part he liked best and found most beautiful, because it seemed to embody some of his own militant spirit, was:

> *There in the heat of battle*
> *I swear to be first in the ranks.*

Even now, when I hear Gounod's music the memory of Vladimir Ilyich singing this aria comes back to me out of the past.

I heard *The Internationale* for the first time in the summer of 1889; hardly anyone in Russia knew it then. We were staying at the farm in Alakayevka in the Samara region. Olga had been playing on the piano and finished with the *Marseillaise*. I hurried over to her and asked her to play it again. Just then Vladimir Ilyich came into the room quite unexpectedly; it was morning and a time when usually wild horses could not drag him from his books. He came over to us and asked us to sing *The Internationale*. He sat down at the piano with Olga and they played the new air through—and then sang it together, very quietly, in French.

Maria told me afterwards that Vladimir Ilyich very much regretted not having continued his studies of the piano or the violin.

Reminiscences of Lenin by His Relatives, Moscow, 1956, pp. 127-29

Ilyich's Favourite Books

I brought with me to Siberia books by Pushkin, Lermontov and Nekrasov. Ilyich arranged them near his bed, alongside Hegel, and read them over and over again in the evenings. Pushkin was his favourite. But it was not only the style that he liked. For example, he was very fond of Chernyshevsky's *What Is To Be Done?* despite the fact that its style is somewhat naïve. I was surprised when I saw how attentively he read this book and how he noticed its finest points. Incidentally, he was very fond of Chernyshevsky, and his Siberian album contained two photographs of this writer, on one of which he had written the dates of the writer's birth and death. This album also contained a photograph of Émile Zola and of Russian writers, Herzen and Pisarev. At one time, Ilyich was very fond of Pisarev and read many of his works. In Siberia we also had a copy of Goethe's *Faust,* and a volume of Heine's poems, both in German.

Upon returning to Moscow from exile Ilyich went to the theatre to see *Der Kutscher Hanschel.* He said afterwards that he had greatly enjoyed it.

Among the books he liked while in Munich I remember Gerhardt's *Bei Mama,* and *Büttnerbauer* by Polenz.

Afterwards, during our second emigration in Paris, Ilyich found pleasure in reading Victor Hugo's *Châtiments,* dealing with the 1848 revolution; Hugo wrote it while abroad, and copies were smuggled into France. Although there is a naïve pomposity in this verse, one feels, nevertheless, the breath of revolution. Ilyich eagerly frequented the cafés and the suburban theatres in Paris to hear the revolutionary chansonniers, who, in the working-class districts, sang about everything — about how intoxicated peasants elected a travelling agitator to the Chamber of Deputies, about the bringing up of

children, unemployment and so on. Ilyich was particularly
fond of Montégus. The son of a Paris Communard, he was a
great favourite in the working-class districts. True, in his
improvised songs — richly garnished with the flavour of
life — there was no definite ideology of any kind, but there was
much in them that appealed. Ilyich often hummed his
Greeting to the 17th Regiment, which had refused to fire on
strikers: "*Salut, salut á vous, soldats du 17-me.*" Once, at Russian
social evening, Ilyich conversed with Montégus and it was
strange to see these two men who differed so vastly — when the
war broke out Montégus sided with the chauvinists — dreaming of world revolution. But things like that happen — you
meet someone in a railway carriage whom you have never
known before, and to the accompaniment of the grinding
wheels you talk in serious vein and say things that you would
never say at another time, and then you part and never meet
again. And so it was here. Moreover, the conversation was in
French, and it is easier to dream aloud in a foreign language
than in one's own. We had the services of a French charwoman
a couple of hours a day. Once Ilyich heard her singing a song
about Alsace. He asked her to sing it over again, and,
afterwards, upon memorising the words, he often sang it
himself. The song ended with the words:

Vous avez pris l'Alsace et la Lorraine.
Mais malgré vous nous resterons français,
Vous avez pu germaniser nos plaines,
Mais notre coeur — vous ne l'aurez jamais!

("You have seized Alsace and Lorraine, but in spite of you
we shall remain French; you have managed to Germanise our
fields, but never will you have our hearts.")
That was in the year 1909, when reaction was rampant and
the Party lay defeated. But its revolutionary spirit had not been
broken. And the song suited Ilyich's mood. One should have
heard the feeling he put into the words:

Mais notre coeur — vous ne l'aurez jamais!

During those very hard years in emigration, concerning
which Ilyich always spoke with a feeling of sadness (when we
returned to Russia he repeated once more what he had often
said before: "Why did we ever leave Geneva for
Paris?") — during those grim years he dreamed and dreamed,

whether in conversation with Montégus, or fervently singing the song about Alsace, or during the sleepless nights when he read Verhaeren.

Still later, during the war, Ilyich was attracted by Barbusse's *Le feu*, which he regarded as an extremely important book — a book which was in tune with his own feelings.

We seldom visited the theatre. On the rare occasions that we did, the insipidness of the play and the bad acting got on Ilyich's nerves. Usually we left the theatre after the first act. The other comrades laughed at us and asked why we wasted our money.

On one occasion, however, Ilyich sat through a play; this I think was at the end of 1915 in Berne, and the play was Tolstoy's *The Living Corpse*. Although it was acted in German, the man who took the role of the prince was a Russian and he succeeded in putting over Tolstoy's idea. Tense and excited, Ilyich followed every detail of the play.

And lastly, in Russia. To Ilyich the new art seemed somehow to be alien and incomprehensible. Once we were asked to a concert in the Kremlin for Red Army men. Ilyich was given a seat in the front row. The actress Gzovskaya, declaiming something by Mayakovsky — "Speed is our body and the drum our heart!" — was gesturing right in front of Ilyich, who was taken aback by the suddenness of it all; he grasped very little of the recitation and heaved a sigh of relief when Gzovskaya was replaced by another actor who began to read Chekhov's *Evil-doer.*

One evening Ilyich wanted to see for himself how the young people were getting on in the communes. We decided to visit our young friend Varya Armand who lived in a commune for art school students. I think that we made the visit on the day Kropotkin was buried, in 1921. It was a hungry year, but the young people were filled with enthusiasm. The people in the commune slept practically on bare boards, they had neither bread nor salt. "But we do have cereals," said a radiant-faced member of the commune. With this cereal they boiled a good porridge for Ilyich. Ilyich looked at the young people, at the radiant faces of the boys and girls who crowded around him, and their joy was reflected in his face. They showed him their naïve drawings, explained their meaning, and bombarded him with questions. And he, smiling, evaded answering and parried by asking questions of his own: "What do you read? Do you read Pushkin?" "Oh no," said someone, "after all he was a bourgeois; we read Mayakovsky." Ilyich smiled. "I think," he

said, "that Pushkin is better." After this Ilyich took a more
favourable view of Mayakovsky. Whenever the poet's name was
mentioned he recalled the young art students who, full of life
and gladness, and ready to die for the Soviet system, were
unable to find words in the contemporary language with which
to express themselves, and sought the answer in the obscure
verse of Mayakovsky. Later, however, Ilyich once praised
Mayakovsky for the verse in which he ridiculed Soviet red tape.
Of the books of the day, I remember that Ilyich was
enthusiastic about Ehrenburg's war novel. "You know," he
said triumphantly, "that book by Ilya the Shaggy (Ehrenburg's
nickname) is a fine piece of work."

We went to the Art Theatre several times. On one occasion
we saw *The Deluge*, which Ilyich liked very much. The next day
we saw Gorky's *The Lower Depths*. Ilyich liked Gorky the man,
with whom he had become closely acquainted at the London
Congress of the Party, and he liked Gorky the artist; he said
that Gorky the artist was capable of grasping things instantly.
With Gorky he always spoke very frankly. And so it goes
without saying that he set high standards for a Gorky
production. The over-acting irritated him. After seeing *The
Lower Depths* he avoided the theatre for a long time. Once the
two of us went to see Chekhov's *Uncle Vanya*, which he liked
very much. And finally, the last time we went to the theatre, in
1922 — we saw a stage version of Dickens's *Cricket on the Hearth*.
After the first act Ilyich found it dull; the saccharine
sentimentality got on his nerves, and during the conversation
between the old toymaker and his blind daughter he could
stand it no longer and left in the middle of the act.

During the last months of his life I used to read him fiction at
his request, usually in the evenings. I read him Shchedrin, and
Gorky's *My Universities*. He also liked to hear poetry, especially
Demyan Bedny, preferring his heroic verse to his satirical.

Sometimes, when listening to poetry, he would gaze
thoughtfully out of the window at the setting sun. I remember
the poem which ended with the words: "Never, never shall the
Communards be slaves."

As I read, I seemed to be repeating a vow to Ilyich. Never,
never shall we surrender a single gain of the Revolution....

Two days before he died I read him a story by Jack
London — the book is lying now on the table in his
room — *Love of Life*. This is a powerful story. Over a snowy
waste where a human being had never set foot, a man, sick and
dying from hunger, makes his way towards a pier on a river.

His strength is giving out, he no longer walks, but crawls, and close behind him, also crawling, is a famished and dying wolf; in the ensuing struggle between man and wolf, the man wins; half-dead, and half-crazed, he reaches his goal. Ilyich was carried away by this story. Next day he asked me to read another London story. However, with Jack London the powerful is mixed with the exceedingly weak. The second story was altogether different — one that preached bourgeois moral: the captain of a ship promises the owner that he will sell the cargo of grain at a good price; he sacrifices his life in order to keep his word. Ilyich laughed and waved his hand.
That was the last time I read to him.

Reminiscences of Lenin by
His Relatives, Moscow, 1956, pp.
201-07

NADEZHDA KRUPSKAYA

Lenin and Chernyshevsky

Comrades, I want to say a few words about the influence which Chernyshevsky had on Vladimir Ilyich. Vladimir Ilyich never made direct mention of this influence in his articles or books, but every time he spoke of Chernyshevsky a note of excitement used to come into his voice. Looking through his works one notices that the passages where he mentions Chernyshevsky are written with particular fervour. There is an indirect indication of Chernyshevsky's influence in Lenin's pamphlet *What Is To Be Done?* Speaking of the period preceding the formation of the Party, that is the period between 1894 and 1898, when the workers' movement was beginning to develop rapidly and assumed a mass character, Lenin says that the young people who had joined this movement had been brought up and their ideas had developed under the spell of the revolutionary activity of former revolutionaries, and that it had cost them a great inner battle to free themselves from this influence and embark on a different road, the road of Marxism. This statement has its autobiographical basis.

As a personality, Chernyshevsky impressed Vladimir Ilyich with his irreconcilability, his staunchness, and the dignity and pride with which he endured the unbelievable hardships allotted him by fate. And everything Vladimir Ilyich says of Chernyshevsky is imbued with deep respect for his memory. When times were hard and difficult moments had to be weathered in Party work, Vladimir Ilyich often used to quote Chernyshevsky's words, "revolutionary struggle is not the pavement of Nevsky Prospekt". Vladimir Ilyich wrote about this in 1907 during a period of particularly oppressive reaction when the Party was forced to retreat. He recalled Chernyshevsky's words again in 1918 when the difficulties confronting

Soviet power reached unprecedented heights, when we were compelled to conclude the Brest-Litovsk treaty and fight the Civil War.

He drew strength from Chernyshevsky's example, and reiterated that a revolutionary Marxist had to be always prepared for any contingency.

But Chernyshevsky's influence on Vladimir Ilyich was not merely confined to his personality. If we glance through Vladimir Ilyich's first illegal work *What the "Friends of the People" Are...* we can see Chernyshevsky's influence with particular clarity. The generation of whom Vladimir Ilyich was speaking, the youth that had joined the revolutionary Social-Democrats in 1894, had grown up in an atmosphere, where — in literature and elsewhere — the peasant reform was being eulogised on all sides. Chernyshevsky, however, evaluated it correctly. And Vladimir Ilyich pointed out that one had to be a genius in the full sense of the word to come to such an evaluation of liberalism at the very time of the peasant reforms and to expose the treacherous role of this liberalism and its class essence.

If we look at Lenin's subsequent activity, we can see that Chernyshevsky had infected him with his uncompromising attitude to liberalism. A marked distrust of liberal phrases and of the liberal position in general permeates the whole of Lenin's work. If we take his Siberian exile, his protest against the "Credo",[173] his break with Struve, and the uncompromising stand which he adopted towards the Cadets and the Menshevik liquidators who were prepared to make a deal with the Cadets — we shall see that Vladimir Ilyich pursued the same uncompromising line as Chernyshevsky had done in his attitude to the liberals who betrayed the peasantry at the time of the 1861 reform. If we seek to draw useful conclusions from Lenin's activity at this period and from this uncompromising stand of his, we shall see that it was thanks to this uncompromising stand taken up by the Party that it managed to win the political struggle. The attitude to the liberal bourgeoisie is a question which is inextricably linked with the question of democracy. In his *What the "Friends of the People" Are... etc.* Lenin wrote: "In Chernyshevsky's epoch the struggle for democracy and the struggle for socialism merged in one inseparable whole." In his appraisal of bourgeois-liberal democracy and the democracy of the bourgeois-influenced Narodniks of the eighties, who by then had reconciled themselves to tsarism, Lenin counterposed to these the democracy of revolutionary Marxism. Chernyshevsky had provided an example of uncompromising struggle against the existing system, a struggle in which democracy was indissolubly linked with the struggle for socialism.

Lenin thought highly of Chernyshevsky's activity and of his genuine democracy, which he regarded to be in keeping with the Marxist attitude towards the masses. Marxist teaching did not merely light the way for the struggle on economic grounds waged between the working class and the capitalists, but it embraced the struggle as a whole and in all its manifestations; it elucidated the whole capitalist system, analysed it and at the same time showed how to link the struggle for democracy with the struggle for socialism. Let us recollect how Marx fought Lassalle, what this struggle was about, and how Marx was infuriated by Lassalle's refusal to appreciate the importance of the independent revolutionary activity of the masses, and we shall understand the socialist essence of revolutionary Marxism. The so-called "legal Marxists",[174] for instance, utterly failed to understand it, forgetting all the time that Marx always focussed his attention on the working class and on the masses. In Marxism, democracy and the struggle for socialism are inseparably linked together. Neither is it accidental that, whenever Vladimir Ilyich touched upon problems of democracy, he invariably recalled Chernyshevsky, from whom he had first learnt that the struggle for democracy had to be linked with the struggle for socialism. If we examine his teaching on Soviets and Soviet power, we shall see that it is in this very context that the fusion of the struggle for democracy with the struggle for socialism is best realised and receives its fullest reflection. I remember that in 1918, as I was preparing to write a popular pamphlet on Soviets and Soviet power, Vladimir Ilyich brought me a clipping from the French newspaper l'Humanité—I have forgotten the name of the French comrade who had written the article—but in this clipping it was written that Soviet power was the most profoundly and consistently democratic power. Vladimir Ilyich told me, as he handed me the clipping, to give particular stress to this fact and to reveal in detail the nature of this genuine democracy which is embodied in the basic structure of Soviet power under which the proletariat is working towards a new and broader democracy.

Marx's writings were translated into Russian as far back as the 1860s, but they also had to be translated into the language of Russian facts. And this Lenin did in his book *The*

Development of Capitalism in Russia.... He mentioned several times how well Chernyshevsky was acquainted with Russian reality and how well he knew the facts concerning the redemption of serfs, etc.

In the early stages of his revolutionary career, Vladimir Ilyich did not pay so much attention to Chernyshevsky's philosophical ideas, although he had read Plekhanov's book *About Chernyshevsky* where particular attention is paid to this aspect of his writings, but at the time he was not so interested in this question. It was only in 1908 when a wide struggle was launched on the philosophical front that he re-read Chernyshevsky once again and referred to him as a great Russian Hegelian and a great Russian materialist. And then in 1914, when owing to the imminence of war the national question assumed urgent importance, Vladimir Ilyich in his article "On National Self-Determination" * firmly underlined the fact that Chernyshevsky, like Marx, had understood the full significance of the Polish insurrection.

...In Siberia Vladimir Ilyich kept an album containing photographs of those writers who exerted a particularly strong influence on him. These included pictures of Marx, Engels, Herzen, Pisarev, and two of Chernyshevsky. He also kept a photograph of Myshkin who had attempted to free Chernyshevsky. And then later, in the Kremlin, he had a complete collection of Chernyshevsky's works among the authors always at hand in his study, standing on the shelves next to the works of Marx, Engels and Plekhanov. In his spare moments he used to read Chernyshevsky over and over again.

There is another detail I would like to mention. In his book *What the "Friends of the People" Are...* Vladimir Ilyich points out how right Kautsky was in saying that Chernyshevsky lived in an epoch when every socialist was a poet and every poet a socialist. Vladimir Ilyich read fiction, studied it and enjoyed it. But there was one thing about his reading — for him an author's social attitudes and artistic representation of reality merged into one. He did not separate the two somehow, and just as Chernyshevsky liked to express his ideas in detail in his novels, so Vladimir Ilyich liked books which vividly reflected social ideas and he chose his fiction accordingly.

This is all I wanted to say on this subject. The little I have said does not include personal recollections. I do not

_____

* The title of Lenin's article is "The Right of Nations to Self-Determination".— *Ed.*

remember any conversations on the subject. One forgets many things with the years, for after all something new happens every day, and one only remembers scraps of conversation, isolated moments and even then often not the exact words. But I think that in Vladimir Ilyich's works, articles and pamphlets the tremendous influence which Chernyshevsky exerted on him is sufficiently clear for us all to appreciate.

N. K. Krupskaya,
Recollections of Lenin,
Gosizdat, 1931, pp. 180-86

MAXIM GORKY

V. I. Lenin

(Excerpts)

...I expected Lenin to be different. There was something missing in him, I thought. He spoke with a burr and stood there looking cocky with his hands thrust in his armpits somewhere. And altogether he was somehow too ordinary, there was nothing of the "leader" in him. I'm a writer. My profession obliges me to make note of little things, and this duty has become a habit, already a tiresome one sometimes.

When I was "led up to" G. V. Plekhanov he stood with his arms crossed and gave me a stern, somewhat bored look, the way a teacher, wearied by his duties, looks at yet another new pupil. He said a most commonplace thing to me: "I am an admirer of your talent." Apart from this I don't remember anything he said. And while the congress lasted, neither he nor I felt any wish to have a "heart to heart" talk.

And this bald, thickset, vigorous man, speaking with a burr immediately began talking about the imperfections of *Mother*, rubbing his Socratic brow with one hand, tugging at my hand with the other, and looking at me with a friendly twinkle in his amazingly lively eyes. He had read the book in the manuscript borrowed from I. P. Ladyzhnikov. I told him that I wrote the book in a hurry, but before I could explain why I had hurried, Lenin nodded and explained it himself: it was very good that I had hurried with it, the book was needed, many of the workers had joined the revolutionary movement impulsively, spontaneously, and they'd find it very useful reading *Mother*.

"A very timely book," he said. This, his only compliment, meant a great deal to me. Then he asked me in a brisk, business-like manner, if *Mother* was being translated into foreign languages and how far the Russian and American censors had spoilt the book. When I told him that it was decided to prosecute the author, he first frowned and then, throwing back his head and closing his eyes, burst into an amazing sort of laughter. His laughter attracted the workers, and a man, I believe it was Foma Uralsky, and three others came up....

* * *

...We happened to be free one night in London, and so a small crowd of us went to the music hall — a small democratic theatre. Vladimir Ilyich laughed readily and infectiously at the antics of the clowns, watched everything else indifferently except the tree-felling in British Columbia which engaged his particular attention. The small stage was converted into a forest camp, and in the forefront two hefty young chaps showed how they could cut a tree with a circumference of about a metre in two, taking no more than a minute to do it.

"Oh well, that's for show, of course," Ilyich said. "They can't keep up that speed in actual work. But one thing is clear: there, too, they use axes, reducing a lot of good timber to worthless chips. So much for your cultured Englishmen!"

He began speaking of the anarchy of production under the capitalist system, of the enormous percentage of raw material wasted, and finished by saying it was a pity no one had yet thought of writing a book on this subject. I wasn't quite clear about what he meant, but before I could ask him, he was already saying something interesting about "clowning" as a peculiar form of theatrical art.

"It shows a sort of satirical or sceptical attitude to the commonly accepted, a striving to turn it inside out, distort it slightly, and demonstrate the illogicality of the commonplace. Intricate but interesting!"

About two years later, in Capri, speaking with A. A. Bogdanov-Malinovsky on the subject of the utopian novel, he said:

"Why don't you write a novel for the workers about how the capitalist plunderers have robbed the earth, squandering all the oil, all the iron ore, timber and coal. It would be a very useful book, Signor Machist!"

* * *

Once I came to see him and found a volume of *War and Peace* on the table before him.

"Yes, Tolstoy! I was going to read the scene of the hunt, but then I remembered that I had to write a letter to a comrade.

I've absolutely no time for reading. I only read your book about Tolstoy last night."

Smiling and narrowing his eyes, he stretched out with relish in his armchair and, dropping his voice, said quickly: "What a rock, eh? What a giant of a man! Now that, my friend, is an artist.... And do you know another amazing thing? Before this Count there was no authentic muzhik in literature."

And then, looking at me with his little eyes screwed up, he asked: "Who, in Europe, can be ranked with him?" And answered himself: "No one."

Rubbing his hands he laughed, well-pleased.

I often noticed this trait in his character — a pride in Russia, in Russian people, in Russian art. Sometimes this trait seemed strangely alien to Lenin and even naïve, but then I learnt to discern in it an echo of his deeply hidden, joyful love of the working people.

In Capri, watching with what great care the fishermen disentangled the nets that a shark had torn and tangled, he remarked:

"Ours work more smartly."

And when I voiced my doubt on this score, he said, not without annoyance:

"Hm-hm, aren't you forgetting Russia, living on this bump?"

V. A. Desnitsky-Stroyev told me how once he travelled by train with Lenin in Sweden. He was reading a monograph about Dürer in German.

Some Germans sharing the compartment with them asked him what book that was. It transpired that they had never heard of their great painter. Lenin was quite delighted and said proudly to Desnitsky, repeating the words twice: "You see, they don't know their artists, but we do."

At Yekaterina Peshkova's in Moscow one evening, listening to Isaiah Dobrovein playing Beethoven's sonatas, Lenin said:

"I don't know of anything better than the 'Appassionata', I can listen to it every day. Amazing, superhuman music! I always think with a pride that may be naïve: look what miracles people can perform!"

And screwing up his eyes and chuckling, he added without mirth:

"But I can't listen to music often, it affects my nerves, it makes me want to say sweet nothings and pat the heads of people who, living in a filthy hell, can create such beauty. But today we mustn't pat anyone on the head or we'll get our hand bitten off; we've got to hit them on the heads, hit them without mercy, though in the ideal we are against doing any violence to people. Hm-hm—it's a hellishly difficult office!"

* * *

His attitude to me was that of a strict teacher and kind "solicitous friend".

"You're an enigma," he once said to me jokingly. "In literature you seem to be a sound realist, but in your attitude to people you're a romantic. With you all people are victims of history, aren't they? We know history, and we tell the victims: overturn the altars, smash the temples, down with the gods! And you'd like to convince me that the militant party of the working class must make the intellectuals comfortable before anything else."

I may be wrong, but I think Vladimir Ilyich enjoyed talking to me. He almost always said to me at parting: "Next time you come, telephone and we'll have a chat."

Once, he said: "A chat with you is always interesting, your range of impressions is wider and more varied."

He asked me about the sentiments of the intelligentsia, the scientists especially. At that time I was working with A. B. Khalatov on the Commission for the Welfare of Scientists. The problem of proletarian literature interested him, and he would ask: "What do you expect from it?"

I would tell him that I expected a lot, but that I considered it absolutely imperative to set up a literary institute with chairs of linguistics, foreign languages—East and West, folklore, the history of world literature, and Russian literature separately.

"Hm-hm," he would say, squinting and chuckling. "Scopeful and dazzling! I don't mind the scope, but then will it be dazzling, eh? We've no professors of our own in this field, and the bourgeios ones will give us such history! No, we couldn't cope with it just now. We'll have to wait three or five years."

"I've absolutely no time for reading," he complained.

He stressed, insistently and frequently, the importance of Demyan Bedny's work from the point of view of propaganda, but said: "He's a bit crude. He follows the reader whereas he should be a little ahead of him."

Mayakovsky, on the other hand, he treated with distrust and was even irritated by him.

"He shouts, makes up some crooked words, but everything he writes is just not the thing, to my mind, just not the thing and hardly understandable. It's all so scattered, it's difficult to

1/4 8*

read. You say he's gifted? Even very much so? Hm-hm, we'll see! Don't you find that too much poetry is being written? There are whole pages of poetry in the magazines, and collections come out practically every day."

I answered that in days such as ours it was natural for young people to be drawn to poetry and that, in my opinion, mediocre verses were easier to write than good prose and took less time besides. What was more, we had very many fine teachers to instruct the young poets in the technique of poetry writing.

"Now, don't tell me that poetry is easier to write than prose! I can't imagine it. I couldn't produce two lines even if you skinned me alive," he said and frowned. "We must spread all the old revolutionary literature there is, as much as we have here and in Europe, among the masses."

M. Gorky,
Collected Works, Russian
edition, Vol. 17, pp. 7, 16-17,
38-40, 44-45

CLARA ZETKIN

My Recollections of Lenin

(An Excerpt)

Lenin found us three women discussing art, education and upbringing. I happened at that moment to be voicing enthusiastically my astonishment at the unique and titanic cultural work of the Bolsheviks, at the unfolding in the country of creative forces striving to blaze new trails for art and education. I did not hide my impression that much of what I observed was still conjectural, mere groping in the dark, just experimental, and that along with zealous searches for new content, new forms and new ways in the sphere of culture one encounters at times an unnatural desire to follow the fashion and blindly imitate western models. Lenin at once plunged with keen interest into the conversation.

"The awakening of new forces and the harnessing of them to the task of creating a new art and culture in Soviet Russia are a good thing, a very good thing. The hurricane speed of their development is understandable and useful. We must make good the loss incurred by centuries of neglect and make good is what we want to do. Chaotic fermentation, feverish hunt for new slogans, slogans acclaimed today with shouts of 'hosanna' in relation to certain trends in art and fields of thought, and rejected tomorrow with cries of 'crucify him'—all this is inevitable.

"Revolution unleashes all forces fettered hitherto and drives them from their deep recesses of life to the surface. Take for example the influence exerted by fashion and the caprices of the tsarist court as well as by the tastes and whims of the aristocracy and the bourgeoisie on the development of our painting, sculpture and architecture. In society based on private property the artist produces for the market, needs customers. Our revolution freed artists from the yoke of these extremely prosaic conditions. It turned the state into their

½ 2 8—7o

defender and client providing them with orders. Every.
artist and everyone who considers himself such, has the
right to create freely, to follow his ideal regardless of
everything.

"But then, we are Communists, and ought not to stand idly
by and give chaos free rein to develop. We should steer this
process according to a worked-out plan and must shape its
results. We are still far, very far from this. It seems to me that
we too have our Doctors Karlstadt. We are too great
'iconoclasts in painting'. The beautiful must be preserved,
taken as an example, as the point of departure even if it is 'old'.
Why turn our backs on what is truly beautiful, abandon it as
the point of departure for further development solely because
it is 'old'? Why worship the new as a god compelling submission
merely because it is 'new'? Nonsense! Bosh and nonsense!
Here much is pure hypocrisy and of course unconscious
deference to the art fashions ruling the West. We are good
revolutionaries but somehow we feel obliged to prove that we
are also 'up to the mark in modern culture'. I however make
bold to declare myself a 'barbarian'. It is beyond me to consider
the products of expressionism, futurism, cubism and other
'isms' the highest manifestation of artistic genius. I do not
understand them. I experience no joy from them."

I could no longer restrain myself and admitted that my
perception likewise was too dull to understand why an inspired
face should be artistically expressed by triangles instead of a
nose and why the striving for revolutionary activity should
transmute the human body, in which the organs are linked up
and form one complicated whole, into an amorphous soft sack
hoisted on two stilts and provided with two five-pronged forks.

Lenin burst into a hearty laugh.

"Yes, dear Clara, it can't be helped. We're both old fogies.
For us it is enough that we remain young and are among the
foremost at least in matters concerning the revolution. But we
won't be able to keep pace with the new art; we'll just have to
come trailing behind.

"But," Lenin continued, "our opinion on art is not the
important thing. Nor is it of much consequence what art means
to a few hundred or even thousand out of a population
counted by the millions. Art belongs to the people. Its roots
should be deeply implanted in the very thick of the labouring
masses. It should be understood and loved by these masses. It
must unite and elevate their feelings, thoughts and will. It
must stir to activity and develop the art instincts within them. Should

we serve exquisite sweet cake to a small minority while the worker and peasant masses are in need of black bread? It goes without saying that the following is to be understood not only literally but also figuratively: we must always have before our eyes the workers and the peasants. It is for their sake that we must learn to manage, to reckon. This applies also to the sphere of art and culture.

"For art to get closer to the people and the people to art we must start by raising general educational and cultural standards. How are things with us in this regard? You grow enthusiastic over the immense cultural progress we have achieved since our advent to power. We undoubtedly can say without boasting that in this respect we have done quite a lot. We have not only 'chopped off heads', as charged by the Mensheviks of all courntries and by Kautsky of yours, but have also enlightened many heads. 'Many' however only in comparison with the past, in comparison with the sins of the classes and cliques then at the helm. Immeasurably great is the thirst we have instilled in the workers and peasants for education and culture in general. This applies not only to Petrograd and Moscow, and other industrial centres, but far beyond their confines until the very villages have been reached. At the same time we are a poverty-stricken people, completely beggared. We of course wage a real and stubborn war against illiteracy. We establish libraries and reading rooms, in the towns and villages, big and small. We organise all kinds of training courses. We present good shows and concerts, send 'mobile exhibitions' and 'educational trains' all over the land. But I repeat: what does this amount to for a multimillion population who lack the most elementary knowledge, the most primitive culture? Whereas today ten thousand and tomorrow another ten thousand are enraptured in Moscow for instance by the splendid performances of our theatres, millions of people are striving to learn how to spell their names and count, are trying to attain enough culture to know that the earth is round, not flat, and that the world is not governed by witches and sorcerers and a 'heavenly father' but by natural laws."

"Comrade Lenin," I remarked, "don't be so aggrieved by illiteracy. In some respects it has made the revolution easier for you. It has prevented the brains of the workers and peasants from being stuffed with bourgeois notions and thus from going to seed. Your agitation and propaganda are sowing virgin soil. It is easier to sow and reap where you do not first have to clear away a whole primeval forest."

1/2 8

"Yes, that's true," Lenin rejoined. "However only within certain limits or, to be more exact, for a certain period of our struggle. We could stand illiteracy during the fight for power, while it was necessary to destroy the old state machinery. But are we destroying merely for the sake of destroying? We are destroying for the purpose of creating something better. Illiteracy goes badly, is absolutely incompatible with the job of restoration. After all the latter, according to Marx, must be the task of the workers and, I add, of the peasants themselves if they want to attain freedom. Our Soviet system facilitates this task. Thanks to it thousands of ordinary working people are today studying in various Soviets and Soviet bodies how to expedite restoration. They are men and women 'in the prime of life', as they are wont to say in your country. Most of them grew up under the old regime and hence received no education, acquired no culture; but now they crave for knowledge. We are fully determined to recruit ever new contingents of men and women for Soviet work and give them a certain degree of practical and theoretical education. Nevertheless we are unable to meet in full our country's demand for personnel capable of creative leadership. We are compelled to engage bureaucrats of the old type, as a result of which bureaucracy has cropped up here. I absolutely hate it, but of course I have no particular bureaucrat in view. He might be a clever man. What I hate is the system. It has a paralysing and corrupting effect from top to bottom. Widely disseminated education and training of the people is a decisive factor for overcoming and eradicating bureaucracy.

"What are our prospects for the future? We have built splendid institutions and adopted really fine measures to enable the proletarian and peasant youth to study, learn and assimilate culture. But here too we are confronted with the same vexatious question: what does all this amount to when you consider the size of our population? What is worse, we are far from having an adequate number of kindergartens, children's homes and elementary schools. Millions of children grow into their teens without an upbringing, without education. They remain as ignorant and uncultured as their fathers and grandfathers were. How much talent perishes on that account, how much yearning for light is crushed underfoot! This is a terrible crime, when considered in terms of the happiness of the rising generation. It amounts to robbing the Soviet state, which is to be transformed into communist society, of its wealth. This is fraught with great danger."

Lenin's voice, usually so calm, quavered with indignation. "How this question must cut him to the quick," I thought, "if it makes him deliver an agitational speech to the three of us." Someone, I do not remember exactly who, began to speak about a number of particularly obnoxious occurrences in the spheres of art and culture, attributing them to the "conditions of the times". Lenin retorted:

"I know all about that. Many are sincerely convinced that the dangers and difficulties of the present period can be coped with by dispensing *panem et circenses* (bread and circuses, spectacles). Bread — as a matter of course. As for spectacles — let them be dispensed! I don't object. But let it not be forgotten that spectacles are not really great art. I would sooner call them more or less attractive entertainment. Nor should we be oblivious of the fact that our workers and peasants bear no resemblance to the Roman lumpen-proletariat. They are not maintained at state expense but on the contrary they themselves maintain the state by their labour. They 'made' the revolution and upheld its cause, shedding torrents of their blood and bearing untold sacrifice. Indeed, our workers and peasants deserve something better than spectacles. They are entitled to real great art. That is why we put foremost public education and training on the biggest scale. It creates a basis for culture, provided of course that the grain problem has been solved. On this basis a really new, great, communist art should arise which will create a form in correspondence with its content. Noble tasks of vast importance are waiting to be solved by our intellectuals along this line. By learning to understand these tasks and accomplishing them they would pay the debt they owe to the proletarian revolution, which to them too opened wide the portals that led from the vile conditions of life, described in such masterly fashion in the *Communist Manifesto,* to the grand open spaces."

That night — the hour was already late — we had broached other themes as well, but the impression these discussions left was but faint in comparison with that produced by Lenin's remarks on art, culture, public education and upbringing.

* * *

Lenin, who interpreted the mass in the spirit of Marx, naturally attached great importance to its all-sided cultural development. He considered it the greatest gain of the revolution and a sure guarantee that communism would be achieved.

"The Red October," he told me once, "opened wide the road to a cultural revolution on the grandest scale, which is being brought about on the basis of the incipient economic revolution and in constant interaction with it. Imagine millions of men and women of various nationalities and races and of various degrees of culture all striving on towards a new life. A superb task confronts the Soviet Government. In a few years or decades it must redress the cultural wrong of many centuries. In addition to the agencies and institutions of the Soviet Government, cultural progress is promoted also by numerous organisations and societies of scientists, artists and teachers. Vast cultural work is carried on by our trade unions at different enterprises and by our co-operative organisations in the villages. The activity of our Party is very much in evidence everywhere. A great deal is being done. Our successes are great compared with what there was, but they look small considering what remains to be done. Our cultural revolution has only just begun."

Casually referring to a splendid ballet being performed in the Bolshoi Theatre, Lenin remarked with a smile:

"Our ballet, theatre, and opera, and our exhibitions of what is new and newest in painting and sculpture are proof to many people abroad that we Bolsheviks are not at all such horrible barbarians as was believed there. I do not deny the significance of such and similar cultural manifestations of our society. I do not underrate their import. But I admit I am more gratified by the setting up of two or three elementary schools in some out-of-the-way villages than by the most magnificent exhibit at some art show. A rise in the general cultural standards of the masses will provide the sound and solid basis needed for the training of the powerful and inexhaustible forces that will develop Soviet art, science and technology. Our aspiration to establish culture and to disseminate it here in our country is extraordinarily great. It must be admitted that we are experimenting a lot. Alongside of serious work there is much that is puerile, immature, that consumes a great deal of our energy and means. Creative life evidently requires extravagance in society as well as in nature. We already have the most important requisites for the cultural revolution since the conquest of power by the proletariat, namely: the awakening of the masses, their aspiration to culture. New people are growing up, produced by the new social order and creating this order."

C. Zetkin, *My Recollections of Lenin*, Moscow, 1956, pp. 17-23, 90-91

ANATOLY LUNACHARSKY

Lenin and the Arts

In the course of his life Lenin had no time to engage in anything like a close study of the arts, and since dilettantism had always been hateful to him and alien to his nature he did not like to make any statements on art. Still, he had very definite tastes. He loved the Russian classics, and liked realism in literature, dramaturgy, painting, etc.

In 1905, during the first revolution, he once had to spend the night at the house of D. I. Leshchenko who had a large collection of Knackfuss editions of the world's greatest writers. The next morning Vladimir Ilyich said to me: "What a fascinating thing is the history of art! The amount of work there is here for a Marxist! I couldn't fall asleep till morning, I looked through one book after the other. And I felt sorry that I never had and never will have any time for art." I remember those words very clearly.

I had several meetings with him in connection with various art competitions, already after the revolution. One time, I remember, he called me in and together we went to an exhibition of monument designs from which a substitute had to be chosen for the figure of Alexander III which had been pulled down from its gorgeous pedestal near the Church of the Saviour. Vladimir Ilyich examined all the designs very critically. And he did not like any of them. One design, done in a futuristic manner, seemed to amaze him particularly, but when his opinion was asked he said: "I'm quite in the woods here. Ask Lunacharsky." He was very glad when I told him that I didn't see a single worthy design there, and said: "And I was afraid you'd erect some futuristic monstrosity."

Another time the matter concerned a monument to Karl Marx. The well-known sculptor M. was especially insistent in his claims. He presented his design of a large monument entitled "Karl Marx Supported by Four Elephants". This unexpected motif struck all of us, and Vladimir Ilyich too, as most peculiar. The sculptor then began to alter his design, and did it over three times, adamantly refusing to give up the first prize to anyone else. When the jury, with myself presiding, rejected his design irrevocably and decided on one proposed by a group of artists headed by Alyoshin, the sculptor M. appealed to Vladimir Ilyich, complaining about the decision. Vladimir Ilyich took his appeal to heart, and rang me up to have a new jury convened. He told me he would come to see the designs presented by Alyoshin and the sculptor M. He liked Alyoshin's very much, and rejected the one by the sculptor M.

That same year, on May Day, Alyoshin's group erected a small-scale model on the spot where the monument to Marx was to stand. Vladimir Ilyich went there specially to see it. He walked round the monument several times, asked how big it was going to be, and finally gave his approval, saying to me however: "Anatoly Vasilyevich, be sure to tell the artist that the hair must be lifelike, so one would have the same impression of Karl Marx as one has from his better portraits, because there doesn't seem to be much likeness."

Once in 1918 Vladimir Ilyich called me in and spoke to me about the need to promote art as a means of agitation. He set out two plans he had. The first was to have revolutionary slogans inscribed on the walls of buildings, fences and other places where posters were usually hung. He suggested some of the slogans right then and there.

His second plan was to erect temporary plaster monuments to great revolutionaries both in Petrograd and Moscow, and to do it on an extremely large scale. Both cities readily agreed to implement Lenin's idea, and it was proposed that there should be an unveiling ceremony for each monument with a speech made about the revolutionary to whom it was dedicated, and that elucidating inscriptions should be made on the pedestal. Vladimir Ilyich called it "monumental propaganda".

In Petrograd this "monumental propaganda" was quite a success. The first such monument was Shervud's "Radishchev". A copy was put up in Moscow. Unfortunately, the Petrograd original fell to pieces and has not been renewed. In general most of those Petrograd monuments collapsed because they were made of such fragile material, and yet I remember some that were very good indeed: the busts of Garibaldi, Shevchenko, Dobrolyubov, Herzen, and a few others. Those made by leftist artists were worse. For instance, when the cubistically stylised head of Perovskaya was unveiled, some people actually jumped back in horror. The monument to Chernyshevsky too, I seem to remember, struck many as rather contrived. The best one was the monument to Lassalle * erected in front of the former City Duma where it stands to this day.** I believe it has since been cast in bronze. Another admirable monument was the standing figure of Karl Marx made by sculptor Matveyev. Unfortunately, it got broken, and in its place (near the Smolny) there is now a bronze head of Marx of a more or less conventional type with none of the originality of Matveyev's plastic interpretation.

In Moscow — the very place where Vladimir Ilyich could see them — the monuments were rather poor.

Altogether there were few satisfactory monuments in Moscow. The one to the poet Nikitin was perhaps better than the rest. I don't know if Vladimir Ilyich examined them very closely, but anyway he once said to me with displeasure that nothing had come of the monumental propaganda. I mentioned the Petrograd experience, at which he shook his head in doubt and said: "Do you mean to say that all the gifted are assembled in Petrograd and the giftless in Moscow?" It did seem strange, and I had no explanation to offer him.

He also had his doubts about Konenkov's memorial plaque. It did not seem particularly impressive to him. Konenkov himself, as a matter of fact, called this work of his, not without humour, a "mnimo-real" *** plaque.

I also remember the artist Altman giving Vladimir Ilyich a portrait of Khalturin done in bas-relief. Vladimir Ilyich liked it very much but afterwards asked me if it wasn't a futurist piece. He disapproved of futurism in general. I was not present at the conversation he had with the students of the Higher Art Technical Studios at their hostel where he once came with Nadezhda Konstantinovna. I was told afterwards that big issues had been raised by the art students, "leftists" all of them, of course. Vladimir Ilyich had replied jocularly, making mild fun of them, but to them, too, he declared that he did not feel competent enough to go into a serious discussion on art. He found the young people themselves a very fine lot, and was delighted that they were communist-minded.

In the last period of his life Vladimir Ilyich rarely had a chance to indulge his interest in the arts. He went to the theatre several times, always to the Art Theatre I believe, which he

---

* By Zelit.— A. L. (The sculptor was Sinaisky and not Zelit, as mistakenly written by Lunacharsky.— Ed.)
** These recollections were written in 1924.— Ed.
*** "Mnimo" means "pseudo" in Russian.— Ed.

thought very highly of. Its shows invariably left a wonderful impression on him.

Vladimir Ilyich loved music. At one time some really good concerts were held in my house. Chaliapin sang sometimes, Meichik, Romanovsky, the Stradivarius quartet, Kusevitsky and other musicians played for us. I often invited Vladimir Ilyich, but he was always busy Once he told me frankly: "Of course, listening to music is very pleasant but, imagine, it upsets me. I take it very hard, somehow." I remember Comrade Tsyurupa, who managed to entice Vladimir Ilyich to one or two recitals given by the pianist Romanovsky in someone's house, telling me that Lenin had greatly enjoyed the music but had obviously felt disturbed.

More than once I had the task to prove to Vladimir Ilyich that the Bolshoi Theatre was costing us very little, relatively speaking, but still, on his insistence, a cut was made in the allocations. He was guided by two considerations, one of which he explained at once. "It won't do to spend so much money on the upkeep of a theatre as sumptuous as the Bolshoi when we have none for the maintenance of the most ordinary schools in the villages." His other consideration he disclosed at a meeting when I disputed his attack on the Bolshoi Theatre and pointed to its obvious cultural importance. And then Vladimir Ilyich twinkled slyly and said: "And still it's a piece of purely landed-gentry's culture, and no one can dispute the fact."

It does not follow from this that Vladimir Ilyich was hostilely disposed to the culture of the past as a whole. It was the entire pompously courtly tone of the opera that seemed to him to have a specifically landed-gentry ring. But art of the past as such, Russian realism especially (including the *peredvizhniki* *), he held in high esteem.

Well, these are the factual data which I can offer from my recollections of Vladimir Ilyich. I repeat, Vladimir Ilyich never made guiding principles out of his aesthetical likes and dislikes.

A. V. Lunacharsky,
Recollections of Lenin,
Partizdat (Russ. ed.), 1933,
pp. 46-50

---

* The name given to realist artists and sculptors associated with the Russian progressive democratic society "Association of Travelling Art Exhibitions" set up in 1870.

The exhibitions arranged by the society in St. Petersburg were subsequently moved to other major cities of Russia. The society existed till 1922, having organised 48 large exhibitions.— *Ed.*

* * *

...In 1918 members of the Proletcult launched a strong attack against the Alexandrinsky Theatre. I myself was closely connected with the organisation, and finally I became somewhat perplexed by their insistent demands to put an end to the "nidus of reactionary art".

I decided to seek counsel from Vladimir Ilyich himself.

...And so, when I came to see him in his office — I don't remember the exact date but anyway it was during the 1918-19 season — I told him that I intended making every effort to preserve the country's best theatres. To this I added: "They're still playing their old repertoire, of course, but we'll quickly purge it of any filth. Audiences, and proletarian audiences in particular, attend their shows readily. Time itself, as well as these audiences, will eventually compel even the most conservative theatres to change. And I think this change will come about quite soon. In my opinion a radical breaking-up would be dangerous here: we have no replacements in this field as yet. And the new that will develop may snap that cultural thread. After all, while taking it for granted that the music of the near future after revolution's victory will be both proletarian and socialist, we can't, after all, imagine that conservatoires and music schools can be closed down and the old 'feudal-bourgeois' instruments and sheet music be burnt."

Vladimir Ilyich listened attentively to what I had to say and then replied that this was the line to adhere to, but that I must also remember to support the new that was born under the influence of the revolution. Never mind if it was weak at first: it must not be judged from the aesthetic point of view alone, otherwise the old, more mature art would retard the development of the new, and though this old art itself would undergo a change the process would be the slower the less vigorously it was spurred on by the competition offered by its young rival.

I hastened to assure Vladimir Ilyich that I would be careful not to make that mistake, and said: "Only we must not allow the maniacs and charlatans who, in rather great numbers, are trying to board our ship to make use of our own means and play a role for which they are not cast and which would do us harm."

To this Vladimir Ilyich made a reply which I remember word for word: "You are profoundly right about the maniacs and charlatans. A class that has conquered, and moreover a class whose own intelligentsia is as yet a quantitatively small force, inevitably falls victim to these elements unless it guards itself against them. It is by way of being both an inevitable result and even a sign of victory," Lenin added, laughing.

"Well then, to sum up," I said "Everything that is more or less sound in old art is to be safeguarded. Art — I do not mean museum pieces, but effective art such as the theatre, literature and music — is to be influenced, but not crudely, to complete its evolution as quickly as possible to meet the new requirements. New trends are to be treated with discrimination. They must not be allowed to seize the field by mere aggression, but are to be given an opportunity to win prominence by real artistic merits. In this respect they are to be given every possible assistance."

To this Lenin said: "This puts it rather precisely, I think. Now try to bring it home to our audiences, and to people in general for that matter, in your public speeches and articles."

"Can I quote you?" I asked.

"No, why? I don't claim to be an expert in the arts. Since you're a People's Commissar you ought to be enough of an authority yourself."

And on that our conversation ended.

A. V. Lunacharsky,
"For the Centenary of the
Alexandrinsky Theatre".
In the book: Konstantin
Derzhavin, *Epochs of the
Alexandrinsky Theatre,*
Lengikhl (Russ. ed.),
1932, pp. IX-XI

ALEXANDER SERAFIMOVICH

Visiting Lenin

I often heard Vladimir Ilyich Lenin at congresses and conferences. It always amazed me that as a rule he needed less time than the speakers who took the floor before and after him, and yet his speeches left such a tremendous impression.

I spoke to him in private only once. And today I'd like to tell about that unforgettable day when Lenin invited me to his flat.

That memorable evening I saw quite a different Lenin, quite unlike the leader and tribune I had seen at the congresses and conferences. This was a new Lenin—a wonderful friend, a jolly person who took a lively, tireless interest in the whole world and who had an amazingly gentle and loving regard for people.

"Are you writing anything just now?" he asked me.

"It's difficult to write just now: there's so much organisation work to do."

He frowned.

"Yes, there's plenty of organisation work in our country just now. But you, writers, must draw the workers into literature. You've got to direct all your efforts towards this. Every short story written by a worker must be heartily welcomed. Do workers publish their stories in your magazine?"

"It could be more, Vladimir Ilyich. They lack knowledge, or culture, I suppose."

He glanced at me with his narrowed, laughing eyes, and said:

"Oh well, never mind, they'll learn to write and we'll have an excellent proletarian literature, the first in the world...."

These words rang with a fervent faith in Man, in Russian art; there was in them an affection for the working people and an unquenchable, active faith in them.

Krasnoarmeyets, 1946,
No. 2, p. 10

Notes

[1] *Russkoye Bogatstvo* (Russian Wealth)—a monthly magazine published from 1876 to the middle of 1918. In the beginning of the 1890s it became the organ of the liberal Narodniks and was edited by Krivenko and Mikhailovsky. The magazine renounced revolutionary struggle and opposed Marxism and Russian Marxists.   p. 9

[2] *Land redemption payments*—payments made by the peasants to the landowners for the land allotments they received after the abolition of serfdom in Russia (1861). The sum total of these payments exceeded several times the real price of the land received by the peasants. The former landowners' peasants, for example, paid the tsarist government about 2,000 million rubles, whereas the market price of the land that passed into their possession did not exceed 544 million rubles. Since the peasants did not all come under the land redemption scheme at once, but at different stages during the period 1861-83, the land redemption payments would have been completed only by 1932. This heavy and intolerable burden caused financial ruin and mass impoverishment of the peasants. The peasant movement during the first Russian Revolution of 1905-07 compelled the tsarist government to abolish the land redemption payments as from January 1907.   p. 9

[3] In 1889, the tsarist government, in an effort to strengthen the landowners' power over the peasants, introduced the administrative post of Zemsky Nachalnik. The Zemsky Nachalniks, who were appointed from among the local landowning nobility, were given tremendous powers, both administrative and juridical, to deal with the peasants. These powers included the right to arrest peasants and administer corporal punishment.   p. 11

[4] *Nedelya* (Week)—a liberal Narodnik weekly, which appeared in St. Petersburg from 1886 to 1901. It advocated the so-called theory of "minor matters", i.e., it appealed to the intelligentsia to renounce revolutionary struggle and to engage in "cultural activity".   p. 12

[5] *Novoye Vremya* (New Times)—a newspaper which appeared in St. Petersburg from 1868 to October 1917. At first it was moderately liberal, but from 1876 onwards it became the organ of reactionary circles among the aristocracy and the bureaucracy.   p. 12

[6] A reference to French utopian socialism, which was widespread in the first half of the nineteenth century.   p. 12

[7] A reference to V. V.'s (V. P. Vorontsov's) *Our Trends*, which appeared in 1893.   p. 12

[8] N. K. Mikhailovsky replied to V. V. in the article "Literature and Life" published in *Russkoye Bogatstvo* No. 10, 1893.   p. 12

[9] *Sotsial-Demokrat* (Social-Democrat)—a literary political review published abroad (London-Geneva) by the Emancipation of Labour group from 1890 to 1892. It played an important role in spreading Marxist ideas in Russia. In all, four issues appeared. The main contributors to the review were G. V. Plekhanov. P. B. Axelrod and V. I. Zasulich.   p. 13

[10] *Svoboda* (Freedom)—a journal published in Switzerland from 1901 to 1902 by the *Svoboda* group that was formed in May 1901. Two issues appeared: No. 1 in 1901 and No. 2 in 1902.

The *Svoboda* group "had no stable or serious principles, programme, tactics, organisation and no roots among the masses" (Lenin, *Collected Works*, Vol. 20, p. 357). In its publications the *Svoboda* group advocated the ideas of Economism and terrorism and supported the anti-*Iskra* groups in Russia. The group ceased to exist in 1903.   p. 16

[11] The demonstration of December 6 (18), 1876 was organised by the workers and students as a protest against the tyrannical actions of the autocracy. G. V. Plekhanov, who took part in the demonstration, delivered a revolutionary speech. The demonstration was broken up by the police; many participants were arrested and sentenced to exile and penal servitude.

p. 17

[12] The slogan *"Land and Freedom"* was released at that time by the illegal organisation of the same name (Zemlya i Volya), set up by the Narodniks in Russia in 1876. Members of this organisation considered the peasants the chief revolutionary force in Russia and sought to bring them to revolt against tsarism. They carried out revolutionary work in a number of gubernias. In 1879 a terrorist grouping was formed within Zemlya i Volya which considered terrorism to be the main means of fighting tsarism. At the congress that same year Zemlya i Volya split into two groups: Narodnaya Volya (People's Will) and Chorny Peredel (General Redistribution).

In addition the reference alludes to the Provisional Regulations for the Organisation of Student Bodies in Higher Educational Establishments under the Ministry of Public Education adopted on December 22, 1901 (January 4, 1902) by Vannovsky, Minister of Public Education. Dissatisfied with these regulations, which put their organisations under constant administrative control, the students refused to recognise them. Even liberal professors opposed the Provisional Regulations, which imposed on them the duty of police surveillance over their students.   p. 17

[13] A reference to the allegory used by N. A. Dobrolyubov in his article "When Will the Real Day Come?" dealing with I. S. Turgenev's novel *On the Eve*.

p. 18

[14] *Rabocheye Dyelo* (Workers' Cause)—an Economist magazine, non-periodical organ of the Union of Russian Social-Democrats Abroad. It was published in Geneva from April 1889 to February 1902 under the editorship of B. N. Krichevsky and others. Twelve issues appeared in all.   p. 19

[15] D. I. Pisarev, "Blunders of Immature Thinking".   p. 20

[16] The article was published in November 1905, in issue No. 12 of *Novaya Zhizn* (New Life), a Bolshevik legal newspaper, when Lenin came to St. Petersburg after the exile.

Novaya Zhizn appeared daily from October to December 1905 in St. Petersburg. Upon his return to St. Petersburg Lenin became the editor of the newspaper which was then virtually the Central Organ of the R.S.D.L.P. Its contributors included V. V. Vorovsky, M. S. Olminsky and A. V. Lunacharsky. Active on the newspaper was Maxim Gorky, who also gave it financial support.

Novaya Zhizn was constantly being harassed by the authorities. Fifteen issues out of 27 were confiscated and destroyed. The paper was closed down after issue No. 27. Issue No. 28, which was the last, came out illegally.

                                                                        p. 21

[17] A reference to the general political strike of October 1905 which compelled the tsar to issue the Manifesto of October 17, 1905, which granted the people civil rights. The Bolsheviks made use of the new freedom of the press to bring out their newspapers legally. After the December armed uprising of 1905 was put down, the autocracy launched an offensive against workers' organisations and their press.   p. 21

[18] *Izvestia Soveta Rabochikh Deputatov* (Bulletin of the Soviet of Workers' Deputies) — the organ of the St. Petersburg Soviet of Workers' Deputies, published from October to December, 1905. Ten issues appeared in all; issue No. 11 was seized by the police while it was being printed.   p. 21

[19] *Proletary* (Proletarian) — an illegal Bolshevik weekly newspaper, Central Organ of the R.S.D.L.P., founded by decision of the Third Party Congress; it was published in Geneva from May to November, 1905 under Lenin's editorship; 26 issues were put out (Nos. 25 and 26 appeared under V. V. Vorovsky's editorship, after Lenin's departure for Russia). Permanent members of the editorial board included A. V. Lunacharsky and M. S. Olminsky.   p. 22

[20] *Oblomov* — a landowner, the chief character in a novel of the same name by the Russian writer I. A. Goncharov. Oblomov came to personify petty routine and mental and physical stagnation.   p. 23

[21] *Cadets* (Constitutional-Democratic Party) — the chief party of the liberal-monarchist bourgeoisie. It was founded in October 1905, its membership included representatives of the bourgeoisie, landowners and bourgeois intellectuals. Hiding behind pseudo-democratic slogans and calling themselves the party "of people's freedom", the Cadets actually betrayed the people's interests, supported tsarism on the main matters of foreign and home policy. They advocated a constitutional monarchy in Russia. After the October Socialist Revolution the Cadets organised conspiracies and revolts against the Soviet Republic. When the interventionists and whiteguards were defeated, the Cadets fled abroad, where they continued their anti-Soviet counter-revolutionary activity.

Balalaikin — a character in Saltykov-Shchedrin's novel *A Modern Idyll*, a liberal adventurist, windbag and liar.   p. 26

[22] *Rech* (Speech) — a daily newspaper, central organ of the Cadet Party was published in St. Petersburg from February 1906 until it was closed down by the Revolutionary Military Committee under the Petrograd Soviet in October 1917.   p. 26

[23] Lenin is quoting the song *Rus* from the last part of Nekrasov's poem "Who Can Be Happy in Russia?"   p. 27

[24] *Trudoviks, Trudovik group* — the group of petty-bourgeois democrats in the State Dumas, consisting of peasants and intellectuals of Narodnik leanings. The trudovik group was formed in April 1906 from among peasant deputies in the First Duma.

In the Duma the Trudoviks wavered between a Cadet and a Social-Democrat line. Owing to the fact that the Trudoviks represented to a certain extent the peasant masses, the Bolsheviks in the Duma pursued a policy of compromise with them on particular points in the interests of the joint struggle against tsarism and the Cadets.   p. 29

[25] *Narodnaya Volya* (People's Will) — the secret political organisation of Narodnik terrorists formed in August 1879 as a result of the split in the Narodnik organisation Zemlya i Volya. Its members fought heroically against the tsarist autocracy. But proceeding from the erroneous theory of "active" heroes and a "passive" mob, they expected to achieve the transformation of society without the participation of the people, by their own efforts, that is through acts of individual terrorism aimed at intimidating and disorganising the government. After the assassination of Alexander II on March 1, 1881, the government was able, through savage reprisals, death sentences and acts of provocation, to crush the organisation.

While criticising Narodnaya Volya's erroneous, utopian programme, Lenin expressed great respect for its members' selfless struggle against tsarism and had a high opinion of their conspiratorial technique and their highly centralised organisation.   p. 31

[26] The article was published in issue No. 50 of *Proletary*, November 28 (December 11), 1909.

On November 26 (December 9), 1909 issue No. 42 of *Utro Rossii* published a letter from *Proletary's* editorial board refuting the report of Gorky's expulsion from the Social-Democratic Party. The editors of *Proletary* asked all the papers, which had published the report, to reprint this refutation.   p. 31

[27] *Vorwärts* (Forward) — a daily newspaper and central organ of the German Social-Democratic Party; by decision of the Halle Congress of the party it was published in Berlin from 1891 under the name of *Vorwärts. Berliner Volksblatt* as a continuation of the newspaper *Berliner Volksblatt* issued since 1884. F. Engels used the columns of this paper to combat all manifestations of opportunism. In the late nineties, after the death of Engels, *Vorwärts* fell into the hands of the Right wing of the party and regularly published opportunist articles.   p. 31

[28] *Otzovism* (from the Russian word *otozvat* — recall) — an opportunist trend which arose among a section of Bolsheviks in 1908. Under cover of revolutionary phrases, the otzovists (A. A. Bogdanov, G. A. Alexinsky, A. V. Lunacharsky and others) demanded the recall of the Social-Democrat deputies from the Third Duma and the cessation of work in legal organisations. They held that in conditions of reaction the Party should conduct only illegal work, and therefore they refused to work in the Duma, workers' trade unions, co-operatives and other mass legal and semi-legal organisations.   p. 31

[29] *God-building*—a religious philosophical trend hostile to Marxism, which arose in the period of the Stolypin reaction (1907-10) among a section of the Party's intellectuals, who abandoned Marxism after the defeat of the 1905-07 revolution. The "god-builders" (A. V. Lunacharsky, V. Bazarov and others) advocated the creation of a new, "socialist" religion, and tried to reconcile Marxism and religion. The meeting of the enlarged editorial board of *Proletary* that took place in June 1909 condemned "god-building" and declared in a special resolution that the Bolshevik group had nothing in common "with this sort of distortion of scientific socialism" (*KPSS v rezolyutsiyakh i resheniyakh syezdov, konferentsii i plenumov TsK* [The C.P.S.U. in the Resolutions and Decisions of Congresses, Conferences and C.C. Plenary Meetings], Part I, 1954, p. 222).   p. 31

[30] *Proletary*—an illegal newspaper founded by the Bolsheviks after the Fourth (Unity) Congress of the R.S.D.L.P. It appeared from 1906 to 1909 at first in Finland, then, by decision of the Bolshevik Centre, its publication was transferred abroad (Geneva, Paris). At the January 1910 plenary meeting of the Central Committee of the R.S.D.L.P. the conciliators managed to carry through the decision to close down *Proletary*. Lenin was its permanent editor.   p. 31

[31] *Vekhi* (Landmarks)—a Cadet collection of articles by N. Berdayev, S. Bulgakov, P. Struve, M. Herschensohn and other representatives of the counter-revolutionary liberal bourgeoisie, which appeared in Moscow in the spring of 1909. In articles on the Russian intelligentsia these writers tried to discredit the revolutionary-democratic traditions of the finest representatives of the Russian people, including Belinsky and Chernyshevsky; vilified the revolutionary movement of 1905 and thanked the tsarist government for having, "with its bayonets and prisons", saved the bourgeoisie "from popular fury". They called upon the intelligentsia to further the interests of the autocracy.   p. 34

[32] *Moskovskiye Vedomosti* (Moscow Recorder)—a daily newspaper which was first published in 1756; in the 1860s it expressed the views of the most reactionary monarchist sections of the landowners and clergy; from 1905 onwards it was one of the chief organs of the Black Hundreds. It was closed down after the October Socialist Revolution in 1917.   p. 34

[33] Belinsky wrote this letter in Salzbrunn on July 15, 1847 after Gogol published his "Selected Passages from Correspondence with the Friends". For Lenin's appraisal of the letter, see his article "From the History of the Workers' Press in Russia" p. 90 of this book.   p. 34

[34] See Note 55.   p.34

[35] *Duma, State Duma*—a representative assembly in tsarist Russia convened as a result of the 1905-07 revolution. Though formally a legislative body, it actually had no effective power. The elections to the Duma were neither direct, equal nor universal. The electoral rights of the working people and the non-Russian nationalities of the country were considerably curtailed. Most of the workers and peasants were not entitled to vote at all.
    The First Duma (April-July 1906) and the Second Duma (February-June 1907) were dissolved by the tsarist government. The Third (1907-12) and the Fourth (1912-17) Dumas were composed mainly of reactionary deputies, who supported tsarist autocracy.   p. 35

[36] The "*four-point electoral system*" — designation of the democratic electoral system, which consists of four basic demands: universal, equal and direct suffrage and secret ballot.   p. 37

[37] See Note 5.   p. 37

[38] *June 3 constitution* — an electoral law issued by the tsarist government at thé time the Second Duma· was dissolved. This was a gross violation of the Manifesto of October 17, 1905 and the Fundamental Law of 1906 which decreed that no laws could be passed by the government without the Duma's approval. The new electoral law led to a considerable increase in the representation of the landowners and the commercial and industrial bourgeoisie and to a drastic curtailment in the number of workers' and peasants' representatives small as it already was. The law disfranchised a large section of the population in the Asian part of Russia and halved the Polish and Caucasian representation. The Third Duma, which was elected on the basis of this law and convened in November 1907, was a Black-Hundred Cadet institution.   p. 38

[39] With the words "Enrich yourselves, gentlemen, and you will become electors" Guizot, head of the French Government in 1840-48, replied to the demand to reduce the high property qualification. The words that the government "put its stake on the healthy and strong, and not on the crippled and drunk" belong to P. A. Stolypin (see Name Index).   p. 38

[40] On August 6 (19), 1905 the tsar's Manifesto was published instituting the Duma as a consultative body under the tsar, with no legislative powers. The Duma derived its name from A. G. Bulygin, Minister of the Interior, who drew up the draft for the convocation of the Duma. The Bolsheviks called upon the workers and the peasants actively to boycott the Bulygin Duma and concentrated their election propaganda on the armed uprising, the revolutionary army and a provisional revolutionary government. The elections to the Bulygin Duma were not carried through: the mounting tide of revolution and the all-Russia October political strike of 1905 swept the Bulygin Duma away before it was convened.   p. 39

[41] This refers to the visit by a group of Duma members to Britain. P. N. Milyukov, the leader of the Cadet Party and a member of the delegation, declared at a luncheon given by the Lord Mayor of London that "so long as there is in Russia a legislative chamber, which controls the budget, the Russian opposition will remain the Opposition of His Majesty and not to His Majesty". The Duma deputies' statement facilitated the tsar to obtain loans abroad.   p. 39

[42] See Note 28.   p. 40

[43] See Note 50.   p. 40

[44] A reference to the Third Duma (1907-12).   p. 40

[45] The All-Russia (December) Conference of the R.S.D.L.P. (Fifth All-Russia) was held in Paris from December 21 to 27, 1908 (January 3-9, 1909). The representative of the Central Committee of the R.S.D.L.P. was Lenin. He delivered a report at the Conference "The Present Moment and the Tasks of the Party" and also spoke on the Social-Democrat group in the Duma and on organisational and other questions. At the Conference the Bolsheviks waged a struggle against two kinds of opportunism in the Party: the liquidators and the otzovists. On Lenin's proposal the Conference condemned the liquidators and called upon all Party organisations to combat attempts to liquidate the Party.   p. 40

[46] *Machists*—adherents of Machism or empirio-criticism, a reactionary, subjective-idealistic philosophical trend widespread in Western Europe at the turn of the century. It was founded by Ernst Mach, an Austrian physicist and philosopher, and Richard Avenarius, a German philosopher. Machism was all the more dangerous for the working class since it professed to oppose idealism and hold in high esteem contemporary natural sciences, which gave it a "scientific" air. In Russia, in the years of reaction, some Social-Democrat intellectuals came under the influence of Machism. It was particularly widespread among Menshevik intellectuals (N. Valentinov, P. Yushkevich, etc.). Some Bolshevik men of letters (V. Bazarov, A. Bogdanov, A. Lunacharsky and others) took up a Machist position. Under the hypocritical pretext of developing Marxism, the Russian Machists actually tried to revise the fundamental ideas of Marxist philosophy. In his book *Materialism and Empirio-criticism* V. I. Lenin revealed the reactionary essence of Machism, defended Marxism against revisionist attacks and comprehensively elaborated dialectical and historical materialism under the new historical conditions. The defeat of Machism dealt a heavy blow at the ideological principles of Mensheviks, otzovists and "god-builders".   p. 41

[47] The *Vperyod* group—an anti-Party group of otzovists, ultimatumists and "god-builders"; it was organised in December 1909 on the initiative of A. Bogdanov and G. A. Alexinsky. It had its own press organ of the same name.

Having no support among the workers, the group broke up in 1913-14; formally it ceased to exist after the February bourgeois-democratic revolution of 1917.   p. 42

[48] *M. Coupon*—a metaphorical name of capital or capitalists in the literature of the eighties and nineties of the last century. It was first used by the Russian writer Gleb Uspensky in his sketches "Grievous Sins".   p. 46

[49] *Synod*—supreme administrative body of the Orthodox Church in Russia.

p 47

[50] *Black Hundreds*—monarchist gangs set up by the tsarist police to fight the revolutionary movement. They murdered revolutionaries, assaulted progressive intellectuals and staged anti-Jewish pogroms.   p. 47

[51] See Note 31.   p. 47

[52] See Note 5.   p. 47

[53] The reference is to the telegram sent to Astapovo by the Social-Democrat deputies of the Third Duma to V. G. Chertkov, a close friend and disciple of Leo Tolstoy: "The Social-Democratic group in the Duma, expressing the feelings of the Russian and the whole international proletariat, deeply mourns the loss of the brilliant artist, the irreconcilable and unconquered fighter against official clericalism, the enemy of tyranny and enslavement, who loudly raised his voice against the death penalty, the friend of the persecuted."   ·   p. 49

[54] *Cut-off lands*—the lands which were taken away (cut off) from the peasants when serfdom was abolished in Russia.   p. 49

[55] *Narodniks*—followers of Narodism, a political trend in Russia, which arose in the seventies of the nineteenth century. The main points in their world outlook were a denial of the leading role of the working class in the revolutionary movement, the erroneous conception that socialist revolution

can be carried out by petty proprietors, peasants; they regarded the village commune, virtually a survival of feudalism and serfdom in the countryside, as a nucleus of the future socialist society. The socialism of the Narodniks was utopian, because it was not based on the actual development of society and consisted merely of fine phrases, dreams and noble intentions.

In the eighties and nineties the Narodniks sought compromises with tsarism and started to voice the interests of the kulaks and to wage a bitter struggle against Marxism.   p. 55

[56] A reference to K. Marx and F. Engels, *Manifesto of the Communist Party*, Chapter III.   p. 57

[57] K. Marx and F. Engels, *Manifesto of the Communist Party* (see Marx and Engels, *Selected Works*, Vol. I, Moscow, 1973, p. 63).·   p. 57

[58] *Liquidationism*—an opportunist trend, which arose among the Menshevik Social-Democrats after the defeat of the 1905-07 revolution. Its adherents demanded the liquidation of the revolutionary illegal party of the proletariat and for it to be replaced by an opportunist one acting legal under the tsarist order. Lenin and other Bolsheviks unremittingly exposed the liquidators who were betraying the cause of the revolution. The liquidators failed to win the support of the workers and were expelled from the Party at the Prague Conference of the R.S.D.L.P. in January 1912.
                                                                                          p. 57

[59] *Manilov*—a character from Gogol's *Dead Souls*, whose name has become a synonym for unprincipled philistinism, sentimentality and day-dreaming.
                                                                                          p. 58

[60] *Men of December 14* (Decembrists)—Russian revolutionaries who revolted against the autocracy and serfdom in December 1825.   p. 58

[61] Lenin quotes from A. I. Herzen's "Ends and Beginnings".   p. 58

[62] A. I. Herzen, "To an Old Comrade" (Letters Four and Two).   p. 60

[63] *Socialist-Revolutionaries* (S.R.s)—a petty-bourgeois party in Russia, which came into being at the end of 1901 and the beginning of 1902 as a result of a merger of various Narodnik groups and circles. The S.R.s recognised no class distinctions between the proletariat and the petty proprietors, played down class differences and antagonisms within the peasantry and refused to recognise the proletariat's leading role in the revolution.

After the February bourgeois-democratic revolution of 1917 the Socialist-Revolutionaries, together with the Mensheviks and the Cadets, were the mainstay of the counter-revolutionary Provisional Government of the bourgeoisie and landowners. The leaders of the party—Kerensky, Avksentyev and Chernov—were members of the Cabinet. The S.R. Party refused to support the peasants' demand to abolish the big landed estates and ruled that they should be preserved. The S.R. members of the Provisional Government sent out punitive detachments against peasants who had seized landed estates.

At the end of November 1917 the Left wing of the S.R. Party formed an independent party of Left Socialist-Revolutionaries. In an endeavour to preserve their influence among the peasants, the Left S.R.s formally recognised Soviet power and entered into an agreement with the Bolsheviks, though soon afterwards they began to campaign against the Soviets.

During the years of foreign intervention and the Civil War the S.R.s
carried on subversive counter-revolutionary activity, supported the interventionists and whiteguards, took part in counter-revolutionary plots and
organised terroristic acts against leaders of the Soviet state and the
Communist Party. After the Civil War they continued their anti-Soviet
activities within the country and in the camp of the White émigrés. p. 60

[64] See Note 24.   p. 61

[65] *All-Russia Peasant Union*—a revolutionary-democratic organisation,
formed in 1905. It demanded political liberties, an immediate convocation
of a constituent assembly, abolition of private property in land, confiscation
and transfer to the peasants of monastery, crown and state lands. The
Union's policy was a half-hearted, vacillating one. The organisation was
persecuted by the police and ceased to exist early in 1907.   p. 61

[66] *Kolokol* (The Bell)—a political journal; its motto was: "Vivos voco!" (I call
on the living); it was published by A. I. Herzen and N. P. Ogaryov from
1857 to April 1865 in London and from 1865 to December 1868 in Geneva
once or twice a month. In 1868 the journal appeared in French, while a
supplement in Russian was published simultaneously. Exposing the tyranny
of the autocracy, the extortion and embezzlement practised by government
officials and the ruthless exploitation of the peasants by the landowners,
Kolokol issued revolutionary appeals and contributed to the struggle against
the tsarist government and the ruling classes.   p. 61

[67] *Polyarnaya Zvezda* (The Polar Star)—a literary political collection; the first
three books were published by A. I. Herzen and subsequent ones by A. I.
Herzen and N. P. Ogaryov in London in 1855-62. The last book came out in
Geneva in 1868. In all, eight books appeared.   p. 61

[68] *Raznochintsi* (Commoners)—Russian intellectuals drawn from the petty
townsfolk, the clergy, the merchants and peasantry, as distinct from those
coming from the nobility.   p. 61

[69] The article was written by N. P. Ogaryov.   p. 62

[70] Lenin is quoting from A. I. Herzen's article "N. G. Chernyshevsky". p. 62

[71] Lenin quotes from A. I. Herzen's article "Gossip, Soot, Grime, etc." p. 62

[72] From A. I. Herzen's letter to I. S. Turgenev of April 10, 1864. p. 62

[73] Lenin quotes from A. I. Herzen's article "Primordial Bishop, Antediluvian
Government and Deceived People".   p. 63

[74] See Note 25.   p. 63

[75] See pp. of this book.   p. 65

[76] *Russkaya Mysl* (Russian Thought)—a monthly literary and political journal
of liberal Narodnik leanings, published in Moscow from 1880 to 1918. After
the 1905 revolution, under the editorship of P. B. Struve, it became the
organ of the Cadet Party and advocated nationalism, Vekhism, and
clericalism and defended landlordism.   p. 65

[77] Lenin is quoting from Nekrasov's poem "Who Can Be Happy in Russia?"
                                                                      p. 66

[78] Lenin is quoting from Nekrasov's poem "To the Unknown Friend Who has Sent Me the Poem 'It Cannot Be'".   p. 67

[79] The expression is from Saltykov-Shchedrin's satirical fairy-tale "The Liberal".   p. 67

[80] *Neo-Kantianism*—a reactionary trend in bourgeois philosophy preaching subjective idealism under the banner of a revival of Kant's philosophy.
                                                                                p. 67

[81] *Russky Vestnik* (The Russian Herald)—a political and literary journal, published in Moscow and St. Petersburg from 1856 to 1906. From 1856 to 1887 its editor and publisher was M. N. Katkov. At first it was of liberal leanings, but in the sixties of the last century it became an organ of serf-owning reactionaries.   p. 67

[82] *Marshal of the Nobility*—the representative of the nobility of a gubernia or uyezd in tsarist Russia. He was elected by the Assembly of the Nobility for the gubernia or uyezd, and was in charge of all the affairs of the nobility. He occupied an influential position and took the chair at meetings of the Zemstvo.   p. 67

[83] See Note 38.   p. 68

[84] *Union of the Russian People*—an ultra-reactionary, Black-Hundred organisation of monarchists, formed in October 1905 in St. Petersburg to combat the revolutionary movement.

It was abolished during the February bourgeois-democratic revolution of 1917.   p. 69

[85] See Note 50.   p. 69

[86] *General Association of German Workers*—a political organisation of the German workers set up at a congress of workers' societies in Leipzig in 1863, with the active participation of Ferdinand Lassalle. The fact that the Association was set up was of positive significance for the working-class movement, but Lassalle, who was elected president, led it along an opportunist path. It confined its aims to campaigning for a general franchise and carrying out parliamentary activity. The Association existed up to 1875.   p. 72

[87] *The Anti-Socialist Law* was promulgated in Germany in 1878 by the Bismarck government with the object of combating the labour and socialist movement. This law banned all the Social-Democratic organisations, mass working-class organisations, and the labour press; socialist literature was confiscated; Social-Democrats were persecuted and deported. These repressions, however, did not break the Social-Democratic Party, which readjusted its activities to the conditions of illegal work. Karl Marx and Frederick Engels gave tremendous assistance to the German Social-Democrats. In 1890 under pressure of the mounting mass labour movement, the Anti-Socialist Law was repealed.   p. 72

[88] *Russkoye Slovo* (Russian Word)—a daily bourgeois-liberal newspaper which appeared in Moscow from 1895; it was closed down in November 1917.
                                                                                p. 74

[89] *Severnaya Pravda* (Northern Truth)—one of the titles of *Pravda*, a legal Bolshevik daily newspaper.   p. 77

9*

[90] The *Bundist*—a member of the Bund, the short form of the title of the General Jewish Workers' Union of Lithuania, Poland and Russia, founded in 1897. It united mainly semi-proletarian elements in Russia's western regions. It brought nationalism and separatism into the Russian working-class movement. In March 1921 the Bund was dissolved after a voluntary decision of its members.   p. 77

[91] *Pale of Settlement*—districts in tsarist Russia where Jews were permitted permanent residence.   p. 82

[92] *Numerus clausus*—a numerical restriction imposed in tsarist Russia on admission of Jews to the state secondary and higher educational establishments, to employment at factories and offices, and the professions. p. 82

[93] *Dzvin* (The Bell)—a monthly legal nationalist journal of Menshevik sympathies, published in Ukrainian, in Kiev, from 1913 to 1914.   p. 93

[94] *Dyen* (The Day)—a daily newspaper of a liberal-bourgeois trend, published in St. Petersburg from 1912 to October 1917. Among its contributors were Menshevik liquidators, who took over complete control of the paper after February 1917.   p. 88

[95] See Note 66.   p. 90

[96] *The Emancipation of Labour group*—the first Russian Marxist group founded by G. V. Plekhanov in Geneva (Switzerland) in 1883; it existed up to the Second Congress of the R.S.D.L.P. in 1903. The group played a tremendously important role in the dissemination of Marxism throughout Russia. Plekhanov and other members of the group translated into Russian, published abroad and then illegally distributed in Russia works by the founders of Marxism. The group dealt a heavy blow to Narodism. p. 91

[97] *Economism*—an opportunist trend within Russian Social-Democracy at the turn of the century. The Economists asserted that the political struggle against tsarism should be conducted by the liberal bourgeoisie, and that the workers should confine themselves to economic struggle for better working conditions and higher wages. Denying the leading role of the Party and the importance of revolutionary theory for the working-class movement they declared that it should develop only along spontaneous lines. Lenin proved in his book *What Is To Be Done?* the complete untenability and harmful nature of Economist views.   p. 92

[98] *Iskra* (The Spark)—the first all-Russia illegal Marxist newspaper founded by Lenin in 1900. The first issue of *Iskra* came out on December 11 (24), 1900 in Leipzig; subsequent issues were published in Munich, from April 1902 in London, and in Geneva from the spring of 1903 onwards.
The Second Congress of the R.S.D.L.P. (1903) recognised *Iskra* as the Central Organ of the Party. Soon after the Congress, however, the Mensheviks took over control of the editorial board and turned *Iskra* into their own organ.   p. 92

[99] *Rabotnik* (The Worker)—a non-periodical symposium, published in Geneva from 1896 by the Union of Russian Social-Democrats Abroad.   p. 93

[100] *Vperyod* (Forward)—an illegal Bolshevik newspaper, published in Geneva from December 1904 to May 1905. Eighteen issues were published. Lenin was its organiser and guiding spirit. Other members of the editorial board were V. V. Vorovsky, M. S. Olminsky and A. V. Lunacharsky.   p 93

[101] See Note 19.   p. 93

[102] *Nachalo* (The Beginning)—a legal Menshevik daily published in St. Petersburg from November to December 1905.   p. 94

[103] *Volna* (The Wave)—a legal Bolshevik daily published in St. Petersburg from April to May 1906. Twenty-five issues were put out. Beginning with No. 9, May 1906, the paper was virtually edited by Lenin. Other members of the editorial board included V. V. Vorovsky and M. S. Olminsky. *Volna* was subjected to frequent police repressions and was eventually closed down by the government. Its place was taken by the legal Bolshevik paper *Vperyod*.   p. 94

[104] *Ekho* (The Echo)—a legal Bolshevik daily published in St. Petersburg from June to July 1906 in place of the newspaper *Vperyod*, suppressed by the government. Fourteen issues appeared. Lenin was the virtual editor of the paper and his articles appeared in every issue.
    The paper was closed down on the eve of the dissolution of the First Duma.   p. 94

[105] *Narodnaya Duma* (People's Duma)—a Menshevik daily published in St. Petersburg from March to April 1907.   p. 94

[106] A reference to the work of an outstanding Russian bibliographer, N. A. Rubakin, *Sredi Knig* (Among Books), containing vast reference material from all fields of knowledge. Lenin's article "On Bolshevism" was included in the second volume.   p. 94

[107] A reference to the proclamation "From Writers, Artists and Actors" imbued with bourgeois patriotism, which set out to justify the war being waged by tsarist Russia against Germany. Among those who signed it were Honorary Academicians, well-known artists A. Vasnetsov, V. Vasnetsov, K. Korovin, sculptor S. Merkulov, F. Chaliapin and other prominent actors of Moscow theatres, writers Maxim Gorky, A. Serafimovich, Skitalets, newspaper editors P. Struve, N. Mikhailov and D. Tikhomirov.   p. 96

[108] *Council of the United Nobility*—a counter-revolutionary organisation of landowners, founded in May 1906. It existed until 1917. Its main object was to protect the autocratic system, the big landed estates and the privileges of the nobility. The Council had a great influence on government policy. During the Third Duma a considerable number of its members were on the Council of State and in the leading centres of the Black-Hundred organisations.   p. 98

[109] Lenin is quoting from N. G. Chernyshevsky's novel *The Prologue*. p. 98

[110] See F. Engels, "Flüchtlingsliteratur".   p. 99

[111] *Bednota* (The Poor)—a daily newspaper for the peasants published in Moscow from March 1918 to January 1931. After February 1, 1931 it merged with the newspaper *Sotsialisticheskoye Zemledeliye* (Socialist Agriculture).

[112] See Note 63.   p.107

[113] *Kolupayev* and *Razuvayev*—types of capitalist sharks portrayed in the works of the Russian satirist M. Y. Saltykov-Shchedrin.   p.110

[114] Lenin is referring to the anti-Marxist views that were spread under the guise of "proletarian culture" by the members of the so-called *Proletcult*

(Proletarian Culture Organisation). The members of the Proletcult in effect rejected the cultural legacy of the past and, cutting themselves off from reality, tried to create a special "proletarian culture" by "laboratory methods". While playing lip service to Marxism, Bogdanov, the main Proletcult ideologist, advocated subjective idealism and Machism. Proletcult was not a homogeneous organisation. Together with the bourgeois intellectuals who made up the leadership of many of its organisations, there were also young workers who sincerely wished to promote the cultural development of the Soviet state. The Proletcult organisations flourished in 1919 but early in the twenties they went into decline, and in 1932 ceased to exist.

In his draft resolution on "Proletarian Culture" (see pp. 141-42 of this book) and in a number of other works, Lenin sharply criticised the erroneous principles of the Proletcult.   p.118

[115] A reference to a decree on "*The Mobilisation of the Literate and the Organisation of Propaganda of the Soviet System*" issued by the Council of People's Commissars on December 10, 1918 and published in *Izvestia* No. 272 on December 12. The decree proposed to register the entire literate population and select public speakers from among them with a view to organising them into groups which must, "first, inform the illiterate population of all the measures taken by the government, and, secondly, promote the political education of the entire population in general".
                                                                        p.119

[116] On May 18, 1919, the Central Executive Committee of the Ukrainian S.S.R. resolved to integrate the armed forces of all the Soviet republics to fight the enemies of Soviet power. Similar proposals were made by the Soviet Government of Latvia, Lithuania and Byelorussia. In compliance with this, on June 1, 1919, the All-Russia Central Executive Committee issued a decree on "The Union of the Soviet Republics — Russia, the Ukraine, Latvia, Lithuania and Byelorussia — for a Struggle against World Imperialism".   p.123

[117] A reference to Vladimir Mayakovsky's poem "Incessant Meeting Sitters". One of the poet's contemporaries recalled Mayakovsky saying: "... if Ilyich himself recognises that my political line is correct, this will show that I am making strides in communism. This, for the likes of us, is the most essential, the most important."   p. 145

[118] A reference to the words in Engels's "Flüchtlingsliteratur".   p.145

[119] See F. Engels, "Flüchtlingsliteratur".   p.119

[120] *Pod Znamenem Marksizma* (Under the Banner of Marxism) — a philosophical and socio-economic journal founded to propagate militant materialism and atheism. It was published monthly in Moscow from January 1922 to June 1944 (from 1933 to 1935 it appeared once every two months).
                                                                        p. 148

[121] The original text here was: "The other day I happened to be scanning through Upton Sinclair's book *The Profits of Religion*. Undoubtedly, the author has some flaws in the way he approached the problem and the manner he treated it. But the book is of value because it is written in a lively tone and gives many concrete facts and comparisons...."

Nadezhda Krupskaya recalled that the author had sent the book to her together with a letter in which he wrote about the struggle he was waging with the help of his novels. Lenin "availed himself of an English dictionary and began reading it in the evenings. The book did not satisfy him as regards its anti-religious propaganda, but he liked its critique of bourgeois democracy" (*Pod Znamenem Marksizma*, 1933, No. 1, p. 148).   p. 148

[122] *The Second International*—an international association of socialist parties founded in 1889. With the outbreak of the First World War (1914-18) the leaders of the Second International betrayed socialism and went over to the side of their imperialist governments; thus the Second International collapsed. The Left parties and groups, former members of the Second International, joined the Communist (Third) International founded in Moscow in 1919. The Second International was reinaugurated at a conference in Berne (Switzerland) in 1919; it included only the parties of the Right opportunist wing in the socialist movement.   p. 149

[123] This, evidently, is a reference to the Paris Commune as a supremely flexible political system in Marx's *The Civil War in France* (see Karl Marx and Frederick Engels, *Selected Works* in two volumes, Vol. I, Moscow, 1962, p. 522) and the high appraisal of the "flexibility of the Parisians" given by Marx in a letter to L. Kugelmann on April 12, 1871 (ibid., Vol. II, pp. 463-64).   p. 149

[124] See K. Marx's letter to F. Engels of April 16, 1856 (Marx and Engels, *Selected Correspondence*, Moscow, 1965, pp. 91-92).   p. 149

[125] *The Brest Peace Treaty* was signed at Brest-Litovsk in March 1918 between Soviet Russia and Germany on terms extremely harsh for Russia. The Soviet Government had to sign it because the old tsarist army had fallen into disruption and the Red Army was only just coming into being. Harsh as it was, the treaty gave Soviet Russia the respite she needed, enabled her to withdraw from the war for a time and to muster forces to rout the counter-revolutionary bourgeoisie and interventionists in the Civil War that started shortly afterwards.

After the revolution in Germany (November 1918) the Brest Peace was annulled.   p. 152

[126] *The New Economic Policy* (NEP)—a policy of the young Soviet state in the period of transition from capitalism to socialism.

It was called "new" in contrast to the economic policy which had been conducted by Soviet Russia in the period of foreign military intervention and the Civil War, which went down in history as the policy of War Communism (1918-20).

[127] See Note 30.   p. 153

[128] A reference to I. F. Dubrovinsky.   p. 153

[129] Maxim Gorky's article "Notes on Philistinism" was published in the legal Bolshevik newspaper *Novaya Zhizn* (New Life) in October and November 1905.   p. 153

[130] At the beginning of 1908 Gorky was completing his short story "Confession".   p. 153

[131] A reference to a statement Maxim Gorky intended to make for the press in connection with the arrest of N. A. Semashko in Geneva.   p. 154

[132] Gorky wrote the article "On Cynicism" for the French periodical *Documents du progrés*. At first it was printed in the symposium *Literaturny*

Raspad, Zveno Publishers, St. Petersburg, 1908 (it came out in January), and then in the March issue of the above-mentioned French periodical. The article contained a number of erroneous ideas of a "god-building" trend.   p. 154

[133] Gorky's letter of January 30, 1908, to Henryk Sienkiewicz was a reply to the opinion poll organised by the latter on the attitude to the seizure of the Poznan landowners' estates by the Prussian government.

The 252 replies to Sienkiewicz's questionnaire were published by him in a book issued in Paris, but Maxim Gorky's letter was omitted.

Gorky's letter was a document of accusation directed against the defence of large-scale private landownership in the Poznan province.

Gorky wrote to Sienkiewicz that he had a high opinion of his talent as an artist, but believed that the artist "should know who the enemies of the people are"; he protested against Sienkiewicz's appeal to Wilhelm II of Hohenzollern with such arguments as the "peaceful" behaviour of the Poles, who were "not kindling the fire of revolution", were punctually paying taxes and providing soldiers for the Prussian army. "These words give me reason to doubt the strength of your love for the Polish people," Gorky concluded (Gorky's Archives).   p. 154

[134] *Kwakalla*—a jocular name for the village Kuokkala in Finland, where Lenin lived from September 1906 to November 1907.   p. 155

[135] The reference is to the refusal of E. Ferri, then leader of the Centrist majority of the Italian Socialist Party, to edit *Avanti!*, the central organ of the party.   p. 157

[136] On Gorky's initiative it was arranged for Lenin to meet A. Bogdanov and his supporters' residing abroad. The meeting took place in April 1908, when Lenin visited Gorky at Capri.   p. 158

[137] Inok (Innokenty)—I. F. Dubrovinsky.   p. 159

[138] *Golos Sotsial-Demokrata* (A Social-Democrat's Voice)—a newspaper of the Menshevik liquidators, put out abroad; it was published from February 1908 to December 1911 first in Geneva and then in Paris.   p 160

[139] *Die Neue Zeit* (New Times)—a theoretical publication put out by German Social-Democrats which appeared in Stuttgart from 1883 to 1923. In the late 1890s after Engels's death, the journal made a practice of publishing revisionist articles.   p. 160

[140] See Note 80.   p. 160

[141] Lenin refers here to the article "Destruction of the Personality", the first version of which Gorky intended to publish in *Proletary* in the form of a series of "items". The article was first published in the collection *Ocherki filosofii kollektivizma* (Essays on the Philosophy of Collectivism), Znanive Publishers, St. Petersburg, 1909.   p. 161

[142] Lenin refers to the collection of articles written by V. Bazarov, Y. Berman, A. Lunacharsky, P. Yushkevich, A. Bogdanov, I. Helfond and S. Suvorov, *Studies in the Philosophy of Marxism*, St. Petersburg, 1908.   p. 161

[143] *Zarya* (Dawn)—a Marxist scientific and political journal, published legally in 1901 and 1902 in Stuttgart by the *Iskra* Editorial Board. Four issues (in three books) appeared. *Zarya* criticised international and Russian revisionism ("legal Marxism" and "Economism") and defended the theoretical foundations of Marxism.   p. 161

[144] A reference to Lenin's book *One Step Forward, Two Steps Back* published in Geneva in May 1904.   p. 161

[145] A reference to A. Bogdanov's book *Empirio-monism*, Issue I, Moscow, 1904.
                                                                    p. 161

[146] A collection of articles written by A. Lunacharsky, V. Bazarov, A. Bogdanov, P. Maslov, A. Finn, V. Shulyatikov, V. Fritche and others, published in St. Petersburg in 1904. Articles by Plekhanov and Lenin were not included in the collection.   p. 162

[147] "*Notebooks*" — "Notes of an Ordinary Marxist on Philosophy" — written by Lenin in 1906 in connection with A. Bogdanov's book *Empirio-monism* (Issue III), have not been found.   p. 162

[148] At that time Lenin was starting to write his *Materialism and Empirio-criticism*.   p. 163

[149] A reference to the school organised by A. A. Bogdanov, G. A. Alexinsky and A. V. Lunacharsky, with Gorky's participation, at Capri (Italy) in 1909. Lenin refused to lecture there, because it was a factional centre of otzovists, ultimatumists and "god-builders".

The school existed about four months. In November 1909, a section of the students, headed by Vilonov, made a clean break with the Bogdanovites. They sent the *Proletary* editorial board a protest against the lecturers' anti-Party behaviour, and were explelled from the school for this. Lenin invited them to come to Paris, where they heard a series of lectures, including those read by Lenin. In December 1909 those who remained at Capri and their lecturers founded an anti-Party *Vperyod* group.

The meeting of the extended editorial board of *Proletary* condemned the Capri school as "a new centre of a faction breaking away from the Bolsheviks".   p. 166

[150] *Rabochaya Gazeta* (Workers' Gazette) — a popular organ of the Bolsheviks published in Paris from 1910 to 1912. Pro-Party Mensheviks (Plekhanovites) contributed to it. The Prague Conference of the R.S.D.L.P. (January 1912) declared *Rabochaya Gazeta* an official organ of the C. C. of the R.S.D.L.P.(B.). Gorky gave it financial assistance.   p. 168

[151] *Sovremennik* (The Contemporary) — a monthly literary and political journal published in Paris from 1911 to 1915. Centred around it were Menshevik liqudators, Socialists-Revolutionaries, Popular Socialists and Left liberals. The journal had no ties whatever with the working-class mass movement.

In his letter to I. A. Bunin (after November 19 [December 2], 1910) Gorky wrote: "*Sovremennik* is hardly a serious enterprise, my 'regular' contribution to it is, of course, an invention, though to be honest an unpleasant one for me" (*Letopis zhizni i tvorchestva A. M. Gorkogo* [Chronicles of Gorky's Life and Work], Part 2, p. 167). In his letters to A. V. Amfiteatrov Gorky repeatedly and persistently asked him to delete the words "regular contributor".   p. 168

[152] *Vestnik Yevropy* (European Messenger) — a monthly magazine published in St. Petersburg from 1866 to the summer of 1918. It advocated the views of the Russian liberal bourgeoisie; from the early 1890s onwards it waged a systematic struggle against Marxism.   p. 168

[153] See Note 76.   p. 168

[154] See Note 1.   p. 168

[155] *Sovremenny Mir* (The Modern World)—a montly literary, scientific and political journal, which appeared in St. Petersburg from 1906 to 1918. The chief contributors to the journal were Mensheviks, including G. V. Plekhanov. The Bolsheviks also contributed to it during the period of their collaboration with the Plekhanovite group of the pro-Party Mensheviks.
                                                                      p. 168

[156] *Krasnoye Znamya* (Red Banner)—a bourgeois political and economic journal published in Paris in 1906.   p. 169

[157] *Zhivoye Dyelo* (Vital Cause)—a daily legal newspaper of the Menshevik liquidators, which appeared in St. Petersburg in 1912. Sixteen issues came out.   p. 170

[158] *Zvezda* (The Star)—a Bolshevik legal newspaper, which was published in St. Petersburg from December 1910 to April (May) 1912 (first once a week, then two or three times a week). Until the autumn of 1911 the pro-Party Mensheviks (Plekhanovites) contributed to *Zvezda*. Lenin gave the paper ideological guidance, while living abroad.
   Zvezda paved the way for the Bolshevik paper, *Pravda*; it was closed down by the government on the day the first issue of *Pravda* appeared.
                                                                      p. 170

[159] *Irkutskoye Slovo* (Irkutsk Word)—a newspaper with Menshevik liquidationist leanings (1911-12).   p. 170

[160] Reference is being made to the article "Cultured People and a Sullied Conscience" by M. S. Olminsky (A. Vitimsky) published in *Pravda* No. 98, August 23, 1912.   p. 160

[161] *Luch* (Ray)—a legal daily newspaper put out by Menshevik liquidators in St. Petersburg from 1912 to 1913. It survived thanks to "the donations of the rich friends of the bourgeoisie".   p. 173

[162] Demyan Bedny established contacts with the Bolshevik press in 1911 when he began working for *Zvezda*. The Pravdist, M. Olminsky, recalls: "Demyan Bedny was not a novice to the world of literature. His poems published under the name Y. Pridvorov appeared in Narodnik and Cadet publications. He was not a Marxist but inclined towards the extreme Left. When a purely Bolshevik paper *Zvezda* made its appearance, he felt a special sympathy for it: at first the editors received his poems by post and then the author came to visit them in person. Soon afterwards he started to come almost every evening to the printing shop, and here, in the friendly talks, while rush editorial work was going on in the vital hours before going to press, he felt a strong yearning for militant literary activity, and a fable writer, Demyan Bedny, came into being. He soon earned Lenin's high praise, though many other comrades cast slanting glances at the newcomer for a long time."   p. 174

[163] In the articles "On the Karamazov Attitude" and "Once Again on the Karamazov Attitude", Maxim Gorky expressed his protest against the Moscow Art Theatre's staging of Dostoyevsky's reactionary novel *The Possessed*. The paragraph that aroused Lenin's criticism formed the conclusion of the second article published in the newspaper *Russkoye Slovo*

on October 27, 1913. When, in 1917, the article was reprinted in the collection *Articles of 1905 to 1916,* Gorky deleted this paragraph.

Progressive-minded workers and intellectuals backed Gorky's protest against the staging of Dostoyevsky's *The Possessed* in numerous letters published in *Pravda* in November and December and at discussions organised on this subject. Reactionary publicists (D. S. Merezhkovsky and others) then began a slanderous campaign against Gorky.   p. 175

[164] Lenin refers to the novel *Paternal Testaments* by the Ukrainian writer V. Vinnichenko, a bourgeois nationalist.   p. 178

[165] Reference is to a pamphlet for working-class women that Inessa Armand intended to write. The pamphlet was not written, however.   p. 179

[166] Reference is to the anti-Party "Baugy" group (Bukharin, Rozmirovich, Krylenko) which took its name from the town of Baugy (Switzerland).
                                                                                                           p. 183

[167] The revolt at the Krasnaya Gorka Fort (Red Hill) started in the early hours of June 13, 1919 and was prepared by the so-called National Centre, a counter-revolutionary organisation which united the forces of a number of anti-Soviet and espionage groups. By capturing the Krasnaya Gorka Fort, the conspirators hoped to weaken the Kronstadt fortifications and, by co-ordinating the revolt with the general offensive at the front, to seize Petrograd.

In the morning of June 16, the revolt was put down.   p. 190

[168] Reference is to the *Explanatory Dictionary of the Living Russian Language* by V. I. Dahl, published in four volumes, 1863-66 (it has twice been republished since the revolution). In accordance with Lenin's instructions, the People's Commissariat for Education began work on compiling a new dictionary, but its publication was not realised at that time.   p. 192

[169] In May 1920 the writer A. S. Serafimovich lost his son at the front during the Civil War.   p. 193

[170] Mayakovsky's poem "150,000,000" reveals the poet's early futurist aberrations; it is pompous and complicated in form; in it the traditions of Russian classical poetry are rejected and futurism is praised as the only literary trend able to express the spirit of the contemporary age.   p. 195

[171] The Central Control Commission — a supreme organ of Party control.
                                                                                                           p. 199

[172] The *Clarté* group of progressive writers and cultural workers was organised by Henri Barbusse in 1915 on the basis of *l'Association Républicaine des Anciens Combattants.* Similar groups were set up in other countries, and together they formed the War Veterans International whose motto was: "War on war". The *Clarté* group included supporters of the Third International — Henri Barbusse, Anatole France, Paul Vaillant-Couturier, and pacifist writers — Romain Rolland, Stefan Zweig, H. G. Wells, Thomas Hardy, Upton Sinclair, Jules Romain, and others. The group published a monthly magazine of the same name (in Paris from October 1919 to January 1928), which in its first years was quite popular in France and abroad. However, the ideological disagreements within the group and its organisational weaknesses did not permit it to become a large and influential group. Soon after Barbusse resigned as editor (April 1924), the magazine lost its progressive significance. It ceased publication in 1928 and the group split up.   p. 201

[173] The title of a document published in 1899 which set forth the main principles of Economism. (For details about Economism, see Note 97.)

p. 220

[174] "Legal Marxism" appeared as a socio-political trend among the Russian liberal-bourgeois intellectuals in the 1890s. Its advocates, headed by Struve, tried to distort Marxism in the interests of the bourgeoisie. Lenin said that Struvism took from Marxism all that suited the liberal bourgeoisie, and threw overboard the true essence of Marxism — its revolutionary power, the teaching about the inevitable doom of capitalism, the proletarian revolution, and the dictatorship of the proletariat. p. 221

Name index

A

A. A., Al. Al., see Bogdanov, A.

Akimov (Makhnovets), Vladimir Petrovich (1872-1921) — prominent Economist and extreme opportunist. After the Second Congress of the R.S.D.L.P. (1903) he became a Menshevik. During the years of reaction (1907-10) he broke away from the Social-Democrats — 93

Alexander II (Romanov) (1818-1881) — Russian Emperor (1855-81) — 61, 62

Alexander III (Romanov) (1845-1894) — Russian Emperor (1881-94) — 235

Alexeyev, Pyotr Alexeyevich (1849-1891) — well-known Russian revolutionary of the seventies; a weaver — 91

Alexinsky, Grigory Alexeyevich (b. 1879) — Russian Social-Democrat. During the 1905-07 revolution he sided with the Bolsheviks; in the years of reaction (1907-10) he became an otzovist and an organiser of the anti-Party *Vperyod* group. In April 1918 he fled abroad where he joined extreme reactionaries — 173

Altman, Natan Isayevich (1889-1970) — Soviet painter and sculptor — 237

Alyoshin, Sergei Semyonovich (1886-1963) — Soviet sculptor — 236

Amfiteatrov, Alexander Vasilyevich (1862-1938) — Russian writer and journalist; a contributor to bourgeois-liberal and reactionary newspapers and magazines. After the October Socialist Revolution he became a White émigré — 168, 169, 170

Andreyeva, Maria Fyodorovna (M. F., M. F-na, Maria Fyodorovna) (1868-1953) — member of the Bolshevik Party from 1904; a well-known Russian actress and public figure; Maxim Gorky's second wife — 153, 167, 169, 170

Anthony, Bishop of Volhynia (Khrapovitsky, A. P.) (1863-1936) — head of the extreme Right trend in the Russian Orthodox Church, an exponent of reactionary tsarist policy. Bishop of Volhynia from 1902, subsequently Archbishop of Kharkov. During the Civil War and foreign military intervention he collaborated with Denikin. When the revolution triumphed in Russia he fled abroad, becoming a leader of the monarchist émigrés — 37, 38, 47, 66

Arakcheyev, Alexei Andreyevich (1769-1834) — a favourite of Emperors Paul I and Alexander

262

I; established a régime of reactionary police despotism — 58

Armand, Inessa Fyodorovna (1874-1920) — prominent figure in the international working-class and communist movement; a member of the Bolshevik Party from 1904 onwards — 178, 179, 181

Armand, Varvara Alexandrovna (b. 1901) — Inessa Armand's daughter, a student of the Higher Art Technical Studios from 1920 to 1927 — 216

Averchenko, Arkady Timofeyevich (1881-1925) — Russian writer and satirist. After the October Socialist Revolution he became a White émigré — 143-44

Axelrod, Pavel Borisovich (1850-1928) — Russian Social-Democrat; an active Menshevik from 1903; a leader of the liquidators during the years of reaction (1907-10) and the new revolutionary upsurge; was hostile to the October Socialist Revolution and became a White émigré — 160

B

Babeuf, Gracchus (real name François Émile) (1760-1797) — French revolutionary and outstanding representative of utopian equalitarian communism — 205

Bakunin, Mikhail Alexandrovich (1814-1876) — Russian revolutionary; an ideologist of anarchism — 59, 60, 205

Baranov, N. M. (1836-1901) — Governor of the Nizhni-Novgorod Gubernia (1882-97); well known for his ruthlessness during the 1891-92 famine — 11

Barbusse, Henri (1873-1935) — French writer and Communist — 121, 122, 216

Bauer, Otto (1882-1938) — a leader of the Austrian Social-Demo-crats and the Second International; one of the authors of the bourgeois-nationalist doctrine on "cultural-national autonomy", the opportunist essence of which was repeatedly exposed by V. I. Lenin — 82

Bazarov (Rudnev), Vladimir Alexandrovich (1874-1939) — Russian philosopher and economist, who associated himself with the Social-Democratic movement in 1896. During the years of reaction (1907-10) he abandoned the Bolsheviks and advocated "god-building" and empirio-criticism; was one of the chief Machist revisionists of Marxism — 156, 162, 164

Bebel, August (1840-1913) — a prominent figure in the German Social-Democratic and international working-class movement. In 1869, together with Wilhelm Liebknecht, he founded the German Social-Democratic Party (Eisenachers); was elected member of the Reichstag several times — 72, 205

Bedny, Demyan (Pridvorov, Yefim Alexeyevich) (1883-1945) — Soviet poet — 174, 217, 227

Beethoven, Ludwig van (1770-1827) — German composer — 226

Belinsky, Vissarion Grigoryevich (1811-1848) — Russian literary critic, publicist, materialist philosopher and revolutionary democrat; played an outstanding role in the history of social and aesthetic thought — 33, 34, 35, 66, 90, 205

Berdayev, Nikolai Alexandrovich (1874-1948) — reactionary Russian mystic philosopher. In 1922, as a result of his counter-revolutionary activity, was deported and became an ideologist of the whiteguard émigrés — 32

Berezovsky, A. Y. (b. 1868) — deputy to the Third Duma; landowner and member of the Cadet Party — 39

K

Kachorovsky, K. P. (b. 1870) — Russian economist; although he contributed to its periodicals, he was not formally a member of the Socialist-Revolutionary Party; author of a number of research works on the agrarian question — 169

Kalayev, Ivan Platonovich (1877-1905) — Socialist-Revolutionary. In February 1905 he assassinated the Governor-General of Moscow, Grand Duke Sergei Alexandrovich (uncle of Nicholas II); was executed — 205

Kalinin, Mikhail Ivanovich (1875-1946) — an outstanding figure of the Communist Party and the Soviet state. In 1919 he became chairman of the All-Russia Central Executive Committee and in 1922 chairman of the U.S.S.R. Central Executive Committee; from 1936 until his death he was chairman of the Presidium of the Supreme Soviet of the U.S.S.R. — 186

Kamenev, Lev Borisovich (1883-1936) — member of the R.S.D.L.P. from 1901 onwards. After the Second Congress of the R.S.D.L.P. (1903) he joined the Bolsheviks. During the years of reaction (1907-10) he adopted an attitude of reconciliation towards the liquidators, otzovists and Trotskyites. After the February bourgeois-democratic revolution of 1917 opposed the Party's course for a socialist revolution.

After the October Socialist Revolution he occupied a number of responsible posts. He repeatedly opposed the Party's Leninist policy, and in 1927 was expelled from the Party as an active member of the Trotskyite opposition; was twice reinstated and again expelled for his anti-Party activities — 190

Kant, Immanuel (1724-1804) — founder of classical German philosophy. His philosophy was a variety of subjective idealism and agnosticism, but a materialist element was to be found in his teaching on "things-in-themselves". Kantianism later influenced representatives of classical German idealism (Fichte, Schelling, Hegel), and gave rise to such trends in bourgeois philosophy as neo-Kantianism, positivism and others. The desire to return to Kant and reconcile Marxism and Kantianism was always characteristic of revisionists — 160

Karaulov, Mikhail Alexandrovich (1878-1917) — deputy to the Second and Fourth Dumas; a landowner and monarchist — 39

Katkov, Mikhail Nikiforovich (1818-1887) — Russian landowner and reactionary publicist. He began his political career as a supporter of moderate landowner liberalism. In the early 1860s he went over to nationalism, chauvinism and the Black Hundreds. His name came to stand for extreme reaction — 39, 67

Kautsky, Karl (1854-1938) — a theoretician of German Social-Democracy and the Second International; at first a Marxist and later a renegade and an ideologist of Centrism (Kautskianism), the most dangerous and harmful variety of opportunism — 12, 82, 102, 222, 231

Kavelin, Konstantin Dmitriyevich (1818-1885) — Russian historian and jurist, professor of the Universities of Moscow (1844-48) and St. Petersburg (1857-61); a representative of landowner-bourgeois liberalism. During the preparation and carrying out of the 1861 "peasant" Reform he opposed the revolutionary-democratic movement and supported the autocratic reactionary policies — 61, 62, 66

and organiser of the Cadet Party
—98

Rodzyanko, Mikhail Vladimirovich (1859-1924)—a big Russian landowner; leader of the counter-revolutionary Octobrist Party of the bourgeoisie and landowners; a monarchist. In March 1911 became chairman of the Third and later the Fourth Duma; supported the tsarist government in its struggle against the revolutionary movement—191

Romanovs, the—the dynasty of the Russian tsars (1613-1917) that was overthrown by the February bourgeois-democratic revolution in 1917—62, 99, 100

Romanovsky, G. I.—Soviet pianist—238

Rosanov, Vasily Vasilyevich (1856-1919)—Russian reactionary philosopher, publicist and critic, proponent of idealism and mysticism and supporter of the autocracy—37, 66, 69

Rozhkov, Nikolai Alexandrovich (1868-1927)—Russian historian and publicist. After the defeat of the 1905-07 revolution an ideological leader of liquidationism; contributor to the magazine Nasha Zarya; editor of the Menshevik liquidators' newspaper Novaya Sibir. In 1922 he broke with the Mensheviks—170

Rozmirovich, Y. F. (Troyanovskaya) (1886-1953)—member of the R.S.D.L.P. from 1904 onwards; was one of the editors of Pravda and a contributor to the magazines Prosveshcheniye, Rabotnitsa and others. After the October Socialist Revolution was engaged in Party and government work—172

Rubanovich, Ilya Adolfovich (1860-1920)—one of the Socialist-Revolutionary leaders—97

Rublyov, Andrei (b. c. 1360-d. 1430)—Russian artist—205

Ryleyev, Kondraty Fyodorovich

(1795-1826)—Russian poet and a prominent figure in the Decembrist movement—205

S

Saint-Simon, Henri (1760-1825)—French utopian socialist—205

Scriabin, Alexander Nikolayevich (1871-1915)—Russian composer and pianist—205

Serafimovich, Alexander Serafimovich (Popov, A. S.) (1863-1949)—Soviet writer—193, 241

Serno-Solovyevich, Alexander Alexandrovich (1838-1869)—a prominent figure in the revolutionary-democratic movement of the 1860s, emigrated in 1862; was the author of a pamphlet entitled Our Home Affairs, which criticised Herzen's liberal waverings—61

Shchedrin (Saltykov-Shchedrin, Mikhail Yevgrafovich) (1826-1889)—Russian satirical writer and revolutionary democrat—9, 67, 171, 205, 217

Shchepetev, A.—member of the Cadet Party and a Black Hundred, publicist and contributor to the newspaper Russkaya Mysl—65, 67, 68

Shervud, Leonid Vladimirovich (1871-1954)—Soviet sculptor—236

Shevchenko, Taras Grigoryevich (1814-1861)—Ukrainian poet, artist, revolutionary democrat and a fighter against tsarism and serfdom—205, 236

Shubin, Fedot Ivanovich (1740-1805)—Russian sculptor—205

Sienkiewicz, Henryk (1846-1916)—Polish writer—154

Sinclair, Upton (1878-1968)—American writer—101, 102

Skovoroda, Grigory Savvich (1722-1794)—Ukrainian philosopher and poet, an ardent defender of the oppressed—205

274

Smirnov, Y., see *Gurevich, E. L.*

Sokolovsky (Basok), M. I. (1879-1938) — Ukrainian petty-bourgeois nationalist and a Menshevik — 83

Solovyov, Vladimir Sergeyevich (1853-1900) — Russian idealist philosopher, publicist and symbolist poet; was hostile to Marxism, rejected and distorted it — 33

Sosnovsky, Lev Semyonovich (1886-1937) — a member of the Bolshevik Party since 1904. From 1918 to 1924 (with intervals) was editor of the newspaper *Bednota*; was expelled from the Party for his anti-Party activities in 1936 — 107

Spartacus (d. 71 B. C.) — Roman gladiator and leader of the greatest uprising of slaves in Ancient Rome (73-71 B. C.) — 205

Stolypin, A. A. (b. 1863) — member of the Octobrist Party, brother of P. A. Stolypin; a contributor to reactionary newspaper *Novoye Vremya* — 37

Stolypin, Pyotr Arkadyevich (1862-1911) — Russian statesman and big landowner. From 1906 to 1911 was chairman of the Council of Ministers and Minister of the Interior. His name is connected with the period of the most severe political reaction (Stolypin reaction, 1907-10) when mass executions were widely used to suppress the revolutionary movement — 29, 30

Stradivarius (Stradivari, Antonio) (1644-1737) — Italian violin maker — 238

Struve, Pyotr Berngardovich (1870-1944) — Russian bourgeois economist and publicist, a leader of the Cadet Party. During the 1890s a leading exponent of "legal Marxism", tried to adapt Marxism and the working-class movement to suit the interests of the bourgeoisie. After the October Socialist Revolution — a White

émigré — 32, 36, 65, 67, 68, 69, 79, 85, 96, 220

Sukhanov, N. (Gimmer, Nikolai Nikolayevich) (b. 1882) — Russian economist and publicist of petty-bourgeois leanings, a Menshevik. After the October Socialist Revolution he worked in Soviet economic bodies; was sentenced as the leader of the underground Menshevik organisation in 1931 — 149, 151, 152

Suvorin, Alexei Sergeyevich (1834-1912) — Russian reactionary journalist and publisher. From 1876 to 1912, publisher of *Novoye Vremya*, a corrupt bourgeois newspaper, the organ of reactionary circles of the nobility and bureaucracy — 69

Suvorov, S. A. (1869-1918) — Russian Social-Democrat, man of letters and statistician. After the defeat of the 1905-07 revolution he joined a group of Party intellectuals, Machists, who waged a campaign against Marxist philosophy; he contributed to the revisionist symposium *Studies in the Philosophy of Marxism* (1908). After 1910 he withdrew from the Party and worked as a statistician — 162

T

Todorsky, Alexander Ivanovich (1894-1965) — member of the C.P.S.U. since 1918, who fought with the Red Army as a commander of a brigade and then a division, in the Civil War, later occupying high commanding posts in a number of military establishments. In 1955 he resigned with the rank of Lieutenant-General and took up literary work — 107

Tolstoy, Leo (1828-1910) — Russian writer — 26-30, 44-48, 49-51, 52-53, 54-57, 88, 205, 207, 216, 225, 226

Tonkov, Vladimir Nikolayevich (1872-1954) — Soviet scientist, anatomist. From 1917 to 1925 chief of the Military Medical Academy. He visited Lenin many times and discussed the question of improving the living conditions of scientists — 190

Tretyakov, Pavel Mikhailovich (1832-1898) — founder of the famous art gallery, who, together with his brother (Tretyakov, Sergei Mikhailovich (1834-1892), presented their collection to the city of Moscow. In 1918 it was nationalised and renamed the State Tretyakov Gallery — 204

Trotsky (Bronstein), Lev Davidovich (1879-1940) — an enemy of Leninism. In 1912 he organised the anti-Party August bloc. After the October Socialist Revolution he held several government posts. In 1918 he opposed the conclusion of the Brest peace and from 1920 to 1921 headed the opposition in the trade union discussion; from 1923 onwards he waged a bitter factional struggle against the Party's general line and Lenin's programme for the building of socialism, spreading the idea that the victory of socialism was impossible in the U.S.S.R. In 1927 was expelled from the Party and in 1929 deported from the U.S.S.R. for anti-Soviet activities — 93, 143, 159, 160

Troyanovskaya, see *Rozmirovich, Y. F.*

Troyanovsky, Alexander Antonovich (1882-1955) — Bolshevik and prominent Soviet diplomat — 172

Tsyurupa, Alexander Dmitriyevich (1870-1928) — Member of the Party from 1898 onwards. Since 1918 was the People's Commissar for Food; since the end of 1921 was Deputy Chairman of the Council of People's Commissars and the Council of Labour and Defence — 238

Turgenev, Ivan Sergeyevich (1818-1883) — Russian writer — 62, 88

Tyutchev, Fyodor Ivanovich (1803-1873) — Russian poet — 205

U

Ulyanov, Dmitry Ilyich (1874-1943) — one of the veterans of the Bolshevik Party; Lenin's brother — 211

Ulyanova, Maria Alexandrovna (1835-1916) — Lenin's mother — 211

Ulyanova, Maria Ilyinichna (1878-1937) — one of the veterans of the Bolshevik Party; Lenin's younger sister — 213

Ulyanova, Olga Ilyinichna (1871-1891) — Lenin's sister — 211, 213

Uspensky, Gleb Ivanovich (1843-1902) — Russian writer — 205

V

V. V., see *Vorontsov, V. P.*

Vaillant, Edouard Marie (1840-1915) — French socialist, member of the Paris Commune and the General Council of the First International (1871-72); one of the founders of the Socialist Party of France (1901) — 205

Verhaeren, Emile (1855-1916) — Belgian poet — 216

Vilonov, Nikifor Yefremovich (Mikhail) (1883-1910) — Russian Social-Democrat, a Bolshevik, was an organiser of the Capri School, but on seeing its anti-Party character broke away from the otzovist factionalists and on Lenin's invitation departed for Paris together with a group of students — 166, 167

Vinnichenko, Vladimir Kirillovich (1880-1951) — Ukrainian writer and bourgeois nationalist. After

CPSIA information can be obtained at www.ICGtesting.com
Printed in the USA
VOW061845060212

LV00001B/49/P